OUT OF FOCUS

OUT OF FOCUS

NETWORK TELEVISION AND THE AMERICAN ECONOMY

BURTON YALE PINES

WITH TIMOTHY LAMER

Foreword by L. Brent Bozell III

REGNERY PUBLISHING, INC.
Washington, D.C.

Library of Congress Cataloging-in-Publication Data

Pines, Burton Yale.
Out of focus : network television and the American economy /
Burton Yale Pines : with Timothy Lamer : foreword by L. Brent Bozell III.
p.   cm.
Includes bibliographical references and index.
ISBN 0-89526-490-0
1. Television broadcasting of news—United States.   2. Journalism,
Commercial—United States.   3. United States—Economic conditions—1981–
I. Lamer, Timothy, 1968–   .   II. Title.
PN4888.T4P56   1994
070.1′95—dc20   93-46426
                                          CIP

Published in the United States by
Regnery Publishing, Inc.
An Eagle Publishing, Inc. Company
422 First St., SE, Suite 300
Washington, DC 20003

Distributed to the trade by
National Book Network
4720-A Boston Way
Lanham, MD 20706

Printed on acid-free paper.

Manufactured in the United States of America.

10   9   8   7   6   5   4   3   2   1

*This book is dedicated
to the independent and innovative spirit
of American entrepreneurs.*

ACKNOWLEDGEMENTS

A MOUNTAIN OF data was required for the analysis in this book. Piling up the data were Joe Busher, Brant Clifton, Chris Crowley, Nick Damask, Andy Gabron, Sally Hood, Cameron Humphries, Steve Kaminski, Marian Kelley (now Marian Wallace), Mario Lopez, and David Muska of the Media Research Center's News Division. They did all of the original analysis of 1992 news programs. Entertainment program analysis was done by Michael Byrne, Jeff Johnson, Tom Johnson, William Smith, and David Tosatti of the MRC's Entertainment Division. Brent Baker and Tim Graham supervised the news analysts and Sandy Crawford supervised the entertainment analysts. Baker, Graham, and Crawford offered valuable advice and guidance to the authors.

Particularly valuable was the work of Kristin Johnson and Tammy Smyth, media analysts for the Free Enterprise & Media Institute. From the research of the News and Entertainment Divisions, they identified all the year's economic stories and programs. Then they counted and categorized the seconds in every news story and analyzed the plots of every entertainment show. They also did background research and fact-checking for the book and designed the graphs that appear periodically throughout these pages.

Richard Kimble, Lawrence Gourlay, and Todd Martin identified the funding for this book, while Leif Noren oversaw the fiscal management of the institute. Brent Bozell, the chairman of the Media Research Center, has guided the institute since its founding. Patricia Bozell of Regnery Gateway edited the book with typical care and patience.

Economists Bruce Bartlett and Stephen Moore of the Cato

Institute, Chris Frenze and Ed Hudgins of the Joint Economic Committee, and Marvin Kosters of the American Enterprise Institute were kind enough to view economic news stories and pick the best and the worst of 1992, which supplied the material for chapters XIII and XIV.

We are also thankful for the generosity of those who have contributed financially to make possible this book and the Free Enterprise & Media Institute, with special thanks to Gratia Montgomery and Marge Mahler.

BURTON YALE PINES

CONTENTS

FOREWORD

ARTHUR OCHS SULZBERGER, former publisher and president of the *New York Times*, spoke before the Detroit Economic Club in 1977 to defend his industry against charges of biased reporting on business matters. "We give more space to a plane crash than to a report on thousands of safe landings made every day," he explained, adding, "I would never suggest that 'good news is no news,' but I would suggest that bad news is often big news."

The same cannot be said for good news. IBM laying off thousand of workers has human drama; not so the explosive growth of Intel and Microsoft, which dwarf the losses at IBM. The decline of the Rustbelt makes for powerful visuals; the growth of the Sunbelt doesn't. Stories on global warming are frightening and exciting; scientific evidence refuting these charges is dull. The abundance of the one without emphasis on the other makes for distorted news, and distortions have consequences in the public policy arena as government mobilizes to address a crisis that may not even exist.

When the bad news in and of itself is inaccurate the results are far worse. In 1989 actress Meryl Streep came before the cameras of CBS's popular "60 Minutes" to charge that Alar in apples was causing cancer in humans. The resulting panic cost the apple industry $150 million in losses before it was demonstrated the charges were false. In the 1970s much was reported concerning the acid rain catastrophe in the United States and led to the National Acid Precipitation Assessment Project launched by Congress in 1980. Nine years and $550 million later the results of the study were made public: no such catastrophe existed. Paul Ehrlich's environmental hysterics in the 1970s launched massive public policy debates; his track record of pathetically inaccurate predictions did not stop him from landing regular production assignments on NBC in the 1980s.

Billions of taxpayer dollars have been spent to tackle the homeless problem in America. Regularly we are told by the media that there are 3 million homeless. Some say 5 million. One network said the figure would be 19 million by the year 2000. Another suggested 40 million "on the knife-edge of homelessness." And yet there is no truth to any of these numbers. Three national studies as well as the National Census have placed the total number at between 250,000 and 600,000. Why the discrepancy? The press believed the 3 million figure offered by the late homeless advocate and gadfly Mitch Snyder, who later admitted the figures were fabricated as a publicity stunt. How the seven-digit estimates were arrived at is anyone's guess.

On a regular basis the media guess, and guess wrong. They readily accept as fact the allegations of the American Left, always suspicious of and hostile to business. It matters not that seldom is there empirical evidence to buttress the charges, and the false data are rarely corrected. Good news is not big news.

Socialism is on the run worldwide while the world wonders why the leader of the free world lurches toward it with the media as its Pied Piper. Sad but true: The American experiment which created the most vibrant economic powerhouse in history is today emasculated; sheepishly we accept as inevitable the regulatory stranglehold which not only paralyzes commerce but the spirit of the entrepreneur as well.

One hundred and fifty years ago the clarion call of economic opportunity was issued as news filtered back that gold had been discovered in a land called California. Men sold their homes, gathered their meager belongings, and with family in tow mounted their rickety Conestoga wagons for the treacherous, mysterious, frightening three thousand mile adventure west. No government guidelines controlled the sojourn; the enterprise succeeded or failed on its merits. It might lead to fortune and future; it could mean death.

Today that same trip takes but hours in the relative luxury of an airline governed by thousands of regulations of which but a fraction are publicized in the endless preflight monologue offered passengers. We are told government regulations require that all our carry-on items be placed in the overhead compartment or under the seat in front of us; given special instructions for those seated in the exit rows; told not to use portable electronic devices such as tape players, audio/video recorders or players, portable computers, calculators, radio or TV receivers, or hand-held electronic games or portable telephones and CD players during taxi, takeoff, and landing; given explicit direction in the insertion of a belt buckle, the tightening of the strap, the removal of a seat cushion, the location of the exit doors, the use of oxygen masks, the precise position required for seat backs and tray tables; and smoking is against the law. Given the opportunity today to travel on Delta, Lewis and Clark would probably opt to stay with the canoe.

Some regulation is necessary and acceptable. Some of it is downright foolish, and one wonders what next will be offered to the public policy arena as a "problem," be given a hearing in the press, and result ultimately in a new regulation passively accepted by a public resigned to such things. On the June 9 CBS Evening News, Dan Rather offered a suggestion. "The deregulated airline industry has come up with another way to save money and boost profits," he warned ominously. "This time they're not cutting jobs or in-flight meals. No, this time they're cutting fresh air. Flight crews and passengers say it's enough to make you sick."

Ironically, Mr. Rather comes from a state that symbolizes the glory of the entrepreneurial spirit, and in the 1970s Dallas was the free enterprise heart of Texas. On a visit there in 1991 I met with business leaders who bemoaned the city's growing infatuation with statism. Why, they wondered, did the once fiercely independent and proud Dallasites no longer understand their success was a result of a culture which championed the freedom of the individual, and that a handcuffed free enterprise system cannot deliver the goods and services on which its citizenry depend?

It is so, I think, because we as a nation no longer understand the culture of free enterprise, and neither do the media. By the time the average child is graduated from high school he will have spent more time being entertained in front of a television than lectured in a classroom. Who then is the teacher and what lessons are taught? The typical businessman on entertainment television is a J. R. Ewing: ruthless, dishonest, selfish, destructive. Similarly, 79 percent of Americans get their economic news from television. One need only study the media's assault on Ronald Reagan's legacy to see their disdain for the free enterprise culture.

The media, of course, will roundly deny this charge. They might point to surveys of the industry demonstrating that while their political leanings are far to the left on the spectrum, the majority of journalists support the tenets of capitalism. Moreover they will accuse the media critic of gross overgeneralization: there is no empirical evidence to support the charges.

There is now. In 1992 the Media Research Center launched the Free Enterprise and Media Institute. Under the direction of Senior Fellow Burton Yale Pines, FEMI set forth on the mission to educate the media about free enterprise. But before affecting change it is of critical importance that the problem be substantiated. Thus the first priority was to accumulate the evidence necessary to demonstrate the media's anti-free enterprise tilt. *Out of Focus: Network Television and the American Economy* is the culmination of the most sophisticated study ever conducted on the issue of free enterprise and the media, the launching ground for what we hope will be a constructive effort to restore a sense of balance to the media's coverage of the free enterprise system.

L. BRENT BOZELL III
November 1993

OUT OF
FOCUS

INTRODUCTION

TV, ECONOMICS, AND TARANTULAS

IT'S THE ECONOMY, STUPID.

A determined focus on this dictum, it is said, won Bill Clinton the presidency. That advice, given to the Clinton presidential campaign staff, was apparently good.

And it would be just as good advice to Americans who seek to be informed about their society. Nothing else (save, perhaps, defense) so profoundly affects so many Americans as does economics.

Rising living standards. Expanding opportunities. New products. Technological advances. Greater and more differentiated leisure. Social mobility. Extra resources to care for the least fortunate. Ever greater options and ever greater choices for an ever greater number of Americans.

All of these—and the list could go on—depend upon a growing and healthy economy.

And American economic health depends to a large extent on how much Americans know about their economy and how well they understand it. Individual Americans must know enough, for example, to take advantage of the economy and the opportunities it offers.

More important, since government actions extensively affect the economy, Americans must know enough about their economy to

3

monitor, influence, and check what their government does to it. A knowing, intelligent American who understands the economy can hold Washington accountable and press Washington to take or avoid actions to keep the economy healthy.

The problem is that Americans do not know much about their economy, how it operates, the forces driving it, or even its key components. A 1992 survey by the National Council on Economic Education finds that "the general public was able to answer correctly only 39% of the questions on economic concepts, relationship, and ideas that are frequently used in discussions of economic matters." Example: "Only 36% knew the basic purpose of profits in an economy."[1]

From the poll's findings, the council concludes: "For most people, the knowledge base for understanding or discussing most economic issues is inadequate. This economic illiteracy has the potential to misshape public opinion on economic issues and to lead to economic policies that have negative or perverse effects on the economy."

Who or what is at fault for this economic illiteracy? According to the council, a key culprit is television. Indeed, when the pollsters asked, "What is your source of information about the economy," 79 percent of Americans answered: Television.

That should come as no surprise. More than 98 percent of all American households have a TV set. In fact, more Americans own TV sets than have telephones or indoor plumbing, and Americans are thirteen times more likely to be watching TV than reading a magazine or a newspaper.

While they were watching TV in 1992, what kind of economic information did Americans receive?

To answer this, the staff of the Free Enterprise and Media Institute monitored and analyzed every minute of the year's ABC, CBS, CNN, and NBC morning and evening newscasts and newsmagazines. In addition, the FEMI staff analyzed twelve weeks' worth of 1992 prime-time entertainment TV—one week selected randomly from each month—for plots, characters, and portrayals that possibly taught an economic lesson or sent an economic message or signal.

From this monitoring and analysis, unprecedented in its scope, a very worrisome conclusion emerged: Television treats America's free enterprise economy in the same way that television treats the tarantula—by massive distortion.

How the hapless tarantula has fared at TV's hands is described by Cornell University psychologist John Condry in *The Psychology of Television*. He writes:

> We have knowledge about tarantulas [from TV] . . . A person who had never seen a real tarantula could still learn what they look like, could learn to discriminate tarantulas from other spiders, and a person watching films on television could learn to fear tarantulas too . . .
>
> How many people know that although these *are* very large and photogenic spiders (making them useful for film and television), they are also quite harmless and delicate animals? . . . They do sting occasionally, but it is usually no worse than a bee sting . . . The fact that they are much more fearful than [a honey bee] we can attribute to movies and television where tarantulas are portrayed as more fearful than they are in reality.
>
> Clearly, we learn some attitudes from television, perhaps especially about things like tarantulas where we have little or no experience.[2]

Just as American attitudes toward the tarantula have been distorted by TV, so too has TV distorted and misrepresented the fundamentals and workings of the economy. In 1992, to a great extent, network newscasts and prime-time entertainment made businesspersons, businesses, business transactions, and free enterprise principles something as fearful and as far from reality as TV's depiction of what in actuality is that hairy, large, delicate—and harmless—spider.

The evidence:

During the year, according to the data compiled by the Free Enterprise and Media Institute, network TV viewers were about 50 percent more likely to hear a newscast segment that distorted free enterprise or was antagonistic to it than one that portrayed it accurately or was favorable to it.

In that year, network newscasts aired 68 hours, 34 minutes on economic policy and business matters. Most of this, some 56 hours, 32 minutes, was background material, often factoids of little importance. But much of the reporting was explicitly or implicitly didactic. Of this, 6 hours, 59 minutes misinformed viewers about the facts or principles of the American economy and business compared to 5 hours, 3 minutes which portrayed the free enterprise economy accurately and fairly.

This meant that a random tuning-in of TV was more likely to give a viewer information that distorted or undermined free enterprise than supported it. If a viewer, for example, happened to be interested in the Los Angeles riots, he or she would have had a nearly two-to-one chance of hearing and seeing an inaccurate description or analysis of economic concepts. If a viewer were interested in health care, there was a more than two-to-one chance of receiving information and analysis misrepresenting free enterprise. Specifically, for every minute of 1992 newscast about health care coverage that was accurate or favorable to free enterprise, 2 minutes, 16 seconds were inaccurate and antagonistic.

The single economic issue covered most intensively in 1992 was regulation. On it, a viewer had a one-third greater chance of watching coverage that misstated free market economic principles and facts than coverage that was accurate.

The only time that network news reporting on economic issues did not tarantulize America's free enterprise economy was in stories dealing with taxes. For every minute of news reporting or analysis devoted to tax matters in 1992, the viewer could have heard 32 seconds accurately dealing with free enterprise concepts versus 28 seconds misrepresenting or distorting them.

A viewer was most likely to receive distorted information about free enterprise in 1992 from CNN and most likely to watch balanced news coverage of free enterprise matters on ABC.

Criteria for assessing the message of TV's economic reporting differ somewhat from those assessing political reporting. While political reports should be measured by how fairly or unbiased they treat a politician or party, the measure of economic reports is how fairly and balanced they deal with the principles on which America's free enterprise system rests and how well they advance Americans' understanding of free enterprise.[3] Herewith the scorecard for network newscasts portraying free enterprise facts, developments, and principles in 1992:

On regulation—101 minutes inaccurate portrayal of free enterprise facts, developments, and principles versus 71 minutes accurate.

On taxes—31 minutes inaccurate versus 36 minutes accurate.

On federal budget and spending—113 minutes inaccurate versus 94 minutes accurate.

On health care—43 minutes inaccurate versus 19 minutes accurate.

On environment—56 minutes inaccurate versus 43 minutes accurate.

Defying quantification was TV's treatment of what could be called the culture of free enterprise—those characteristics in a society that create the framework and incentives for healthy economic activity. For free enterprise these characteristics include the work ethic, a propensity to defer gratification by saving and investing rather than consuming, personal discipline, readiness to take risks, high rewards for entrepreneurial success coupled with penalties for failure, and an attitudinal climate which does not presume that seeking profits is the equivalent of greed.

Though TV's portrayal of the culture of free enterprise did not lend itself to second-by-second measurements, extensive analysis of the contents of newscasts and prime-time entertainment, supported by scores of examples, finds that very little on network newscasts and on prime-time entertainment in 1992 reinforced the culture of free enterprise. At times, comments were explicitly hostile to the culture. On an episode of "Civil Wars," for example, thrift was ridiculed. On "Roc," an unemployed slacker usually ended up on top despite poor work habits.

Most often, however, the notions that high profits created high incentives for risk taking, for savings, and even for hard work were ignored or implicitly slighted by network TV. This did less damage than an outright assault on free enterprise, but it did damage nonetheless. A thriving American economy requires citizens who understand something of how their economy functions and, perhaps more important, are encouraged to work hard, save, invest, seek profits, and take risks—or, if they do not, then at least understand and appreciate those who do.

By failing to reinforce the culture of free enterprise, TV in 1992 was derelict in its role as teacher—just as derelict as if TV signalled that taking drugs or discriminating against African-Americans were okay.

THE TARANTULA ECONOMY

Americans received a huge helping of economics on TV in 1992. In a typical week, newscasts served up a smorgasbord of economic statistics and stories about companies, labor unions, foreign trade, congressional bills, national debt, personal finances, innovations, and new products. Viewers received consumer advice and even some fairly explicit economics lessons. Together these numerous stories, as in a painting by numbers, comprised a portrait whose features made it the economic cousin of a tarantula.

This portrait depicted firms bilking the U.S. government for millions in food stamp frauds, cheating the Pentagon, mislabelling foods and suntan lotion, making (according to CBS "This Morning") "profits the old-fashioned way—by gouging consumers," disposing toxic wastes illegally, manufacturing flawed jaw implants, misleading doctors in medical journal advertising, making dangerous baby-walkers, recalling hundreds of thousands of cans of chicken soup because of glass particles in the rice, overcharging borrowers, and selling counterfeit Picasso prints.

To be sure, most, if not all of those stories probably were factually true—as would be stories about a tarantula's size and other intimidating physical characteristics. But in the aggregate, the stories about the American economy were false because such stories were almost all that viewers in 1992 heard and saw about it. Missing almost completely were accounts, equally true and vastly more representative of reality, of businesses, businesspersons, and economic developments that created jobs, satisfied customers, increased national competitiveness, and advanced living standards.

Without these other stories, more typical of how the economy works, the viewer was left with a composite picture of the American economy as ugly and dangerous, like the supposed tarantula—an economic system harboring companies that overcharge, fail, and fake, and that are bossed by executives who swindle, are vastly overpaid, are crazy, or end up in jail, or all of the above. Almost blacked-out for viewers was the truth: that nearly all American businesses are honest and contribute enormously to the nation's standard and quality of living.

TEACHING ECONOMIC LESSONS

TV newscasts in 1992 taught the American public several lessons about their free enterprise economy:

1. They should have little faith in the dynamics of the marketplace
2. Consumers are stupid
3. New inventions and economic developments generally create serious problems; and, above all,
4. The best answer to economic problems and difficulties is government.

Marketplace dynamics was, for example, a secret that TV kept from viewers. Few TV reporters conveyed the notion that in free enterprise, the dynamics of the marketplace (including the forces of competition) were the central economic factor. Typifying the reporting was CBS' Ray Brady, who talked about economic growth as if it were a matter of luck or whimsy. Said Brady near the end of 1992: "If America's business leaders like Mr. Clinton's economic policies, their own business policies could bring on an expanding economy and above all more jobs." He added that Clinton's economic success would be a matter of "whether President-elect Clinton will get much help on jobs from corporate America."

In the economic world painted by Brady, businesspersons and investors made their decisions not, apparently, to increase sales or market share or profits, but to "help" or not "help" Clinton because they either "liked" or "disliked" his policies. Brady gave viewers not even the slightest hint of the market forces that affect economic decisions and outcomes.

That consumers are bumpkins ever ready to be fleeced was another frequent lesson on TV. Several reporters, including ABC's Paula Lyons, CNN's Brian Barger, NBC's Lea Thompson, and CBS's Hattie Kauffman, called for federal action to regulate the freshness of fish. Their assumption was that consumers were so stupid that they would continue to buy rotten fish. Even after Trudy Lieberman of *Consumer Reports* told viewers of "Good Morning America" January 16 that since consumers are "able to choose quality and reject those products that are not good quality, maybe retailers will pay more attention," Lyons still thought government action would be a good idea.

Ignored by reporting was the fact, painfully learned by manufacturers of shoddy or untrendy products, that American consumers are sharp, tough, and unforgiving, and that information flashes from one consumer to another at a speed unmatched by the fastest computer.

The third lesson taught by TV, reflecting the networks' apparent lack of faith in free market forces and the consumer, was that technological and product innovations invariably pose dangers. This carried a strong whiff of Luddism, named after the early nineteenth-century attempt by English weavers to shatter, with huge hammers, the new textile looms which were threatening their traditional jobs.

Typifying such Luddism was a CBS "This Morning" December 11 item about a new device that would use high frequency radio signals to transmit TV. Host Harry Smith told viewers that this would "pose a threat to the cable TV industry." Perhaps it would;

but it also would do much more, such as cutting the cost of receiving cable-like programs for all consumers.

Smith's comment could have been a parody of the classic classroom joke told by economics professors ridiculing Luddite responses to economic and technological developments. The Luddite, say these professors, would have greeted Edison's invention of the light bulb by proclaiming: "Candlemakers are threatened." Smith and his colleagues almost always reported economic developments as threats; seldom did they portray them as benefiting anyone.

The strongest lesson learned from newscasts was that government is the answer to economic problems. Viewers got little sense that the government's role in the economy was a matter of torrid dispute.

For NBC's Irving R. Levine, for instance, the prescription for the troubled American auto industry was federal interference of one sort or another—federal tax credits, low interest loans, and federal pressure to cut auto executives' salaries. When Levine said that American workers had to learn new skills, for him the teacher must be the federal government. Ignored entirely by Levine were the vast and successful job retraining programs run by private firms.

ABC's Stephen Aug too looked almost reflexively to government. Reporting on the year's persistent unemployment, he told viewers that jobs would be created only by "higher spending" by government. To CBS's Ed Bradley, consumers had no one to turn to but the federal government to ensure the safety of auto seats. He ignored the fact that the consumer's decision to buy an auto or every other product was by far the most powerful influence on any business.

Particularly revealing of TV's faith in government effectiveness was its reporting on the efforts to rebuild Los Angeles after the spring riots. Though ABC's Peter Jennings and Bob Jamieson introduced viewers to Enterprise Zones, a potentially useful device to spur economic activity, Jennings defined the zones as "areas mostly in inner-cities where the federal government would create jobs by offering industry new tax breaks to set up shop there." What viewers heard from Jennings was that the jobs in the Enterprise Zones would be created by government. He was wrong. The jobs would come not from government but from investors and other risk-takers who would set up businesses because the zone would remove government-made barriers to entrepreneurial activity.

The reporters' preference for government action also was clear in their treatment of regulation. Newscasts seemed to assume that government officials and bureaucrats had the information, ability, and tools to regulate economic matters effectively. The message seemed to be: If there is a problem, government regulations can fix it.

Typifying this was coverage of cable TV reregulation. No reporter questioned the notion that only the Federal Communications Commission could check the climb in cable rates. Similarly with workplace safety. The assumption was that more federal inspectors and higher federal fines could make work safer. And only government rules and inspectors could ensure quality housing construction.

When it came to the environment, network TV's message again was that pollution and other environmental problems could be solved only by government. ABC's Barry Serafin approvingly cited those who were saying that "more federal funds are needed for monitoring and research" of the "red tides" problem, while ABC's Charles Gibson prodded a guest by asking: "How do we attack the problem? Is it government money?" As for health care, when the Bush administration's private-sector plan was discussed, CBS's Harry Smith said, "It is hard not to be cynical" about it. Yet rarely in the year did Smith express cynicism about government proposals.

TV'S TEN PROBLEMS

Network TV's distorted treatment of business and economics in 1992 probably was not deliberate. Indeed, polls show that, whatever the TV industry's political leanings, the industry strongly supports free enterprise. A 1982 survey, supervised by Robert Lichter, of Hollywood's most influential writers, producers, and executives found 81 percent supporting the basic capitalist premise that big corporations should remain privately owned. The survey also found Hollywood far from egalitarian: 94 percent said that those with more ability should earn more, while 66 percent said that free enterprise was fair to workers.

An earlier 1981 Lichter study had found that reporters tended to agree with their Hollywood counterparts. According to the study, 65 percent of reporters strongly disagreed with the statement that "private corporations should be publicly owned; 86 percent agreed that those with more ability should earn more; and a solid majority were against government-guaranteed jobs."

TV's problem with the economy and business thus may not be bias. Rather the TV community may simply not understand economic matters, particularly how the free enterprise system works and how the profit incentive spurs creativity, risk-taking, savings, postponed gratification, and extraordinarily hard work. TV simply may be economically illiterate.

If TV's problem is ignorance of the free enterprise economy rather than a bias against it, then the solution to the problem could be relatively straightforward: TV could decide to stop its inadvertent depiction of the American economic system as a tarantula. Just as TV newscast reporters and producers and entertainment writers eventually (and under pressure) learned to portray women, blacks, and gays more accurately and with more understanding, so too can they learn to do so with free enterprise economics.

If TV executives, producers, writers, anchors, and reporters decide to end their distorted portrayal of free enterprise, they can start by addressing ten key problems that TV has in covering economics and business.

PROBLEM #1:
Errors of fact and basic interpretation

Reporters at times just get the facts wrong. In 1992, for example:

☒ CBS commentator Ray Brady's statement in his January 14 report on bankruptcies in the retail industry that "Stores could be like the airline industry. The fewer of them around, the less the competition—and the higher prices go for consumers." Brady was wrong. Since airline deregulation, air fares have plummeted, the number of passengers has soared, and the frequency of service to cities has multiplied dramatically.

☒   CBS Reporter Bob Schieffer's statement January 18 that government successfully had helped industry in "mobilizing to fight World War II, building the first atomic bomb, landing on the moon, and Star Wars." Schieffer cited these as examples of successful government-industry collaboration. Schieffer was wrong. While they were warranted (whatever their costs) to protect the nation militarily, they were enormously wasteful, inefficient, and expensive. To be sure, the projects did typify what happens when government and industry work together. But they did not succeed, as Schieffer intended, as models for contemporary government-business cooperation. They showed all the reasons why such cooperation almost always is a mistake.

☒   CBS Ray Brady's message on January 27 and CNN Terry Keenan's message on January 31 that junk bonds were junk. Brady and Keenan were wrong. So-called "junk bonds" generally have proved to be safe and high-yielding investments.

☒   CNN Larry Lamotte's contention January 29 that "America is reluctantly changing to a service economy" and that this is not a healthy development. Lamotte was wrong. Volumes of economic data and analyses confirm that the change has been neither reluctant nor damaging to the economy.

☒   CNN's contention January 30 that Japanese and other foreign purchases of American properties were not good for the American economy. Almost all economists disagree.

☒   NBC commentator Irving R. Levine's statement May 25 that America was losing high-paying jobs. Levine was wrong. The trend in America has not been toward low-end jobs but toward well-paying skilled jobs.

☒   ABC reporter Don Kladstrup's message on "Nightline" June 1 that Third World peasants had no alternative but to slash-and-burn their land even though it was destroying their country's forests. Kladstrup was wrong. They had a choice. An economic system that would give them a stake in the land and a free market in which to sell their crops would create incentives for the peasants to preserve and improve their land.

☒ ABC Forrest Sawyer's statement on "Nightline" June 1 that "the world is a vastly poorer place today than when you were born." Sawyer was wrong. By no economic (or political or social) measure is the world poorer than it was a generation ago.

☒ ABC "World News Tonight" anchor Peter Jennings' statement June 2 that "government would create jobs" in urban Enterprise Zones. Jennings was wrong. Private investors and businesspersons create Enterprise Zone jobs.

☒ CBS Ray Brady's statement December 11 that the success of Bill Clinton's economic program depended upon how much help he would get from "Corporate America." Brady apparently assumed that corporate America, the biggest firms, create jobs. Brady again was wrong. The biggest firms have created few jobs in the past decade; almost all of the millions of new jobs in the 1980s were created by small businesses.

PROBLEM #2:
Squandered opportunities

Often a reporter is given a chance by the theme of a report or by the remark of a Talking Head expert to make a point that could have taught the viewer something about the American economy. Yet reporters almost always fail to do so. In 1992, for example:

☒ NBC's Jeff Madrick, CBS' Bob Kur, and NBC's Keith Morrison, among others, reported that the rich became richer and paid fewer taxes in the 1980s at the expense of the poor. They were wrong. In fact, the rich paid a higher percentage of total taxes in the 1980s than in previous decades. Reporters made the mistake of getting their numbers from groups hostile to Reagan policies; typically such groups included the late 1970s, with its stagnant economy, as part of "the eighties."

⊠   CNN's story that jobs at fast food chains were physically dangerous for teens. Anchor David French squandered the opportunity to tell viewers how such chains were teaching basic work discipline and skills to enormous numbers of inner-city teenagers. Rather than being dead-end, low-skilled employment for these teens, fast food outlets have become apprenticeship launching pads to better jobs.

⊠   ABC's major story about corporations establishing day care centers. Reporter Bob Jamieson squandered the opportunity to explain how the day care centers could boost productivity.

⊠   ABC's story on General Motors launching its own credit card. Stephen Aug, after asking who the "big losers" would be, squandered the opportunity to ask the obvious paired question: Who would the "big winners" be? Had he done so, he could have explained how consumers win when competition forces down credit card interest rates.

⊠   ABC, CBS, and NBC's reporting on the proposal to reform product liability law. These reporters squandered many opportunities to describe how the current product liability process had driven up prices for consumers and even kept some goods off shelves. Addressing this would have informed viewers of the complicated trade-offs in economic matters and warned them that what initially might appear as a sensible solution typically has unwanted consequences.

⊠   All networks' reporting on unemployment rates. Their reporters squandered many opportunities to discuss how jobs are created.

⊠   All networks' reporting on businesses. Their reporters squandered the opportunities even to observe that it is business, and only business, that creates the jobs and wealth that pushes up the nation's living standards. The only time viewers caught a glimpse of this was when a Bush administration official or a businessperson pointed out that small and medium businesses were where job growth had occurred.

☒ All of the networks' massive coverage of the United Nations environmental conference in Rio. Their reporters squandered every opportunity to move beyond the soundbite and conventional questions to explore dissident views on how threatened the global environment actually was and on how to meet the threat.

☒ All the networks reporting on health care. When reporters covered tragic cases of Americans who were sick and lacked health insurance, they missed the opportunity to tell viewers that these were the exceptions and that the vast majority of Americans had health care coverage.

PROBLEM #3:
Panic and gloom

Economics and business stories typically emphasize the negative, focusing particularly on victims. As a result, viewers are told that the economy mainly causes problems. In 1992, for example:

☒ Reporting on the environment seemed to evoke every possible apocalyptical phrase. Said ABC: "The world [is] headed toward environmental catastrophe," and "The world is being poisoned. It is being devoured by ravenous billions of us. And no end is in sight." Said CNN: "The Labrador duck is no more. Extinct. So too the Carolina parakeet, the ivory billed woodpecker," and "The forests are shrinking . . . species are vanishing day by day." Said CBS: "Droughts, storms, floods, even extinction of some species could be the result of global warming." And said NBC: "The world is facing the potential for record heat, record drought, forests going up in flames, sea levels rising creating an unprecedented refugee problem," and "This may be the last chance they have to save the planet."

☒ CBS's Ray Brady consistently portrayed the economy as a miasmic swamp holding nothing but predatory dangers for the average American. He told viewers, among other things, that falling housing prices and lower airfares were bad news, that thousands of Americans were "suffocating under bills," that "insurance companies refuse to pay" claims, that con artists were taking advantage of the unemployed, and that couples who failed to negotiate financial prenuptial agreements could face "a costly breakup."

☒ Victims were paraded across the screen. CNN viewers saw a women suffering from cerebral palsy who lived in a home along "with five disabled housemates [that was] about to be closed. Its residents [were] shipped out to state hospitals." A "thirty-year-old quadriplegic was among the hundreds of homecare residents kicked out when [California] cut off checks, forcing the homes to shut down." Other networks showed that "students from kindergarten to college" as well as hospital patients would suffer from government spending cuts. These cuts would cause an "increase in TB cases . . . people will be going without medical care."

☒ Reporting on the problems of health care was a litany of morbid catastrophes. Ignored completely was the fact that America has the world's finest health care system and that foreigners flock to America for health treatment and medical training.

PROBLEM #4:
Ignoring habeas corpus

TV reporting frequently identifies a problem and calls for a solution without ever citing evidence that a problem actually existed. Doing this violates what could be called journalism's *habeas corpus* standard: Just as in criminal law no crime can exist without the prosecution "having the body," so too in journalism, no problem should be reported to exist without having the body of evidence that the problem does exist. In 1992, this *habeas corpus* standard often was ignored as, for example:

☒ CNN's Brian Barger argued for increased federal inspection of fish—without citing one case of anyone becoming ill from fish under the current regulatory system.

☒ NBC's Betty Furness advocated laws requiring auto manufacturers to make bumpers stronger—without citing or interviewing any auto-buyer who had asked for stronger (and thus more costly) bumpers.

☒ NBC's Jeff Madrick called for tougher federal laws on workplace safety—without offering any evidence that the ostensible lack of regulations had been causing workplace accidents.

☒ Many reporters, most notably NBC's Michele Guillen, ABC's Sylvia Chase, and ABC's Paula Lyons, produced distorted statistics on auto accidents. Chase, for instance, said two thousand had died in grisly truck underride accidents in twenty years. What she did not say was that this represented fewer than two-tenths of 1 percent of all traffic fatalities.

PROBLEM #5:
Suspending inquisitiveness and skepticism

Curiously, in covering economic and business matters, TV reporters seldom wielded two of their craft's most valuable tools—skepticism and persistent (if not irritating) curiosity and inquisitiveness. In 1992, for example:

☒ When contradictory statistics and other evidence about the economy were released, reporters rarely questioned the contradiction nor tried to explain it to viewers.

☒ In the many reports on airline fare wars, TV journalists seldom asked "Why?" As a result, missing from the coverage was a discussion of the economic forces that had prompted airlines to slash fares or of the fierce competition ignited by airline deregulation.

☒ In covering Third World demands for huge sums of extra aid from the West, TV reporters never asked how Third World countries would spend the billions of extra aid or how those countries already had spent the billions in aid received in the past decades.

☒ In covering regulatory matters, TV reporters sought no evidence to support their points. Stories implicitly calling for new regulations thus contained no examples of successes of earlier regulations. Nor did TV reporters seem to look for examples of the effects of deregulation. Had reporters sought them, they could have told viewers about deregulation successes in trucking, telecommunications, and air travel.

☒ Reporters frequently ignored facts and other data that contradicted an argument they were making. In doing this, they resisted a basic journalistic instinct to grow cautious and inquisitive when encountering contradictions. A segment by NBC's Jeff Madrick making a case for more regulation, for instance, discovered that Michigan's strict enforcement of tough workplace regulations had not prevented a determined violator from continuing to violate the law. This should have prompted Madrick to question whether regulations were really the answer to problems like workplace safety. It didn't, and he didn't. Similarly CNN's Carl Rochelle, in a segment on how cable TV overcharged customers, ignored the relevance of the fact (which he reported) that the number of cable subscribers had soared after deregulation. This should have led Rochelle to ask how an industry, that allegedly was serving customers poorly, could see such a jump in the number of its customers.

PROBLEM #6:
Absence of balance

In most of the TV reporting on economics and business, the legions advocating a government-dominated economy are not balanced by free enterprise spokesmen and women. In 1992, for example:

⊠ In the first week of the Rio environmental conference's TV coverage, the network newscasts interviewed thirty environmental experts who were not government officials. Of these, twenty-eight represented environmental groups advocating increased government action; only two suggested nongovernment alternatives.

⊠ Coverage of the product liability issue presented only those opposed to a bill which would limit damages that a court could award a plaintiff. Missing from TV were those who sought the new limits because they had suffered under the existing system. Viewers thus heard nothing from workers who had lost their jobs, businessmen who had closed their plants, and city officials who had seen their tax base shrink because of huge product liability costs. Balance would have required that those seeking no limits on product liability awards because they claimed to be victims of flawed products be offset by those claiming to be victims of a draconian and costly product liability regime.

⊠ In reporting on studies done by such liberal groups as the Children's Defense Fund and the Economic Policy Institute, reporters rarely went to free market think tanks, such as the Competitive Enterprise Institute, the Cato Institute, or Citizens for a Sound Economy, for an opposing analysis.

⊠ In reports on government spending programs, such as those affected by California's budget crisis, reporters typically would go to recipients of government benefits who would lament the possible loss of benefits. Reporters did not interview taxpayers for their view of the programs, nor did they speak of the cumulative effect that spending programs have on the economy.

PROBLEM #7:
Tilting credibility

Though seemingly balanced, some TV reports, in fact, are tilted because one side of an argument is presented more credibly to viewers than the other side. One way of stacking the odds is to pit an official against an "expert." Since experts are presumed to be well-informed neutral observers, they have much higher credibility with viewers than do politicians or officials who are presumedly advancing some self-serving agenda. Thus pairing a "consumer expert" with a "Bush administration official" resulted not in giving equal weight to both sides but in an advantage to the expert. Genuine balance requires pairing not merely liberal against conservative, Democrat against Republican, or critic against the critic's target, but pairing those whom the viewer regards as equally credible. In 1992, for example:

☒ In coverage from the Rio Summit, viewers saw and heard sharp criticisms of America from network reporters, foreigners, and expert Talking Heads. The only statements defending America's actions came from U.S. officials, mainly Environmental Protection Agency chief William Reilly. As a government official, his defense of American policy could not have been as credible to viewers as was the critique of America by the phalanx of ostensibly neutral experts.

☒ CBS's Hattie Kauffman, reporting on product liability, paired Bush administration officials against consumers. Said Kauffman: "Consumer advocates say that the administration wants to protect businesses, not the consumer." Kauffman's opposing Talking Heads were Commerce Secretary Barbara Franklin versus consumer "advocate" Linda Lipsen of Consumers Union and "victim" Jana Rousonno, who had a leaky breast implant.

☒ NBC's Robert Bazell, reporting on a Minnesota state-run health system, paired system-critic Arne Carlson, the state's governor, against a series of nonpoliticians who backed the health system—a man with cancer but no insurance, a family unable to afford to go to doctors because it only had hospitalization insurance, and a family with children and no insurance.

⊠ In what later became the discredited "Dateline NBC" story about side-impact crashes and GM trucks, reporter Michele Gillen interviewed many "experts" who in fact were affiliated with trial lawyers' groups. Such groups gain from attacks on the auto makers. Not only did Gillen not advise viewers of the "experts" link to the trial lawyers, she paired their interview with that of a GM official. Viewers, of course, would discount much of a GM employee's argument as being obviously self-serving.

Problem #8:
Covering the political horserace

TV reports of legislative efforts to deal with economic issues frequently ignored the economic side of the matter. Instead, the reports focused on the political horserace. In 1992, for example:

⊠ CBS's Paula Zahn, in reporting a National Urban League proposal for a Marshall Plan for the cities, discussed only its political and budgetary aspects. Of an Urban League official she asked: "How much do you figure your plan would cost, if you got everything you wanted?" "With our current deficit, how do you propose we come up with $50 billion a year?" "When you say we 'need to look at areas of taxes' what do you mean by that?" "But you're also aware of what you're fighting when it comes to the voters and their reaction to a proposed tax hike." "And do you think that those people would be willing to buy into a tax hike if that's what it takes to bring this program into fruition?" She not only ignored the proposal's economic facets, but never even asked how such a Marshall Plan would revive America's inner cities.

⊠ In covering congressional consideration of the proposed Balanced Budget Amendment, TV reporters focused almost entirely on the political angle. They asked which party's bill would win, which party would gain electoral advantage, and so on. Ignored was the substance of the matter: how such an amendment could cut the federal deficit. Almost all of the experts interviewed were politicians or political pundits; no economists were in the lineup.

⊠ ABC's lengthy profiles of Clinton's incoming economic team were conducted mainly in political terms, asking, for instance, whether Congress would go along with Clinton's economic proposals. There was little discussion of the economic context or merit of the proposals.

PROBLEM #9:
Ignoring the concept of trade-offs

Few notions are as central to understanding the advantages of a free market as trade-offs: that every economic action imposes some price or cost, whether direct or indirect, visible or hidden. This is the profundity of Milton Friedman's legendary "no free lunch" quip. In almost all instances, the free market has demonstrated an ability vastly superior to that of government to balance the trade-offs. Yet TV reporting, with the sole exception of the damage to economic growth inflicted by environmental regulations, has ignored trade-offs. In 1992, for example:

⊠ In covering the heated debate over the family leave bill, reporters did not explain the trade-off between the bill's promised benefit and its cost to the economy. The viewer was not told, for instance, that job creation could be retarded because the bill could hurt the small businesses that create almost all new jobs.

⊠ In covering the Americans with Disabilities Act, reporters did not explain to viewers how compliance with the law could raise the cost of business operations and thus probably reduce American competitiveness and job creation.

⊠   In covering a process that irradiated strawberries, no mention was made that by extending strawberry shelf life, costs to the consumer would be reduced.

PROBLEM #10:
The parade of factoids

TV newscasts devoted considerable time to factoids—tidbits of data and statistics. Seldom are the factoids placed in context. Typically they seem to substitute for reporting and analysis, as if stringing together a requisite number of facts automatically produces a journalistic story. Yet what transforms data into a story is the journalist's ability to provide contexts, to weave together rather than string together facts.

Typifying TV's 1992 factoid reporting was its coverage of the R. H. Macy & Company bankruptcy filing early in the year. While all networks reported on the hard times afflicting the famous retailer, what they gave viewers was almost exclusively unconnected tidbits—Macy's size, its sales volume, its debt, and that its problems, in part, were due to the recession and management mistakes.

Missing from the reporting was the "why" and "how" which not only would have told viewers much more about the Macy's situation, but would have taught something about how the American economy functions. Nothing was said, for example, about how the bankruptcy procedure might salvage Macy's or about other Macy's options. Almost nothing was explained about the "why"—the economic principles and market dynamics that had pushed Macy's and other old-line department stores to the brink of disaster while allowing an entirely new cast of stores (the Bombay Company, the Gap, the Limited, Nordstroms, Wal-Mart, the rejuvenated Woolworths, and others) to thrive.

AND NOW ... THE YEAR'S WORST AND BEST

All or some of TV's ten problems appeared in almost all economic and business stories to a varying extent and in a varying degree. Those in which the extent and degree were extreme were the year's worst stories and greatly misled viewers. Those in which they were slight were the year's best stories and most rewarding to the viewers.

To select the best and worst stories of 1992, the Free Enterprise and Media Institute assembled a jury of respected free market economists: Bruce Bartlett of the Cato Institute, Christopher Frenze of the Joint Economic Committee of Congress, Edward Hudgins of the Joint Economic Committee of Congress, Marvin Kosters of the American Enterprise Institute, and Stephen Moore of the Cato Institute. These jurors viewed a selection of twenty news segments that had been nominated by the staff of the Free Enterprise and Media Institute.

The jurors' collective verdict:

The year's worst story was the NBC "Nightly News" February 7 report by Keith Morrison distorting the economic record of the 1980s. The year's best was the ABC "20/20" report by John Stossel astutely describing for viewers how the marketplace's competitive forces could solve even problems of personnel management.

ENTERTAINMENT'S POWERFUL PUNCH

In teaching TV viewers about America's economy, 1992's prime-time entertainment packed a powerful punch. Entertainment's ability to do so is beyond question. Explains George Gerbner, former dean of the University of Pennsylvania's Annenberg School of Communications and a leading authority on the social impact of television: "If you can write a nation's stories, you needn't worry about who makes its laws. Today television tells most of the stories to most of the people most of the time."[4]

In entertainment TV's stories, businessmen filled a rogues' gallery. In the 1992's dramas and sitcoms, viewers saw car dealers selling stolen cars, bankers robbing banks and murdering, hotel owners killing, oil company executives running drugs and murdering, jewelry store owners murdering, and so forth. Even in a series as creative and cute as "Dinosaurs," explicit economics lessons depicted company bosses callously eating an endangered species, destroying a redwood forest, and quashing a marvelous technological breakthrough because it could have hurt profits.

Though businesspersons were nearly invisible on TV newscasts, they overpopulated TV entertainment's underworld. They comprised 24 percent of all main characters on entertainment TV, though making up (according to the U.S. Census) a smaller share of the population. And they were 43 percent of entertainment TV's criminals in 1992. Yet in the real world, businessmen commit a tiny percentage of crimes.

Entertainment TV's hostility to businesspersons and free market economic concepts, of course, is not new. Pioneering studies discovering this were conducted a decade ago by S. Robert Lichter, Stanley Rothman, and Linda S. Lichter. More recently, Robert Lichter writes in his important book, *Watching America: What Television Tells Us About Our Lives*: "Big business has become television's favorite villain . . . [A] majority of the CEO's portrayed on prime time committed felonies. Businessmen now make up the largest group of murderers on TV apart from gangsters; in TV's executive suite, crime is the bottom line."[5]

The Free Enterprise and Media Institute's survey of 1992 network entertainment TV finds that nothing has improved since Lichter and Rothman's earliest studies. In total, in 1992, businesspersons accounted for sixty-six of the 154 criminals in the twelve sample weeks analyzed. Businessmen were more than four times more likely to be criminals than members of other professions. One in four business characters committed a crime, compared to one in seventeen for characters of all other occupations.

Although businessmen accounted for 24 percent of all characters, they committed 36 percent of the murders and 43 percent of other crimes like drug trafficking, fraud, and robbery.

Not only did entertainment TV criminalize businesspersons in 1992, it trivialized them. In the considerable time that they were on camera, businesses, bosses, and other executives rarely were depicted as they function in the real world—agonizing over competing interests, making payrolls, creating jobs, trying to be inventive, or even making money. Instead, TV entertainment told viewers that:

> If your business has financial problems, you solve them with murder ("Jake and the Fatman").
>
> If you need money for a new business (like a pizza parlor), you head for Las Vegas and gamble ("Hearts Are Wild").
>
> If you try to save money for the future, you are silly ("Civil Wars").
>
> If you have customers, you cheat them ("Vinnie & Bobby," "L.A. Law," "Married With Children").
>
> If you are a banker, you rob banks ("Matlock").
>
> If you run a company, you destroy the forests ("Dinosaurs") or dump toxic wastes into a landfill ("Parker Kane," "Nightmare Cafe").
>
> If you start out as a respected businessman, you become a drug dealer ("Quantum Leap").
>
> If you own a fertilizer company, you manufacture illegal chemical weapons and then attempt to poison a reporter who has found you out ("Quantum Leap").
>
> If you are a car dealer, you front for car thieves ("Tequila and Bonetti").
>
> If you run a truck repair shop, you sell stolen trucks ("In the Heat of the Night").
>
> If you manage a film studio, you distribute pornography ("Lady Boss").
>
> If you are a real estate developer, you bribe city officials, break the arm of an employee, and spit in a cop's face ("Picket Fences").

If you are a corporate executive, you beat your wife ("The Commish").

If you own a store, you change the expiration dates on the dairy products that you sell ("The Simpsons").

If you own a construction company, you defraud pensioners and young people ("Murder She Wrote").

TV Also Gets it Right—Sometimes

Teaching Americans how their economy functions should not be difficult for TV. Just how easy it could be was demonstrated occasionally by some reporters and writers in 1992.

ABC's "World News Tonight" January 30, for example, highlighted the private sector's ability to respond to society's problems. Reporter Kathleen Delaski told viewers how some 120 insurance companies were finding ways to help terminally ill patients by allowing them to cash in their life insurance policies before they died.

A similar private sector response was portrayed in the networks' stories on the efforts by a hundred large corporations to fund day care centers for their employees. From the stories, viewers could learn the useful economic lessons that: (1) if government does not address a genuine need, the private sector can; and (2) private firms do this not only altruistically but in their own self-interest. Other stories explained that private firms were attempting to meet employee needs by offering flexible hours and flexible leave.

In a rare glimpse of what government intrusion can do to the economy, NBC described how California's very costly worker compensation program was chasing businesses and jobs out of the state.

Occasionally viewers received a lesson in basic economics. NBC's Irving R. Levine correctly told viewers that the typical entrepreneur raised money from his or her own savings and from family members. Levine noted too that small businesses had added great numbers of jobs to the economy. CBS's Hattie Kauffman reminded viewers of the enormous power of choice in the free enterprise system and how this unleashed the dynamics of competition. In a simple, but valid, observation she said: "Everyday at the checkout stand we cast our votes. If we want our mascara clear or wine coolers clear, that's just what the manufacturers will give us."

Viewers received the best information on economic topics when reporters personally knew something about them. In 1992, these topics were taxes and silicone breast implants. Since journalists paid taxes, journalists knew that the level and kind of taxes could affect their spending and saving behavior. As for breast implants, many journalists must surely have known women who had implants or feminist activists who insisted that women had a right to control what happened to their bodies and thus had a right to take a chance with a breast implant.

Probably because journalists had some kind of experience with these two topics, TV reporting on them in 1992 did not reflexively support government and regulation. To the contrary, the majority of the reporting was unfriendly to taxes and to more government regulations of implants. On the tax issue generally, ABC's Mike Schneider even became indignant and refused to allow a guest get away with saying that a gasoline tax would be relatively painless. It was rare to find a TV reporter so tenacious in his or her efforts to refute the claims of a critic of free enterprise.

Had TV newscasts handled other regulatory issues as they did breast implants, TV would have served Americans well by teaching them some economic basics—that well-intended regulations could have very painful consequences, that life was full of intelligent risk-taking, that striving for a risk-free society inflicted an extraordinary price, that agonizing and complicated trade-offs were inherent in all economic decisions, and that government was not necessarily the best judge of which trade-offs to make.

DOES IT MATTER?

Should Americans be concerned about what appears on TV? Does it really matter?

To both questions the answer, of course, is yes. What Americans watch on the tube is what Americans, to a significant extent, learn about life, their society, and their nation. Of this there is no dispute. Several decades of studies confirm TV's power as a teacher.

In 1972, the Surgeon General's Scientific Advisory Committee, in its report, *Television and Growing Up: The Impact of Televised Violence*, warned that TV taught violence because of the considerable evidence "of a causal relation between viewing violence on television and aggressive behavior." A decade later, a study by the National Institute of Mental Health, *Television and Behavior*, concluded that television played an important role in the lives of children and adults.

In 1985, the American Psychological Association declared that television violence could cause aggressive behavior.[6] And says psychologist John Condry: there is a "psychological mechanism that permits the information seen on television to affect the viewers actions, thoughts, and beliefs in and about the world of reality."[7]

This "psychological mechanism" operates in entertainment as well as in newscasts and other explicitly informative programming. Writes George Gerbner: "Even when people recognize that the material they are viewing is fictional, its messages and images gradually shape expectations and beliefs about the real world."[8] Nodding agreement is the American Civil Liberties Union's executive director Ira Glasser. Writing in *TV as a Social Issue*, he said: "The perception of what is real, particularly concerning social issues, is determined more and more by what people see on television—and not only on news shows."[9]

Much of the concern about TV as a teacher has focused on fears that TV contributes to violence and to unflattering and even dangerous stereotypes of women, minorities, the elderly, and gays. Stated C. Clark: "Mass media encourage respect for social groups by showing them in roles that are sympathetic and positive . . . Conversely, respect is denied when social groups are portrayed in stereotyped or negatively valued roles."[10]

When sociologists and other experts describe how such "stereotyped" and "negatively valued roles" are imparted by TV, they talk about what some have called the "drip model." The American Psychological Association has described this as "a process of subtle and gradual incorporation of frequent and repeated messages . . . The more television individuals watch, the more they believe and accept its messages about society." Added the Task Force on Television and Society: "People's worldviews are shaped by a gradual, cumulative process of multiple exposures to frequent messages."[11]

Condry agrees, writing: "The 'facts' of the world of television tend to 'creep into' the attitude and value systems of those who are heavy consumers of it, and it does this in a quiet, insidious manner. Most heavy viewers are not aware that their attitudes and values have been influenced."[12] The average American is exposed to this "quiet, insidious manner" for the four hours every day that he or she watches TV—or the seven hours every day that TV flickers in the average household.

The plethora of scholarly studies about TV as teacher prompts a troublesome conclusion:

If TV can influence viewers on racism, sexism, and attitudes towards the elderly and gays, then TV certainly can influence what viewers know about their economic system, about businesses and businesspersons, and about the impulses, trade-offs, and other factors driving the American economy. As such, the portrayal of the free enterprise system on TV newscasts and prime-time entertainment can have consequences as grave, if not graver, for society as TV's portrayal of violence, women, gays, minorities, and the elderly.

Without great effort or difficulty, TV could remove the distortions that have transformed the American free enterprise economy into a tarantula. All TV needs do is to add balance and begin teaching viewers how their economy functions. The first step would be for TV executives to insist that stories on the economy and business answer the six fundamental questions learned by rote by every student journalist: Who? What? When? Where? Why? How?

Posing such questions in 1992 would have forced reporters to express some doubts about the alarmist claims made by environmentalists, about the accusations of cable TV price gouging, about the denunciations of airline deregulation, and about a variety of claims—that regulations were efficacious, that billions of dollars would be saved by going to a single-payer health care system, that the rich became richer at the expense of the poor and middle class in the 1980s, and that spending cuts would hurt the poor.

The second step would be for TV executives to address television's problems by posing the sixteen questions suggested in the conclusion of this book. This too would not be difficult.

These measures would prevent TV from transforming the American economic system into a tarantula. Then, beyond these measures, TV could recognize a special responsibility—to teach Americans how their economic system functions. In doing so, the networks could heed the advice of the American Psychological Association: "Our failure to use the power of television to pursue positive goals deserves at least as much attention as we give to its exploitation by purveyors of socially harmful messages."[13] Surely advancing public understanding of America's free enterprise economy is a worthy and positive goal.

NOTES

1. "A National Survey of American Economic Literacy," National Council of Economic Education, New York, N.Y., 1992, p. 6.
2. John Condry, *The Psychology of Television* (Hillsdale, N. J.: Lawrence Erlbaum Associates, 1989), pp. 121–122.
3. See appendix for methodology.
4. *Newsweek*, December 6, 1982, p. 136.
5. S. Robert Lichter, Linda S. Lichter and Stanley Rothman, *Watching America, What Television Tells Us About Our Lives* (New York: Prentice Hall Press, 1991), p. 20.
6. Althea C. Huston et al., *Big World, Small Screen: The Role of Television in American Society* (Lincoln: University of Nebraska Press, 1992), p. 2.

7. John Condry, *The Psychology of Television*, pp. 81–82.
8. Althea C. Huston et al., *Big World, Small Screen*, p. 22.
9. Ira Glasser, *Television and the Construction of Reality*; S. Oskamp, ed., *TV As a Social Issue* (Newbury Park, CA.: Sage, 1988), p. 46.
10. Althea C. Huston et al., *Big World, Small Screen*, pp. 21–22.
11. Ibid., p. 130.
12. John Condry, *The Psychology of Television*, p. 141.
13. Athea C. Huston et al., *Big World, Small Screen*, p. 5.

PART I

FOUR TYPICAL WEEKS

WHAT TV TELLS AMERICANS

CHAPTER ONE

A TYPICAL WEEK: JANUARY 25-31

423 Squandered Minutes

As January 1992 ended, TV covered those events that would shape the rest of the new year. Most compelling, predictably, was the presidential race and the heated battle for the Democratic nomination. The front runner even then, though no certain thing, was Bill Clinton. Yet the Democratic race was reported as a side-show since almost no one regarded Persian Gulf War Hero George Bush as beatable. Indeed, Bush was acting presidential this week by delivering his State of the Union address. Beyond politics, the Washington Redskins won the Superbowl, while the Mike Tyson and Jeffery Dahmer trials began. Overseas, round three of the Middle East Peace Talks got underway in Moscow.

As TV informed Americans about these events, it was also telling them about happenings in their economy—the recession, business, world economic developments. In total, during this last week of January, the three network morning programs plus the ABC, CBS, CNN, and NBC evening newscasts broadcast 423 minutes on economic matters, accounting for 19.7 percent of all news.

This coverage was Americans' major source of information of

how their free enterprise system worked. What specifically did Americans learn? What facts, accurate and flawed, were they given? What aggregate message was broadcast? How much was their economic understanding advanced?

A GARNISH OF STATISTICS

As in every week, economic reporting at the end of January was a mix of statistics, hard news, consumer advice, profiles, and analysis.

A staple of this reporting was the steady trickle of statistics released by government agencies and private groups. These are reported almost as a ritual, much as restaurants at one time plopped parsley on every plate. No one knew what to do with the green sprig. Almost no one ate it, yet restaurants dared not omit it.

So it has been with reporting routine economic statistics. Apparently an essential garnish, unexplained and often unrelated economic data are dolloped into newscasts.

This week such data told viewers that the gross domestic product barely increased, that consumers were still pessimistic, that personal income moved up only slightly, that the index of leading indicators fell, that sales of new homes were way off, that a record 24.5 million Americans received food stamps in December, that unemployment climbed again, that jobless claims rose 24,000 from the previous week, that orders for durable goods in December fell 5 percent, that two thousand Californians lined up for a job fair, that layoffs were spreading, and that the Big Three auto makers reported $7 billion in losses and were planning to shut ten assembly plants.

In the aggregate, these statistics painted an economy in trouble. The problem was that the statistics never were presented in aggregate and never were pulled together for a composite economic picture. They were reported when released—housing sales on Monday, GDP figures on Wednesday, personal income figures on Thursday, and leading economic indicator figures on Friday.

To confuse the viewer even more, when rosy statistics (such as December's 0.9 percent climb in existing home sales) were reported along with the gloom, viewers were not told whether the conflicting numbers could or should be reconciled. Nor were viewers told how to reconcile December 1991's climb in home sales with the CBS "Evening News" report that 1991 was a grim year for housing. Similarly, when Federal Reserve Board Chairman Alan Greenspan, interviewed on ABC "Good Morning America" and CBS "This Morning" January 30, said that the economy might improve, no commentator sought to explain Greenspan's cheery views in light of the dreadful news.

The week's statistics thus were nothing but a stream of disjointed data left to the viewer to connect.

THE BIG STORIES

Every week has its big economic stories. This week they were George Bush's tax proposals in his State of the Union Address, the mounting trade tensions between Washington and Tokyo, and the impending bankruptcy of venerable retailer R.H. Macy & Company.

State of the Union

TV understandably gave much attention to Bush's State of the Union, before and after the January 28 speech. From network coverage viewers learned that:

1. Bush, after having spent two months building expectations for the speech, was trying to lower them.
2. Bush had recruited Reagan speechwriter Peggy Noonan to help with the speech.
3. Bush could not propose dramatic tax cuts because, it was said, they would break the 1990 budget agreement and scare the financial markets.

4. Some 69 percent of Americans, according to an ABC News poll, did not think the speech's economic proposals went far enough.
5. Most of Bush's proposals already had been rejected by Congress.
6. Many of Bush's proposals, such as changing the income tax withholding tables so that workers would have less deducted from their paychecks but less refunded later, were mere gimmicks.
7. Democrats in Congress and on the presidential primary trail were rejecting the Bush proposals as "more trickle down economics."

While most of this information was accurate, it was dribbled out to viewers in such snippets and left so unexplained that it surely failed to give viewers much understanding of the economy. When ABC's Mike Schneider and Sheilah Kast, for instance, reported on the poll finding that 69 percent of Americans thought Bush had not gone far enough in attacking the recession, they did not even attempt to give viewers answers for the obvious journalistic question: "What had he failed to go far enough with—spending cuts and tax cuts, or certain spending increases?"

Also unexplained was why tax cuts made financial markets nervous. The most that reporters did was to suggest that it had something to do with the deficit and interest rates.

Most of the reporting focused on the political aspects of the speech. This was balanced. On NBC "Today" January 29, host Katie Couric paired a university administrator who was not a Bush supporter with a legal secretary who was. Charles Bierbauer, in his CNN "World News" story January 29, included soundbites from both Republican political consultant Ed Rollins and Democratic political consultant Robert Squier.

But completely missing from the coverage, except for CBS, was what economists thought of the Bush speech. Even when delving deeper than the political level, reporters rarely talked to those who could have taught viewers something about the economy. Example: NBC's Mike Jensen, in his NBC "Nightly News" report January 29, did not talk to economists but took the easy, man-in-the street approach; he asked a home buyer and a home builder what they thought of Bush's call for a tax credit for first time home buyers; and for reactions to the withholding reform proposal, Jensen talked to literally two people on the street.

Better served were viewers of CBS. "Evening News" reporter Ray Brady interviewed economists David Jones, Lacy Hunt, and Nancy Lazar on January 28. Although Brady worried that tax cuts would increase the deficit, he at least gave viewers a statistic rarely heard from newscasts: "The problem: Since Mr. Bush's election in 1988, government spending has soared, pushing the federal deficit even higher." While viewers might have wondered why Brady did not suggest cuts in spending, since it had been tagged as the problem, at least they were given the facts. Lazar, meanwhile, pointed out that this was the first recession in decades in which taxes were actually going up. She applauded Bush's tax cuts.

Even better served were viewers of CBS "This Morning." Before and after the speech, cohost Harry Smith interviewed Martin Feldstein, former chairman of Reagan's Council of Economic Advisers, and Charles Schultz, former chairman of Carter's Council of Economic Advisers. From them viewers at least heard a discussion of some economic principles related to Bush's proposals.

AMERICA V. JAPAN

There were at least nine stories on the deterioration of American-Japanese trade ties in the wake of George Bush's disastrous visit to Tokyo—five on ABC, two on NBC, and one each on CNN and CBS. From these stories, American viewers learned that:

1. Japanese officials, according to ABC, were bashing American workers and ridiculing American managers as inferior, while American and Japanese officials and lawmakers were exchanging insults.
2. Japanese Prime Minister Kiichi Miyazawa, reported CBS,

assured the U.S. that he really did promise Bush that Japan would buy more American-made parts for cars.

3. "Buy American" campaigns, according to NBC and ABC, were sprouting across the U.S. As examples, the networks reported that Los Angeles County was canceling its contract to buy Japanese-made trains, a Cleveland businessman was offering cash to anyone buying American cars, a Cincinnati woman had demolished a Toyota auto, and angry workers at America's factories were forcing foreign-made cars to remote spaces in parking lots.

4. Some American businessmen had succeeded in Japan, reported ABC, such as a Colorado maker of artificial lungs and a Colorado manufacturer of children's furniture.

5. Japanese investors, according to CNN, were buying high-profile American properties, like a Florida racetrack, Hollywood film companies, and more than 120 golf courses.

In several of the reports, Talking Head experts expanded viewer understanding of the issue. Both ABC and NBC pointed out problems with "Buy American" campaigns; some seemingly Japanese products, noted reporters, were made in America while some seemingly American goods (like some John Deere equipment) were made in Japan. NBC, meanwhile, interviewed chief U.S. trade negotiator Carla Hills who warned that Japan-bashing in America did not help her efforts to open more Japanese markets to American goods.

In aggregate, what viewers learned was that there was a trade problem between America and Japan, that Japanese officials and businessmen were saying nasty things about Americans, that "Buy American" campaigns were not all good, and that some Americans were succeeding in Japan.

The trouble with this composite message was that despite the extensive coverage of the issue, little was said about the cause of the trade tensions: Tokyo's determination to keep its markets closed to American goods. Only NBC's interview with Carla Hills obliquely touched this when she stressed that she was trying to open markets in Japan and that this would benefit both American and Japanese economies. And nothing was said by reporters about the real victims of Japanese trade barriers and Japan's closed economy: the long-deprived Japanese consumers who suffer one of the industrial world's lowest living standards.

Troubling too was the coverage of the "Buy American" campaign—the strong implication that it was difficult to determine what precisely was American. No Talking Head challenged the notion that "Buy American" in itself might be flawed and could hurt the American economy. In fact, NBC's Diana Koricke on "Nightly News" January 25 even suggested, incorrectly, that a "Buy American" campaign could rev up the faltering American economy. She would have given viewers more useful information had she said:

"Buying American when it's not the best product at the best price could send the wrong message to American companies. Economists say it's only when American consumers demand the best that American companies remain competitive."

On the matter of Japanese investment in America, the only counterpoint CNN made to the alarmist theme that Japan was buying up America was that British investors actually owned more of America than did Japanese. But this left unchallenged the implication that Americans should be troubled by foreign purchases of American assets. CNN's John Zarella gave viewers no chance to hear the offsetting view, held by almost all economists, that foreign investment creates jobs for Americans. Zarella could have said:

"Most economists argue that investment in the American economy, whether by foreigners or Americans, creates jobs here at home."

At the end of the week, network TV news executives thus should have been troubled that their coverage of American-Japanese trade failed to give viewers much information that they could use to understand or form judgments on that important issue. As a conveyer of data and isolated facts, the networks had succeeded; as a conveyer of news in a useful context and as an educator, the networks had failed.

Macy's in Trouble

The networks succeeded no better in covering the R. H. Macy & Company's impending bankruptcy. From the nine stories on the subject (five on ABC and two each on CBS and NBC), viewers learned that:

1. Macy's, according to ABC "World News Tonight," was in trouble because it was a triple victim: of the recession, of a leveraged buy-out ("Like many American companies, [Macy's is] too heavily in debt"), and of the trend of Americans to shop at smaller malls.
2. Macy's, according to NBC "Today," was $4 billion in debt ($3.5 billion according to ABC), was out of cash and out of merchandise, and had overextended itself by buying several retail chains.
3. Macy's was unlikely to be rescued by Lawrence Tisch.
4. Macy's troubles were a personal tragedy for the store's employees.
5. Every major New York City department store open at the start of the recession, according to ABC "World News Tonight," had closed or sought bankruptcy.
6. Macy's, according to CBS's Ray Brady on the "Evening News," was 134 years old, world famous, had more than 250 stores and $7 billion in sales, and was featured in the movie *Miracle on 34th Street*.
7. Macy's core problems, according to ABC "Good Morning America," were poor management, tough competition, failure to adapt quickly to changing tastes, and very high debt.
8. Macy's stores would remain open despite the bankruptcy.

The coverage of Macy's problems was extensive, probably because the retailer for a century had epitomized the best of American merchandizing. Yet for all of the TV time devoted to Macy's, viewers learned little beyond factoids—Macy's size, its sales volume, its debt—and that its problems, in part, had been due to the recession and management mistakes.

The viewer was told nothing about how the bankruptcy procedure might salvage Macy's or about other options that Macy's had. The viewer thus ended the week knowing a few extra random facts about Macy's, but (with one exception) little more about the economic principles and market dynamics that could push a business—even as large and venerable as Macy's—to bankruptcy and then allow that business to recover.

Typical of the factoid reporting was Ray Brady's January 27 commentary. CBS Anchor Dan Rather, in his introduction, said that Macy's was "the newest example of a retailer gone wrong." This was a promising opening; it offered the viewer some analysis of what was "going wrong" at American retailers. Yet Rather's opening was ignored by Brady in his long segment; he explained neither what had gone wrong at Macy's nor how it had done so. Brady contributed nothing to viewer understanding of how retailing's intense competitiveness had left little room for mistakes while, at the same time, giving American consumers a vast selection at low prices. He would have added to viewer understanding had he said:

> **"In a healthy economy the same companies do not stay on top forever. If they did, it would be a sign of the economy's weakness, not strength."**

The notable exception to the uninformative reporting was ABC's "Good Morning America" January 28 segment. It explicitly tried to expand viewer understanding of economics. It began with reporter Nancy Snyderman interviewing Roger Brinner of DRI\McGraw Hill. From Brinner the viewer heard that a business's fate often was determined by the skill of its managers and by the nature of its competition. Brinner explained that Macy's for too long had stuck with what he called the old department store model which was being replaced by shopping malls. Brinner added that Macy's managers had also taken on too much debt.

And from "Good Morning America" Tyler Mathisen, the show's money editor who is also an editor for *Money Magazine*, viewers heard that though Macy's and other big stores were in trouble, small retailers were doing fine.

This ABC segment taught viewers something about free enterprise; namely, that the ever-shifting, dynamic market constantly imposes new challenges on established businesses; competition cannot be ignored by even the biggest business; good management is a key ingredient of success; and a huge size is not necessarily an asset.

Bankruptcy also was in the news this week because of Trans World Airlines Inc.'s troubles. But as with the Macy's reporting, the TWA stories taught viewers very little. Beyond conveying the useful information to American travellers that TWA would continue flying while under bankruptcy protection, the message was mainly that the carrier was the victim of airline deregulation and of the complicated junk bonds financing schemes used by Carl Icahn to buy TWA some years earlier.

The only two explicit economic points made by the TWA coverage, moreover, were questionable. In the first, CNN reporter Terry Keenan said that "Icahn recouped his $400 million investment, but TWA was left with billions in costly junk bonds." This implied strongly that junk bonds literally were junk. In fact, despite their name, junk bonds have been a sound investment.

The second questionable point was made when CBS's Rita Braver on "Evening News" said that TWA was "brought down by deregulation, recession and huge corporate debts." Here she depicted deregulation as a phenomenon from which only problems had sprung. While airline deregulation indeed has created some problems, it also has cut travel costs, made air travel affordable for millions of Americans, and improved airline service at almost every American city and town. This CBS did not mention.

TV'S PORTRAIT OF BUSINESSES AND BUSINESSPERSONS

Every week TV paints a picture of business, corporations, executives, and entrepreneurs. This week the networks aired nineteen such stories (plus those on the Macy's and TWA bankruptcies). Of the nineteen stories, twelve depicted failures or deplorable excesses in the free enterprise system.

TV viewers learned that:

1. GMAC Mortgage Company overcharged 365,000 borrowers.
2. Dow Corning Wright, according to ABC "World News Tonight" and NBC "Today," was balking at releasing documents on the safety of its silicone breast implants.
3. Bethlehem Steel continued to lose money and was laying off 6,500 workers.
4. Unscrupulous home repair contractors, according to NBC "Nightly News," were bilking many Americans. As examples, reporter Noah Nelson told viewers about a tin man and a finance company that had coaxed Christine and Robert Hill to pay for their home repairs by taking out a $21,000 mortgage which they could ill afford. The message from NBC was that such fraud thrived in states lacking tough home repair industry regulations.
5. Telephone scams, according to CBS "This Morning," were selling inferior, fake, or nonexistent merchandise.
6. Art galleries, according to CBS "Evening News" and NBC "Nightly News," had sold at least 88,000 counterfeit prints by claiming that they had been done by Picasso.
7. Those whom NBC "Nightly News" labelled "Merchants of Greed," the "biggest financial crooks of their time" who "traded Wall Street for prison cells," were doing relatively well after leaving prison.
8. An unidentified congressional researcher asserted that top American executives were paid fifty-three times more than workers.

9. A new book, *Crazy Bosses*, argued that craziness was what it might take to succeed in business.

The aggregate message of these stories was: the American economic system fostered swindlers, failing businesses, galleries that sold fake art, companies that overcharged, and executives who either ended up in jail, were vastly overpaid, or were crazy. As a whole, this picture greatly distorted the American economy. In truth, almost all American businesses are honest and contribute enormously to the nation's standard and quality of living, but this assertion would surprise anyone whose knowledge of the business world has come mainly from TV.

Networks need not distort how the economy functions when they report economic problems. Take the NBC segment on home repair horrors. Alerting consumers to potential fraud was good and useful TV, as was the advice offered by reporter Noah Nelson that homeowners should get references before hiring repair firms and get legal help for problems. But it would have been equally useful for Nelson to add, without diminishing his report's newsworthiness or drama:

"Fortunately, the tin man who bilked his customers was not typical. Most tin men are honest. And home repair is one of America's largest industries, creating tens of thousands of jobs and offering upwardly mobile entrepreneurial opportunities to minorities and those with limited schooling."

Offsetting somewhat the week's insistently negative picture of American business were a half-dozen upbeat stories, three on NBC. The January 29 "Today" interviewed the gadget guru, a regular guest on the show who alerted viewers to potentially useful new gadgets. The next day, the "Nightly News" profiled Pam Resch of San Jose, California, who had been fined for giving piano concerts in her home. Sympathetically portraying Resch, NBC strongly implied that government imposed silly regulations on business activity. The following morning, "Today" gave viewers a peek at an entrepreneurial Connecticut couple. Similarly upbeat was CBS's

"This Morning" January 28 segment on why the "Home Shopping Club" was one of cable TV's biggest successes.

The week's lone positive TV image of a company or industry was ABC's "World News Tonight" January 30 report on how some 120 insurance companies were finding ways to help money-strapped terminally ill patients by allowing them to cash in their life insurance policies before they died.

FIFTEEN STORIES THAT DON'T ADD UP

Every week, TV tells Americans something specifically about how their economy functions. This week, in fifteen separate items, Americans learned that:

1. Housing sales were up because the Federal Reserve Board lowered interest rates.
2. Corporate profits were a good barometer of how the economy was doing.
3. December's 5 percent fall in durable goods orders could mean more layoffs or no new hiring.
4. The world economy was increasingly integrated.
5. A "Buy American" campaign could boost the economy.
6. Big federal deficits could limit George Bush's tax-cutting options.
7. Timidity by banks in making loans was one cause of the sluggish economy.
8. The recession was not stopping Americans from buying soft drinks.
9. The national debt was leading to higher taxes and higher mortgage rates and preventing many federal programs from being funded.
10. An expanding service sector was unhealthy for the economy.
11. The recession was creating a new class of workers: temporary executives.
12. One reason Japan was beating America economically was

that the Japanese were introducing new products every six months, even though the old products were still in demand.

13. Plunging factory orders and hesitant consumer spending were a chicken-and-egg situation; economists were not sure which would come first, yet reversing both was needed to trigger economic growth.

14. One way for realtors to sell houses in the grim California market was to advertise on TV.

15. America's lackluster economy in part was caused by German and Japanese government policies.

Some of these were useful facts that could have expanded Americans' knowledge—particularly that the world economy was increasingly integrated, that there was a demand for temporary executives, that there was a link between durable goods orders and job creation and bank lending. The trouble was that much of the presentation of these facts consisted of questionable accuracy, logical inconsistency, and flawed interpretation, while other data were empty factoids delivered without interpretive context. Taken together, the fifteen stories did not add up to a useful or even reliable economics lesson for viewers.

Some reporting was just silly, such as ABC's "Good Morning America" kicker to its January 28 economic issues roundup. Reporter Richard Davies said that "in spite of the recession, Americans continue to buy more soft drinks. Coke is gaining market share." The first problem was the *non sequitur*. A gain by Coke was no evidence that the soft drink industry was gaining sales; Coke's performance might have been atypical for the industry.

The second problem was Davies' failure to indicate what he meant by "in spite of the recession." This implied that it somehow was strange that soft drinks would gain in a recession. Perhaps it was; more likely it was not strange at all. Soft drinks typically might gain because a recession could prompt Americans to dine and entertain at home more. Then again, soft drinks typically might not gain in a recession. Whatever the case, just a short phrase by Davies about why soft drinks might do well in a recession would have transformed the remark about Coke from an empty statement into one conveying some knowledge about the economy.

GOVERNMENT IS THE ANSWER

At least sixteen of the week's stories dealt directly with the federal government's role in the economy—through taxation, regulation, or spending. Almost every one of these stories took as its premise that when the marketplace created problems only the government had the answer. Rarely were possible nongovernment solutions mentioned.

ABC "Good Morning America," for instance, discussed how budget cuts proposed by the Bush administration would hurt the needy. To make its point, ABC interviewed senior citizens who, if programs were cut, no longer would be visited by federally subsidized nurses; ABC also photographed Washington, D.C., housing projects that would lose federal subsidies. Throughout the segment, ABC reporter Sheilah Kast gave no hint of any alternative to federal help.

Yet without diluting the drama or impact of her story, Kast could have expanded viewer understanding had she said:

"While budget cuts may cause some pain in the short run, some economists say that federal subsidies create their own problems by encouraging the poor to depend on them permanently. And while some housing projects are in trouble, others in Washington have improved dramatically when their tenants took over management control from federal bureaucrats."

One of the week's two stories on the federal deficit was aired by CNN "World News." David French started his report by asking the right question: "How did it happen" that the deficit got so high? Yet the three-minute segment never tried to answer this. Instead,

French used considerable time to make what surely was the obvious point—that the projected $399 billion federal deficit for the year was much larger than the $1 billion price tag on Donald Trump's Taj Mahal casino or the $2.1 billion cost of the space shuttle. This silly comparison added nothing to viewer knowledge of the deficit or understanding of how it had mushroomed.

Four stories in the week, all on ABC, specifically addressed taxes. One short item explained that Maine was beginning to tax Girl Scout cookies. A second item looked at the Bush administration proposal to give each family an additional $500 tax deduction per child. In this story, reporter Sheilah Kast used, without comment, very controversial and questionable statistics about who would benefit from the tax cut and offered viewers only Talking Heads opposing the measure. As bad, Kast ignored the key economic question of the proposal: whether the Bush administration was right when it argued that American families were overtaxed.

Kast's point would have been more useful to viewers had she said:

> **"Bush claims that the value of the dependent deduction has decreased over the years and that families with children thus are overtaxed. To correct this, he wants to add $500 to the child deduction. Critics say that this would benefit the rich more than the poor. But White House supporters have their own statistics to show that even with the new deduction, wealthy Americans would continue to pay an increasing share of the nation's taxes."**

ABC gave much better treatment to the third and fourth tax stories of the week. The third story on taxes was the look of "World News Tonight" at the mounting pressure in Congress to repeal the 10 percent "luxury" tax on yachts. Reporter Steve Shepard told viewers that public outrage and protests about the tax had soared as the tax pushed the American boating industry into a tailspin. His main message was that the tax had not worked as planned. Bush Chief of Staff Sam Skinner explained to viewers that the tax had been designed to raise revenues, but instead had thrown taxpaying shipyard workers out of their jobs and caused the government to lose revenue.

In the week's fourth tax story, "Good Morning America" on two successive days analyzed George Bush's order that withholding tables be revised to reduce the amount of income taxes withheld from paychecks. The lengthy ABC report delivered considerable information and solidly educated the viewer. For one thing, *Money Magazine* editor Tyler Mathisen emphasized that the Bush idea was not a tax cut because the increased weekly pay checks ultimately would be offset by the reduced refunds that taxpayers would get from the IRS. For another, while acknowledging that many taxpayers looked forward every year to a large refund, reporter Jim Hickey correctly explained that this was not wise money management for it was giving the government interest-free use of taxpayer money until April 15.

So Is Regulation

The week's coverage of the federal role in the economy included seven stories on regulation. ABC ran three segments on the vast new rules imposed by the Americans with Disabilities Act—or ADA. "Good Morning America" and "World News Tonight" reported that all Americans soon would see changes like braille menus and lower shelves in supermarkets. The only critique of the new regulations came from businessmen who told Reporter Jim Hickey that the regulations were confusing and vague.

The facts reported by ABC were true. What ABC ignored, however, was what had been the central point in the debate over ADA: its cost to the economy and the avalanche of law suits that it was expected to trigger. Because ABC did not even hint at this, the economic message to the viewer was that ADA-like regulations had many benefits and while they might be confusing, they imposed no serious costs. Completely missing from the reporting was the notion of trade-offs, which is central to every economic relationship.

Viewers would have been better served had Hickey said:

"But don't think that ADA comes cheaply. Some economists reckon that every year it will cost the economy tens of billions—and everyone in one way or another will pay a share. ADA might be worth it, of course, and a country as rich as America might be able to afford improving access and opportunities for the disabled. But it just shows once again that everything has trade-offs."

The concept of trade-off also was ignored by an ABC "Good Morning America" story on Food and Drug Administration hearings about whether new regulations were needed to require foods to be labelled with nutritional information. The 90-second story addressed the valid question of whether labels could be designed in a way that would not mislead or confuse consumers. Ignored was the equally valid issue of whether the attempt to obtain perfect labelling would impose too high a cost on the economy and consumer.

Reporter Richard Davies could have advanced viewer understanding of this economic issue had he added:

"Of course, every new regulation on labelling increases costs—directly or indirectly—to the consumer. Whether the cost is worth it or not is up to consumers. And they can let officials know how they feel."

Another instance was the proposed regulatory change that would allow a business to sell what is called its "right to pollute." This very complicated matter was covered by ABC and NBC. The proposal would permit a business whose exhaust or other polluting emissions fall below the maximum set by law to sell the unused potential to another business which then could emit pollutants above the maximum. Many economists have argued that creating a market in pollution rights ultimately would reduce pollution significantly. The reason: if businesses could make money by selling unused pollution rights, they would build their new plants to exceed pollution standards by as much as possible.

Explaining this complex concept correctly not only required the reporter to stress that the measure would not, as its name seemed to imply, encourage pollution, but would create economic incentives to build the most environmentally appropriate plants possible. Without such an explanation, the viewer probably could not understand how a "right to pollute" could protect the environment.

But viewers did not see or hear such an explanation on ABC "Good Morning America" January 31. Tom Schell noted only that the measure would reduce costs to businesses; he said nothing about the measure's incentives nor about how a "right to pollute" would work. Almost surely, ABC left its viewers befuddled.

By contrast, that same morning, viewers listening to Faith Daniels on NBC "Today" were told clearly that the measure was "a plan to make it profitable for businesses to pollute as little as possible." To illustrate this, reporter David Garcia cited the example of a 3M Company plant in Ventura County, California, that had reduced its emissions and earned $1.5 million by selling 78 tons of pollution credits to the Procter and Gamble Company which needed a larger pollution allowance so that it could expand an existing plant. Garcia even noted that a futures market would be created for smog. Although most viewers probably did not know what a futures market was, the implication was that selling a "right to pollute" was an economic, market-driven concept with many welcome possibilities, including smog reduction.

HINTS FOR CONSUMERS

Every week network viewers received economic and consumer advice. This week's advice told viewers to:

1. Be careful when buying strawberries irradiated by a new process that killed bacteria and delayed ripening to extend the strawberries' shelf life in stores.
2. Get references before hiring home repair firms and get legal help if there were problems with contractors.
3. Look for credit cards with lower rates.

Generally there were two themes in such advice. The first was guidance with which consumers could make wise choices. The second was a subtle, perhaps unintended, statement about how the economy worked.

In this week's three items, the economic message was that it was unwise to delay the process by which strawberries ripened, that regulation was needed to curb repair firm abuses, and that Congress could lower credit card rates set by banks. This message painted an inaccurate picture of the way the economy functioned. Omitted regarding the strawberries, for example, was the notion that delayed ripening extended strawberry shelf life in stores and this, in turn, reduced costs to consumers.

ENTERTAINMENT'S MESSAGE

TV dramas, sitcoms, and other entertainment touched on many economic matters and hence conveyed economic messages.

Businessmen and women were regular characters on sitcoms, crime shows, and other dramas. On some programs, this January week, the message was that businesspersons generally were okay. This was the case in NBC's "Sisters," which portrayed Frankie, a corporation vice-president, as competently handling a tough situation dealing with the possible sexual harassment of one of her staffers. CBS's "Hearts Are Wild," meantime, depicted Caesar's Palace owner Jack Thorpe as kind to his employees (and to his dying friend), ABC's "Baby Talk" featured businesswoman Maggie as touchingly attentive to her child, the NBC movie "Fine Things" had merchant Bernard Fine living what seemed an ideal life in an ideal small town, ABC's "Capitol Critters" portrayed a food company cooperating with a government sting operation, ABC's "Homefront" depicted a black family saving money to start a business, and NBC's "Law and Order" exonerated a businessman wrongly accused of mugging a pregnant woman.

Such upbeat depictions of businesspersons and businesses were more than outweighed, however, by episodes telling viewers that businesspersons were likely to be crooks or otherwise untrustworthy. Examples:

In ABC's "Dinosaurs," the boss ate an endangered species and ordered destruction of a redwood forest to make room for a housing project.

In CBS's "Jake and the Fatman," a casino owner concluded that his business would profit if he had some people murdered.

In CBS's "Tequila and Bonetti," a used car dealer fronted for car thieves.

In Fox's "Herman's Head," Mr. Bracken was a sadistic boss who enjoyed making his employees insecure.

In NBC's "Matlock," the town banker was involved in bank robberies.

In NBC's "In the Heat of the Night," a towing company owner plotted to kill his ex-wife while a truck repair shop owner dealt in stolen trucks.

In NBC's "Different World," a firm's vice-president sexually harassed his staffer.

Entertainment TV's criminalization of businessmen and women was matched by its trivialization of them. Almost nothing this week portrayed them operating in the real world of their businesses or professions. In CBS's "Hearts Are Wild," for instance, when Mickey and Sammy wanted to raise money to open a pizza parlor, they went to Las Vegas to win it at the gaming tables.

Overall, entertainment's message seemed to be: (1) that being a businessperson or entrepreneur was inconsequential; and (2) that businesspersons were likely to be crooked or similarly distasteful.

What might have been entertainment TV's sole positive message in the week about the American economic system was "Sisters"' depiction of Teddy. While flopping in her attempt to sell cosmetics to women at kaffee-klatsch gatherings, she found the women eager to buy the self-designed, hand-painted sweatshirt that she was wearing. Whether intended by the "Sisters" writer or not, this was a pure supply-side message: that creating a supply of a product created its own demand. The episode ended with Teddy happily anticipating a new career designing and manufacturing clothing.

GETTING THE FACTS WRONG

At times in the week, network TV gave the viewer inaccurate facts and data and an illogical discussion of them. Among the most serious mistakes were:

1. ABC "Good Morning America" January 29 with *Money* Magazine editor Tyler Mathisen's statement that taxes were higher because of the national debt. Taxes do not necessarily rise with the debt; they do so only if spending is not cut.
2. CNN Reporter Larry Lamotte's contention January 29 that "America is reluctantly changing to a service economy" and his strong implication that this was not a healthy development. The fact is that America has been shifting from manufacturing towards service for more than a century and that this shift (underway in all advanced industrial nations) has been seen by economists as a sign of economic progress.
3. ABC's Stephen Aug January 30 illogically citing two corporations with falling profits and one with rising profits to make his point that looking at corporate profits was one way of telling how the economy was doing. What conclusion could the viewer draw from Aug's contradictory examples? It would have been much better for him to cite aggregate numbers of how many corporations had rising and how many falling profits.
4. ABC Sheilah Kast's statement January 31 that the Bush proposal to give each family an extra $500 tax deduction for each child would benefit the wealthy most. U.S. Treasury statistics and those by private economists and institutions show the opposite result.
5. CBS commentator Ray Brady's strong implication January 27

and that by CNN's Terry Keenan January 31 that junk bonds were junk. In fact, bonds issued by higher-risk firms generally have proven to be safe and high-yielding investments.

6. ABC reporter Diane Sawyer's January 31 statement on "Prime Time Live" that the average American credit card holder was carrying $1,600 in charges from one month to another. The actual figures according to a Federal Reserve Board statistical release was $2,281 in 1990 and $2,426 in 1991.

NEWSCASTS' MESSAGES

Messages conveyed by TV's economic and business coverage in this January week were that:

1. A "Buy American" campaign, whatever its faults, could help push America out of the recession.

There is no economics basis for these statements by NBC's Diana Koricke and ABC's Nancy Snyderman. The two reporters would have been much more accurate had they told viewers:

"Buying American may make some consumers feel better— that they're doing something to help fellow-Americans whose jobs may be threatened. In fact, they're doing little, if any- thing. To risk over-simplification, if they pay more for American-made goods, they will have less to spend on other goods—and thus could jeopardize the jobs of Americans mak- ing these other goods."

2. One sure way to lower America's trade deficit with Japan would be for the Japanese government to promise that Japan would buy more American-made auto parts and other specifically designated goods. These reports by ABC "World News Tonight" and CBS "Evening News" were incorrect. The fact is that America's trade balance with individual countries is not a matter of trade in

specific goods but of aggregate trade in all goods. The cause of the American imbalance with Japan, to a large extent, has been Japanese barriers to almost all foreign goods. Winning from Japan promises to buy some American goods in slightly greater quantity would not lower the trade deficit with Japan appreciably.

Viewers would have learned more had ABC and CBS said:

"Though Tokyo may be promising to buy more American auto parts, the U.S. trade deficit with Japan will stay very high until Japan moves to lower its myriad of daunting barriers to almost all American—and other foreign—goods and services."

3. Japanese and other foreign purchases of American properties was bad for the American economy.

This report by CNN "World News" would have been judged as incorrect by almost all economists. CNN should have told viewers:

"It is understandable that Americans get irritated when they see foreigners buying up American property. But economists say that this foreign investment actually is good for us. It creates jobs in America and infuses capital used for American business expansion and innovation."

4. Economic problems are solved mainly by government action. This was the bottom line of the ABC "Good Morning America" discussion of potential cuts in federal housing subsidies, of the NBC "Nightly News" story on the home repair industry's need for regulation and on the account that action by Bonn and Tokyo could spur American economic growth, of the ABC "Good Morning America" report on the need to mandate extensive labelling of food products, and of the CNN "World News" story on Senate efforts to regulate cable TV.

5. Only higher taxes, according to ABC "Good Morning America," could cut the federal deficit.

6. Businesspersons mainly were dishonest or untrustworthy since home repairmen (said NBC "Nightly News") defrauded customers, art galleries (said NBC "Nightly News") sold counterfeits, telephone scams (said CBS "This Morning") took advantage of consumers, financiers like Michael Milken and Dennis Levine (said NBC "Nightly News") ended up in jail, executive pay (said NBC "Today") was too high, and bosses (said a book reviewed by ABC "Good Morning America") were crazy.

7. Macy's and TWA got in trouble because they were too heavily in debt, sold junk bonds, and expanded too rapidly.

8. Government regulation (according to ABC "Good Morning America") might be a problem because it was confusing and vague, but not because it imposed great costs on the economy.

9. The right to pollute (said NBC "Today") might be an innovative way to reduce pollution.

No message during the week was less informed and informative about America's economic system than Diane Sawyer's ABC "Prime Time Live" report on credit card rates. Revealing startling economic illiteracy, she said that, while banks charged high rates for borrowing money via their cards, "the banks don't return that favor on the interest they give you on your savings." Sawyer apparently did not understand that banks pay interest not as "favors" to depositors but to attract customers. The economy does not function through mutual favors; it functions as all participants seek the best deal for themselves. If a bank was trying to do anyone or anything a favor, it was to itself—that's what banks do.

Sawyer confirmed her scant understanding of the economy later in her report when she said: "If you're a reliable customer, with a good credit history, did you know there are banks that will reward your good behavior?" Such lower rates, of course, were not a reward to customers, but the result of intense competition by banks for creditworthy customers. If the customer is "rewarded" by lower rates, the reward comes not from the banks but from the economic system's competitiveness. To Sawyer, however, the American economy apparently functions by participants doing each other favors and giving each other rewards.

LETTING OPPORTUNITIES SLIP AWAY

TV's errors of omission generally should be viewed more charitably than those of commission. Broadcasters, even more than the press, operate under severe time and space constraints limiting how much they can cover. But in economic matters, the media should take extra care not to let pass appropriate opportunities to educate the public. When TV economic coverage misses the opportunity to point out basic economic concepts or to identify cause-and-effect linkages, TV squanders opportunities to educate.

Coverage this week that squandered opportunities included:

1. ABC's "World News Tonight" report on Senate attempts to repeal the luxury tax on yachts. Missed was the opportunity to tell viewers that when taxes are increased on items, sales of those items drop and thus revenues from those taxes fall below expectations.

2. ABC's "World News Tonight" report on Macy's bankruptcy. Though reporter Bob Jamieson raised the interesting point that all major New York department stores were in trouble, he never explained why this was so. Viewers would have gained had he mused:

> **"Established institutions grow bureaucratic and slow to adapt. They thus become vulnerable to competition. While Macy's and other old-line department stores therefore are in trouble, the aisles are bustling in newer stores, run by managers with newer ideas."**

3. Stephen Aug's "Good Morning America" commentary that corporate profits were a barometer of how the economy was doing.

Though Aug's point was valid, he never told viewers why profits are a particularly useful measure. He could have added:

"Rising profits not only give firms the money they need to invest or pay dividends or raise salaries. Rising profits also encourage new entrepreneurs to take the plunge and invest in a new business."

4. The networks' routine reporting on jobless claims. Missing was even a phrase explaining what jobless claims were and what the numbers meant.

5. The networks' extensive coverage of the American-Japanese trade dispute. Reporters could have explained that the dispute to a large extent was the result of Japan's trade barriers. Then reporters could have added:

"America does not need a trade surplus with every country— and this includes Japan. Surplus in some countries could offset deficits in others. And, in fact, America has a very large surplus with Western Europe, which shows that American business, when given access to markets, can compete in even the most advanced and competitive markets."

6. ABC's "Good Morning America" analysis of the Bush administration's budget proposals. Reporters could have used the budget story as an opportunity to add:

"Some economists think that Bush has a point, that getting rid of subsidies would be a good thing. These economists point out that subsidies create perverse incentives and end up creating costly and persistent problems."

7. Irving R. Levine's NBC "Nightly News" commentary on the plunge in factory orders and on Bush's proposed investment tax credit. Levine missed the chance to speculate:

"Some economists say that one reason that businesses have been reluctant to expand is that taxes on their earnings are too high. Why take the risk of buying new equipment, ask businessmen, if taxes take a huge chunk of profits? If this is so, then maybe Bush's plan makes some sense."

8. CNN's "World News" report on the federal deficit. Although reporter David French raised the question, "How did the deficit grow so large," he never answered it. He could have said:

"Some say that the deficit is large because taxes have been cut. Others point out that even though taxes were cut, tax revenues have increased greatly. This leads many economists to advise that it has been the huge jump in spending that has pushed up the deficit."

He also could have pointed out that, historically, when tax revenues increase, spending increases even faster, thereby destroying any deficit-cutting potential.

9. NBC's "Nightly News" profile of Pam Resch who had been barred by regulations from giving piano concerts in her home. NBC missed the chance to use Resch as a paradigm for how regulations imposed huge burdens on business and creativity in general and particular difficulties for small businesses. NBC Keith Morrison could have said:

"Maybe we've been overdoing it with regulations when a Pam Resch can't make a few bucks by giving a piano concert. Many small businesses, in fact, plead for relief from the regulations that they say are keeping them from expanding and hiring extra workers."

CHAPTER TWO

A TYPICAL WEEK: MAY 30-JUNE 5

FAILING THE TEST AT RIO

As JUNE 1992 began, Denmark startled the world by rejecting the European Community's Maastricht Treaty, news leaked of a mounting sexual harassment scandal in the U.S. navy (soon known as the Tailhook Affair), and votes were being cast to choose which Elvis was to grace a postage stamp. In the presidential race, Clinton locked up the nomination by winning the primaries in Alabama, California, New Jersey, and Ohio, while Perot drew mounting support.

Economic matters this week rivalled the political for attention, with economic coverage on the network's morning and evening newscasts totalling 7 hours, 55 minutes. The main reason, which accounted for nearly half of it—some 3 hours, 5 minutes—was the gathering in Rio de Janeiro of leaders from 170 nations for the United Nations environmental issues conference, billed as the Earth Summit. What also captured significant coverage this week were unemployment's sharp, and unexpected, jump from 7.2 percent to 7.5 percent, a looming AT&T strike, and the airlines' fare war.

Viewers during the week heard a particularly long list of economic statistics. There were reports on personal incomes (up), consumer spending (up), construction (down), the index of leading economic indicators (up), new home sales (up), the trade deficit (down), employment levels (up to the highest in three years), factory orders (up), American car sales (up), Japanese car sales (down), retail sales (up), food stamp recipients (up), food bank supplies (down)—and unemployment (up sharply).

From all this the networks drew contradictory conclusions, telling viewers that:

The economic news was "mixed" (CNN "World News" June 1);

The economic recovery was "weak" (ABC "Good Morning America" June 2);

There were "more signs that the economy is recovering, but this is a slow, weak climb out of the recession" ("Good Morning America" also on June 2);

The "recovery . . . is better than most analysts expected" ("Good Morning America" also on June 2);

America slowly was coming out of recession (CBS "Evening News" on June 2 and CNN "World News" on June 3);

The numbers showed a recovery (NBC "Nightly News" and CBS "Evening News" on June 4); and

The recovery was extremely sluggish (NBC "Nightly News" on June 5).

Most analyzed was the report of May's 7.5 percent unemployment, the highest in eight years. Generally, viewers were told that joblessness had jumped because the economy's slight upturn was raising the hopes of many who had dropped out of the workforce. Their new optimism was prompting them to look for jobs.

NBC's "Nightly News" Mike Jensen on June 5, however, saw it differently. For him, pessimism not optimism was driving up unemployment. People, he said, "get scared when they hear about things like this—2,000 more pink slips today at McDonnell Douglas in California." Jensen might have been right, but he never explained how such pessimism could increase joblessness.

The rest of Jensen's commentary was even more confused. After first describing the economy as "extremely sluggish," he later advised: "Look behind the headlines. The numbers aren't so bad as they seem at first glance." But his explanation was that the numbers, at second glance, were both bad and good. He said: "After all, 68,000 new jobs mostly in services were created in May. That's the figure analysts consider most important, more people on the payroll." That, apparently, was good. Bad, according to him, was that more jobs were needed.

Jensen surely added to viewers' befuddlement when he said: "There is a need to have many more [jobs created] if the economy is really going to get moving." This reversed the causal order usually accepted by economists: Jobs are the result, not the cause, of economic growth. To add further to the muddle, he ended his story with "unemployment is the last thing to improve in a recovery." That was indeed correct, but it was also inconsistent with his statement that first jobs are created and then the economy starts moving.

THE RIO EARTH SUMMIT

The Rio conference, in preparation for two years, was the big news. The week's coverage included the walk-up to the summit and the first three days of the twelve-day conference. In total, the four networks this week ran forty-nine stories directly on the summit plus thirty-two on related environmental topics.

For TV, this was saturation coverage. With it came the airtime to move beyond soundbites and conventional questions with their predictable answers. In covering the Rio summit, the networks had the financial resources, lead-time, and access to the world's experts to explore a variety of views on how threatened the environment is, and how to meet the threat.

It was, for the networks, an uncommon opportunity. And it was an opportunity squandered. Little new ground was explored. What was worse, reporting from Rio and about Rio was strikingly unbalanced. In the week, by the lopsided ratio of 28 to 2, the networks

ENVIRONMENTAL EXPERTS

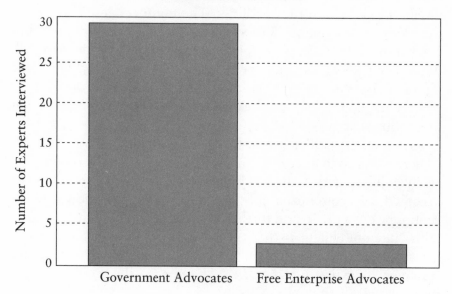

Number of Nongovernment Officials Interviewed
during the Rio Earth Summit

showcased experts who held alarmist views about the environment and sought only governmental solutions to protect the environment over those experts who raised some doubts about both. Missing almost entirely was even a hint that the nongovernment forces of the marketplace could be mobilized, in some fashion, to protect the environment. Missing too was any skeptical questioning of the doomsday predictions for the environment.

Squandered as well was the networks' opportunity to educate viewers about Third World demands for massive extra aid from the West. In covering this, TV reporters were curiously deficient in journalistic skepticism and pluck. Generally, in fact, network reporters sounded more like delegates from Third World countries determined to wring extra foreign aid out of America and the West than like journalists covering an event. Never did a reporter question how Third World countries would spend the billions of extra aid were the West to grant it.

The result: Rather than being exposed to coverage of uncommon breadth and depth on the environment, network viewers this week were repeatedly assailed by the same analyses and arguments.

To be sure, not all the news from Rio required heady analysis. There was, for example, the spectacle of the Rio summit itself, the unprecedented converging in one city of some hundred heads of state or government. This the networks covered well, telling viewers that 35,000 Brazilian troops were patrolling Rio, that police were sweeping the homeless out of the city, that massive traffic jams made travelling by car almost impossible, and other scene-setting tidbits.

Similarly straightforward was their reporting of the summit's American domestic political aspect—the battles inside the Bush administration over whether George Bush would attend the meeting, whether the United States would sign certain summit agreements, and over how much of the U.S. delegation's actions at Rio would be set by the delegation's head, Environmental Protection Agency boss William Reilly.

FAILING THE FIRST TEST AT RIO: THE INTERNATIONAL STORY

The real tests of network reporting were their handling of the other themes of the Rio story: the international politics of the conference, the scientific argument about the environment, and, above all, the economics of environmental protection. In all of these, the networks performed poorly.

As an international story, the meeting in Rio was characterized repeatedly as a conflict between the poor South and the rich North. At issue, viewers were told, was whether the advanced industrial nations would bow to demands of the South for hundreds of billions of dollars in extra aid. This was needed, Third World spokesmen told American TV audiences repeatedly, so that poor countries could develop economically in ways that would not damage the environment.

In TV's reporting of this North-South dispute, the main culprit was America. Typical was Forrest Sawyer on ABC "World News Tonight" May 31 saying: "The U.S. is under fire for standing in the way of efforts to protect the planet." Four days later, Doug Tunnell on CBS "This Morning" reported that Bush "emerged as the villain here in Rio. The self-described environment president forced the UN to water down a global clean air accord and refuses to sign another agreement to further protect endangered species." On ABC "Good Morning America" that day, reporter Mike Schneider observed that though the summit was but one day old, "delegates were already criticizing the U.S."

And for anchor Margaret Larson, in introducing Ed Rabel's segment on NBC "Nightly News" June 5, "the Bush administration seems to be the summit's Enemy #1." Rabel's segment featured foreign officials and environmental experts saying, as similar officials and experts did on NBC "Nightly News" and "Today," that "the president of the United States" had "sharply diminished" the summit agenda and had made "this conference meaningless."

Washington was also the culprit for CNN's Christiane Amanpour on "World News" June 3. After stating that the "rich North and poor Southern countries were on a collision course that could derail the summit," she told viewers that "the U.S.—the world's richest country and its biggest polluter—has either refused to sign or watered down the summit's key treaties."

In using the phrase "watered down," Tunnell and Amanpour invoked what had become a near-mantra of CNN and ABC reporters when discussing America's stand on the proposals at Rio. It was used by them nearly a dozen times in the week and several times by CBS and NBC to criticize U.S. behavior. Yet at no time did any reporter (except NBC's Rabel) explain how the U.S. had "watered down" a treaty or proposal. The message simply was that while other countries were offering "good" treaties at Rio, Uncle Sam the grinch was ruining them by "watering them down."

No reporter, moreover, pointed out that many leaders of the industrialized countries at Rio did not want costly treaties any more than did America. Knowing that the Bush administration would not permit wasteful treaties, these other leaders safely were able to posture as defenders of the environment and critics of Bush. Even without questioning the motives of the critics, reporters would have served viewers better had they said:

> **"While many complain that the U.S. is watering down proposals here, others argue that U.S. officials are merely looking after the interests of American taxpayers, so they won't be forced to subsidize environmental measures of dubious value."**

Throughout the week, viewers saw American network TV reporters, foreigners, and expert Talking Heads all beating up on America; the only statements defending America's actions came from U.S. officials, almost exclusively from EPA chief Reilly. The trouble is that viewers tend to find officials less credible than ostensibly nonpolitical experts and reporters. With but one exception, no nonofficial appeared on the four networks that week to explain or defend U.S. action at the summit.

The Reilly quotes that were selected for broadcast, moreover, tended to confirm the image of America as stingy and unreasonable. Take Reilly's broadcasted response on June 4 to ABC "Good Morning America" reporter Berry Serafin's statement that the United States had "watered down" the global warming treaty and was balking at the "Agenda 21" plan to give $125 billion in extra aid to the Third World. What the TV audience heard Reilly say was: "No one has that kind of money." Surely, Reilly had said vastly more than that to reporters in Rio.

A stingy America was again the impression conveyed by the Reilly soundbite in a May 31 interview with NBC "Nightly News." In it, Reilly told reporter Keith Morrison that "there is no way that this conference or any future conference will serve as a basis for those kinds of North-South financial transfers." On CNN "World News" June 3, Reilly said: "Our own budgetary situation and that of many other developed countries simply do not permit" such increases of aid to the Third World. And the following day CBS "This Morning" broadcasted Reilly saying: "The financing mechanism is not one that we support."

Other reporting reinforced the image of a skinflint America. Example: NBC "Nightly News" reporter John Cochran said that when it came to the environment, Bush had given priority to pocketbook issues, had favored developers and loggers, and had made it harder for cities to protest industrial use of public land.

At times, Reilly's exasperation with the persistent questions about the financial aid aspects of the conference surfaced. On NBC "Nightly News" June 3 he said: "We can only hope that this story or this line on the United States [reluctance to increase aid vastly to the Third World] will become tedious and wear a little thin with time."

He was wrong. Only rarely did TV give viewers a chance to see Reilly talking about the substance of U.S. environmental policy— that U.S. environmental regulations already were tougher than those proposed at Rio and that the U.S. was opposing the Biodiversity Treaty because, among other things, it would endanger American patents and other intellectual property.

Network coverage of the summit also addressed scientific issues, particularly the contentions that the earth's atmosphere was warming and that vast numbers of animal species were facing extinction. Almost all the reporting unquestioningly accepted the gloomiest assertions of the environmental extremists. A rare exception was NBC's "Nightly News" Robert Bazell. After Talking Head Michael Oppenheimer of the Environmental Defense Fund grimly predicted "record heat—record drought—forests going up in flames—sea levels rising, creating an unprecedented refugee problem," Bazell correctly tempered this alarmist litany by stressing that such doomsday claims, including the prediction of global warming, were disputed by many scientists.

In what perhaps was the week's most balanced segment on Rio, ABC "Good Morning America" science Editor Michael Guillen on June 2 stressed that enormous controversies and no easy answers surrounded environmental problems. In illustrating this, he explained that while many environmentalists condemned burning the rain forests, "scientists have found that burning tropical rain forests may actually be good for the environment. It may actually help cool the atmosphere because the smoke from the fires . . . helps reflect the sunlight and cool the earth."

As a result, Guillen told viewers, scientists "are nowhere near figuring out what's going on with the whole global warming issue." To make his point even stronger, Guillen emphasized that "science, by its nature, is uncertain" and that "science is uncertain" about the environment.

FAILING THE SECOND TEST AT RIO: THE ECONOMIC STORY

Most Rio coverage focused on the economics of environmental protection. Here the networks first won and then lost kudos. They won for alerting viewers that at the environmental policy's core was a possibly painful trade-off between environmental regulations and economic growth. They lost for poorly describing this trade-off.

TV served viewers well by explaining that slower economic growth and fewer new jobs might be the price of tough regulations to reduce pollution, protect animal species, and otherwise solve what were seen as environmental problems. On CNN "World News" June 1, for instance, reporter Marina Mirabella rhetorically asked if economies could grow without permanently damaging the environment. She implied that the answer was no by citing nations "in the Southern Hemisphere who say development comes before conservation." That evening NBC's Tom Brokaw said that the task of the Rio summit was "how to save the earth and not go broke in the process."

The important notion that there was tension and a trade-off between stiff environmental regulations and economic development was best depicted this week by NBC's "Nightly News" June 1 profile of Tijuana, the now-booming Mexican city a few miles from San Diego. In his report, Robert Bazell first showed viewers one horror after another: kids playing in toxic waste containers, untreated sewage flowing through streets, and fumes from a lead plant fire blowing through villages. But then he stressed that "despite the environmental dangers, more and more poor people move into the shacks near the factories, hoping for work." This, he said, was the basic question at the Rio Summit: "How can Third World countries lift themselves out of poverty without assaulting their own and the world's environment?"

Though the networks did well by explaining that there was a trade-off between tough environmental regulation and growth, and that controversy raged over how to strike a balance between the two, they floundered in depicting the controversy's two sides. The air was mainly filled with reporters and Talking Heads calling for environmental regulations no matter what their cost. Viewers heard almost nothing from those who could have warned just how painful that cost could be or have suggested innovative ways to protect the environment without costly regulations.

TV's sharp tilt to one side in this debate came through in network reporters' near-apocalyptic language describing the situation that drew the world leaders to Rio. To NBC's Ed Rabel, the battle at Rio was "over how the environment can be saved" and Rio "may be the last chance they have to save the planet." To Christiane Amanpour, "the summit with perhaps the loftiest goals ever [is] to stop us from pushing our own planet towards environmental collapse." And for ABC's Peter Jennings, the nations at the summit "have a very tall order: how to prevent making the place we live an unlivable place."

With the consequences ostensibly so dire, enormous economic pain, including falling living standards, might not be too high a price to pay. This, in fact, was what viewers repeatedly—and almost exclusively—heard. During the week, at least twenty-eight expert Talking Heads advocating tough environmental regulations were presented to American viewers. They were offset by a mere two Talking Heads skeptical of such measures. Much more balanced were interviews with politicians; critic of Bush policies Albert Gore, then senator from Tennessee, appeared on TV ten times during the week, while Bush administration-defender Reilly appeared twelve.

CBS gave viewers two nonexperts who did not push an extremist environmental agenda. But as Chemical Workers Union members, their background imparted no credibility to their refutations of the environmental extremist argument. Their appeal was purely emotional. Appearing June 1 on the "Eye on the Earth" series (CBS "Evening News"), the pair warned that regulations would destroy jobs. Said one: "I believe in clean air. But I also believe in providing for my family and [environmental regulations have] had a devastating impact on our community." The second union member said: "I love clean air and clean water. But if I'm not eating, it doesn't do me a lot of good."

Interviewed also on the CBS program was Mary Allen Summerlin, mayor of Port Arthur, Texas. Said she: "We just wonder if the quality of our air is going to improve to anything like the degree of the pain we suffer by the loss of jobs. There is a balance that has to be maintained."

Reporter Wyatt Andrews on the CBS program addressed the matter of balance and gave the viewer useful information. He pointed out that while most Americans said that they were concerned about the environment, not many were willing to make sacrifices for it; few were willing, he noted, to give up their cars. And, he added, though people wanted to protect the ozone layer, not many would go without their refrigerators or air conditioners. He also told viewers that the Clean Air Act's tough new rules for oil refineries had forced Chevron to fire 650 workers.

The week's only two credible Talking Head experts who were not environmental extremists were a Vatican official who opposed population control and economist Murray Weidenbaum, perhaps America's leading expert on regulation and the first chairman of Ronald Reagan's Council of Economic Advisors. Again it was CBS, this time "This Morning," that gave viewers at least a peek at the dissenting side in the environmental discussion. From Weidenbaum viewers learned that a number of solid scientific reports had debunked the notion of global warming, that America already was spending enormous sums on environmental protection and pollution control, and that the kind of measures being proposed at Rio would devastate the American economy.

Paired with Weidenbaum on the CBS program was the Environmental Defense Fund's Oppenheimer. His organization was an activist group seeking government solutions to environmental problems. He told viewers that the earth was experiencing "a faster warming than ever in the history of civilization. It would make the earth hotter than ever in the history of the human race." Oppenheimer was interviewed at least twice more during the week—by CNN "Prime News" May 31 and by NBC "Nightly News" June 4, on which he said flatly that the world was facing "record heat, record drought, forests going up in flames, sea levels rising, creating an unprecedented refugee problem."

When Oppenheimer presumably was not available, other Environmental Defense Fund spokesmen were interviewed: Bruce Rich on ABC "World News Tonight" June 4, and Michael Bean on CNN "World News" and ABC "World News Tonight" May 30. Bean charged that the U.S. had abandoned its commitment to environmental principles. ABC, meanwhile, interviewed Liz Barrett-Brown of the Natural Resources Defense Council, another activist group demanding huge government programs for the environment. CNN interviewed Bill Barclay of Greenpeace International, Randall Hayes of Rainforest Action Network, and Jacques Cousteau three times. Cousteau also appeared once on CBS. His main message was that the globe's most pressing environmental problem was what he called the "population big-bang," "the population explosion."

ALONG WITH RIO, PROFILES IN PANIC

Reinforcing the message that the earth indisputably edged on environmental catastrophe and that this could be prevented only by the massive and costly action proposed at Rio were the broadcasts of eco-horror stories. On successive evenings, the "Eye on the Earth" series (CBS "Evening News") profiled a crusade to save Philippine forests and what was described as the rapid deterioration of the Florida Everglades, ABC's "Nightline" profiled Madagascar, and ABC "World News Tonight" looked at Namibia and India.

Typical of the panicked tone of these profiles was "Nightline" Forrest Sawyer's introduction of the segment on Madagascar. First he declared, incorrectly, that "the world is a vastly poorer place today than it was when you were born." Then he told viewers:

"[The world] is being poisoned and devoured by ravenous billions of us. And there is no end in sight."

What followed on "Nightline" was a lengthy report on Madagascar by Don Kladstrup. His message was as direct as it was simple: Madagascar demonstrated that man was the great enemy of the environment. As evidence, he described how Madagascar's "unique" rain forest was being chopped and burned by peasants. Kladstrup took great care not to condemn these peasants, stressing that they were so poor that they had no choice but to clear new forest areas when their crops and cattle depleted previously cleared land.

Interviewed by Kladstrup was Patrick Daniels of Conservation International who said: "We're working with villagers who aren't able to do anything other than feed themselves day to day so their choices are to cut down the forests. They don't have any techniques other than slash and burn." Zoologist Alison Jolly told Kladstrup: "If I was locked in the Louvre with my children and they were hungry and cold, sooner or later . . . I'd burn the Leonardos to keep my children warm."

If, however, the peasants were not to blame for their "slash and burn" agronomy devastating Madagascar's forests, who or what was? Kladstrup made no effort to answer this. Instead he offered viewers Talking Heads who merely reinforced the tone of near helpless despair for the survival of Madagascar's unique forests. Interviewed were Conservation International president Russell Mittermeier, biologist Roderic Mast, World Wide Fund for Nature's Nat Quansah, Conservation International's Patrick Daniels, World Wildlife Fund's Sheila O'Connor, and zoologist Alison Jolly. All of these and all of their organizations stand on one side of the environmental debate. They insist on massive and draconian government action. On this program their message was: Madagascar alone could not save its valuable environment; Madagascar needed help from other nations.

Kladstrup did not challenge this. Nor did he offer viewers even one expert voicing doubts about the extreme environmental choices presented by "Nightline" Talking Heads. Yet Kladstrup easily could have solicited such doubts had he interviewed a free market economist. Viewers then could have heard about possible economic measures that Madagascar itself could take to prevent environmental depredations.

Such an economist, for instance, could have asked whether Madagascar government policies, such as tight central controls, might not have been smothering the economy. If so, the economist could have suggested, Madagascar could adopt new policies which would spur economic growth and thus give peasants an alternative to slash-and-burn farming. One such policy would be to give the peasants a property right in their land. After all, the economist could have explained, for centuries farmers worldwide had taken meticulous care to avoid exhausting their land when it had been economically rewarding for them to do so.

A free market economist also could have suggested that economic incentives could be created to protect the Madagascar forest's valuable plants and animals. Example: Western pharmaceutical firms and other industries that make products from forest materials could be given a stake in the forest's survival. Such a stake would be similar, the economist could have told viewers, to that which has prompted timber companies to replace the trees that they cut since the companies' long-term profits depend on a continuous supply and harvest of trees.

It would also be similar to the Deseret Land and Livestock Corporation. This company turns a profit on a ranch by allowing fee hunting, which creates an incentive to maintain a rich habitat. According to the Montana based Political Economy Research Center: "The growth of game animals has been so successful that the ranch has supplied elk to the public hunting lands of the state of Utah."

Such an explanation or any other veering from the apocalyptic outlook of environmental extremists was completely missing from Kladstrup's long report on Madagascar. Only in his kicker did he even hint that economic forces might help Madagascar out of its environmental dilemma. Concluding his segment, Kladstrup said that the lemurs inhabiting the forest might survive if they "could become a major money maker and attract tourists."

This was a fundamental economic point; instead of being an afterthought, it could have been offered to balance those who saw no solution for Madagascar but massive amounts of outside help. Kladstrup could have said, without significantly lengthening the segment:

"If the lemurs become valuable, the communities will benefit from tourism and they will make sure that the lemurs survive and multiply—just as other African countries have learned to reap tourist dollars by protecting their wildlife."

As unbalanced as Kladstrup's report was Bill Whitaker's story on CBS "Evening News" June 2 about the murder of a priest who had been trying to save Philippine forests. The general villain of the segment was trade; booming foreign demand apparently had been creating a market for Philippine wood products. The specific villain was Japan, the major importer of Philippine wood. Critics called Japan a "Godzilla," but Whitaker said: "The Japanese are only buying what the poor nations of South East Asia are all too willing to sell."

What made Whitaker's segment unbalanced was his failure to note one of the most common, and valid, observations about developing countries: that trade is extremely valuable for their economic growth, much more valuable than aid. Typically, in fact, reports about the dilemma of Third World economic development have depicted trade as a white knight. Yet by his seeming determination to label economic growth the environment's enemy, Whitaker made trade into an enemy.

More conventional were the culprits on the CBS "This Morning" June 4 look at the Everglades. Here the culprits were Miami area incinerators releasing mercury vapors and sugar-cane farms encroaching on the Everglades swamps. In this segment, reporter Bob Faw committed a distressingly common error in reporting economic matters: he failed the *habeas corpus* test.

Just as criminal law requires that a body be produced to prove that a murder had been committed, so journalism too should require that a victim of an economic problem be identified to prove that such a problem exists. Without evidence of an ostensible problem's consequences, journalists should say, there is no problem.

Faw produced no evidence of the problem's consequences.
Though he easily identified incinerators and farms as culprits, he
had a hard time identifying the depredations they ostensibly were
creating. Without them, he had no case for his contention that the
"Everglades National Park, the second largest park in the nation, is
under assault." All Faw showed the viewers were incinerator vapors and farmland.

Another illustration of the missing *corpus* was the portion of
Faw's report describing Everglades fish as being contaminated by
mercury. Although Faw dealt with this for some time—interviewing a fisherman, the Everglades National Park superintendent, and
even Carol Browner of the Florida Department of Environmental
Regulation (later named by Bill Clinton to head the federal Environmental Protection Agency)—the segment failed to cite any instances of anyone becoming ill from fish caught in the Everglades.
And though Faw said that sugar cane fields "continue to seep
southward [and] developers are inching closer to the park every
year," he did not say how this was hurting the Everglades.

To Faw's report, therefore, the viewer rightly could demand:
"Where is the corpse?" If no one was becoming ill from Everglades
fish and if the park was not being damaged by expanding farmland,
then the viewer could equally demand: "What is the problem?"

To be sure, the Everglades may be endangered. And sugar-cane
farmers may well be culprits, but Faw did not make the case for
this. Instead, he and CBS "Evening News" seemed to use a presumed Everglades problem to sound an alarmist chord as background music for the Rio conference.

Much more balanced was ABC's June 3 and 4 broadcasts about
India. Here "World News Tonight" recounted how economic
growth in a country as populous as India could increase global
pollution vastly and put other pressures on the environment. "Consider what could happen to the world," said reporter Ned Potter,
"if shantytown cooking fires are replaced by thousands of smoke-
stacks, if the one million cars here grow to half a billion." Despite
painting this terrifying picture of what Indian modernization could
do to world ecology, ABC avoided even hinting that India should
consider forsaking growth as a proenvironment measure. Instead,

"World News Tonight" told viewers about Indian attempts to produce nonpolluting energy: a solar pond to store heat for pasteurizing milk; wind turbines on the shores of the Arabian Sea; and farmers producing natural gas from agricultural waste.

What viewers thus learned from "World News Tonight" was the useful concept that there are no easy answers in the environmental debate—that though growth has environmental consequences, no country can be expected to forsake growth. The trouble was that "World News Tonight" also told viewers that only hundreds of billions of dollars in aid from wealthy nations, much in the form of technology, could help India avert environmental catastrophe. Portrayed as particularly stingy, predictably, was America, which also was implicitly criticized for being reluctant to share its modern technology with the Third World. Potter failed to say that because India offered poor protection for patents, the West has long feared giving new technology to it and similar nations.

In addition to the stories directly dealing with Rio, the summit prompted the networks this week to air more than a half-dozen other segments on environmental issues. From most of them, viewers again correctly learned that tough environmental regulations could threaten economic growth. CBS "Evening News" May 31, for example, analyzed what it called Kansas City's tough choices in fighting air pollution. It explained the trade-off between antipollution measures and growth and also introduced viewers to the complex, but economically sound, concept that pollution could be reduced by allowing businesses to sell to each other the unused portion of their allotment to emit pollutants.

BEYOND RIO

TV coverage of the Rio Summit crowded out many other economic stories this week. The most compelling of those that were broadcast, because of their broad consumer interest, were the looming strike at AT&T and the end of the airline fare wars.

With the conceivable interruption of complete nationwide

phone service, the networks understandably gave extensive coverage to the possibility that 125,000 AT&T workers would walk off the job. The week saw eleven stories on this. Almost all of them, again understandably, updated the status of AT&T-union negotiations. CNN "World News" May 30 told viewers that if there were a strike, temporary workers were ready to fill in; the following day, all four networks reported that negotiations were going into overtime; and the morning of June 1, CNN and NBC reassured viewers that the talks were still going on, while CBS announced that new contracts had been signed and a strike averted.

But the useful status reports aside, viewers learned very little about the issues in the dispute. NBC "Nightly News" said it was a matter of job security and ABC said it was wages, job losses, and pensions. Typical of how the networks approached the issue was the report by David French on CNN "Prime News" May 31; he explained that the unions were seeking better pay and job protection.

In none of the eleven broadcasts on the strike did any reporter explain what AT&T was seeking or why. Nor did any reporter, even fleetingly, look at the extremely competitive economic dynamics of the fast-evolving global telecommunications industry. These might have prompted AT&T to make new demands on its workforce, demands which were being resisted by the unions.

As with the AT&T strike, the airline fare wars was very much a consumer story. The ten newscasts on it this week reported "travel agencies and ticket offices choked with summer bargain hunters," 2 million calls to airline offices, jammed airplanes, 25 million tickets sold, and one American in ten planning to fly during the summer at half-price.

Yet in all the reporting, again as with the AT&T strike coverage, the networks gave viewers scant economic information. The little learned by the viewer was that: the fare wars could force weaker airlines out of business (CBS "Evening News"); hotels, car rental agencies, and other travel-related industries would benefit enormously from the increased number of travellers (CNN "World News"); and travel was a $15 billion industry, employing 200,000 (CBS "Evening News").

Missing from all ten newscasts was even a hint of journalism's mandatory "Why." There was no discussion, for example, of what prompted the airlines to slash fares nor of the fierce competition ignited by airline deregulation.

The week's only other compelling economic-related story was Los Angeles's continuing efforts to recover from its late-April, early-May riots. ABC "Good Morning America" June 2 interviewed Los Angeles Mayor Tom Bradley who, along with California Governor Pete Wilson, was visiting Washington seeking federal aid to rebuild Los Angeles' damaged areas. Bradley's entire message was that only government could rebuild Los Angeles.

Viewers could have heard a different message the following day when CBS "This Morning" interviewed Peter Ueberroth, then in charge of the effort to rebuild Los Angeles. Presumably, this gave CBS host Harry Smith at least a chance to mention some of the private economic forces that could be tapped to reconstruct Los Angeles' damaged areas. But Smith wasted this opportunity. Instead, he focused almost exclusively on the story's horse race aspect—whether partisan politics would get in the way of federal funding.

In their discussion of Los Angeles, Peter Jennings and Bob Jamieson on ABC "World News Tonight" June 2 introduced viewers to Enterprise Zones, a concept calling for the reduction of taxes, regulations, and other government-imposed barriers to economic activity in designated impoverished areas. Enterprise Zone proponents have argued that this would stimulate investment and jobs in the inner city and other chronically underdeveloped communities. Enterprise Zones were being discussed as one solution for Los Angeles.

It was useful for viewers to hear about Enterprise Zones. But it was misleading for Jennings to define them as "areas mostly in inner cities where the federal government would create jobs by offering industry new tax breaks to set up shop there." This incorrectly told viewers that government created jobs and that government would do so in the zones. What would have been correct would have been:

"What advocates expect to happen in Enterprise Zones is that investors and other risk-takers will create jobs after the government-made barriers to entrepreneurial activity are removed."

TV's PORTRAIT OF BUSINESSES AND BUSINESSPERSONS

As with every week, TV this week profiled a number of businesses, though fewer than usual, probably because of the heavy coverage of the Rio Summit. As also in other weeks, the profile seen by newscast viewers was skewed: business was something suspicious and tainted. Not once in the week was a business depicted as creating the jobs and wealth that push up the nation's living standards.

In the week, viewers learned that:

1. Rockwell International, according to CNN "World News" and NBC "Nightly News," would have to pay fines for illegally treating and disposing of waste at Rocky Flats in Colorado.
2. Jaw implants, according to CBS "Evening News" Edie Magnus, could leak artificial particles into the body.
3. Manufacturers of suntan lotion were misleading consumers, according to ABC "World News Tonight" Bettina Gregory, because the lotion's labels said nothing about the potential dangers from Ultraviolet A, which was not blocked by the lotion.
4. Many medical journal advertisements for drugs, according to CBS "This Morning" Paula Zahn, were misleading doctors. A study of the matter, said Zahn, was calling for tighter government regulation of those advertisements.
5. General Electric Company, according to NBC "Today" Keith Morrison, was penalized for violating a ban on the sales of certain engines to Israel.
6. A heart valve manufacturer, according to CBS "This Morning," was being sued for a valve which allegedly had a tendency to break.

7. Fruit juice makers were misleading consumers, according to CNN "World News" Susan Rook, because labels on the fronts of fruit juice containers did not summarize exactly the container's actual contents as listed on the labels on the backs of the containers. Rook cited an unnamed public interest group which was insisting that federal regulations require that front labels, as well as back labels, list the container's content by percentage.

In the week, viewers also were reminded of the troubles of convicted Wall Street financier Michael Milken, when CBS "This Morning" June 3 reported that he had returned to court in an attempt to reduce his ten-year sentence.

The only upbeat news about a business came from ABC "World News Tonight" Stephen Aug who reported on June 2 that the Big 3 American automakers were increasing output, boosting the quality of their products faster than the Japanese, and, for the first time in six years, taking business away from the Japanese. To make its point, ABC interviewed a woman in New York City who had traded her Nissan for a General Motors Saturn. She and other car buyers were finding, according to two Talking Heads, that the quality of American cars had been increasing while the price of Japanese cars had been going up.

What's New on the Market

In network reports on innovations in the marketplace, viewers learned that:

1. Unemployed graphic designer Michael Hernandez of San Francisco, according to Dave Michaels and Linda Joyce on CNN "Prime News" May 31, started a cooperative that was finding odd jobs for unemployed professionals.
2. A new kind of lightbulb had been invented which would last more than ten years and save energy, according to all four

networks on June 1. Reporter Al Hinman on CNN "World News" said that the lightbulb would cost $15 and burn for ten to twenty years; NBC "Nightly News" reporter Robin Lloyd said that it would burn for fourteen years; and ABC "World News Tonight" reporter Jim Slade said that it would cost $20.

These factual discrepancies among the networks, however, were not the main difficulty with the coverage. It was the wasted opportunity by reporters. This technological development could have, but did not, inspired them to ask: "What prompts such inventions?" Even a lone sentence could have revealed to viewers the key contribution of entrepreneurs and risk-takers to progress.

Nor did any reporter mention that though the lightbulb would be expensive at first, the price almost surely would drop as manufacturers refined the product—just as TV sets, computers, VCRs, calculators, and thousands of similar innovations plunged in price after landing on the market.

Consumers this week were told:

1. To be careful when making investments. CBS money editor John Stehr on "This Morning" June 1 cautioned that silver was not likely to be a wise investment and that, despite ostensible government guarantees, "collateralized mortgage obligations" carried considerable risk.
2. Manufacturers of soap, detergent, soft drink, and other goods were removing the color from their products. "Clear," explained Hattie Kauffmann on CBS "This Morning" June 3, was becoming the trendy look for products.
3. To investigate carefully the appropriate kind of life insurance. This caution came in a report by *Money* magazine editor Tyler Mathisen on ABC "Good Morning America" June 3.

ENTERTAINMENT'S MESSAGE

Some entertainment shows understandably pick up on contemporary themes. Sexual harassment and the recession, for instance, both turned up this week in CBS's "Trials of Rosie O'Neill." In the episode, Rosie's daughter Kim felt that she was being sexually pressured by the editor when she sought a job on the school paper. Meanwhile, Rosie, a public defender, complained that she was being overworked because the hard economic times were forcing people to use public defenders rather than private lawyers. Sexual harassment too was a theme in NBC's "Different World."

Businesspersons and the free enterprise economy got a fairer break from entertainment programs this week than from newscasts. In ABC's "Who's the Boss," Angela pressed her son to get a job because she believed that it would give him strength and build character. Said Angela: "If Jonathan finds his own job it will build confidence and strength. And it will give him a better outlook on life." Similarly Roseanne's husband Dan, in ABC's "Roseanne," told his daughter Becky that she would have to get a job to pay for her new car because "it's better to earn something than to have it handed to you." NBC's "In the Heat of the Night" sympathetically depicted the town's banker, while Fox's "Family Matters" featured kind and hard-working Aunt Rachel who owned a restaurant.

Perhaps the most honest portrayal of free enterprise was in NBC's "Law & Order," despite its cops' sarcastic attitude towards businessmen and women (and, it seems, towards almost everything else). A major character in the episode was a woman who owned a garment company. Viewers were taken inside her Manhattan factory and saw her bustling around, harried and hard-working, and heard her say: "Designing clothes. It's a tough business; twenty-four hours a day and then some." When one cop implied that she might be ignoring her son, she retorted: "I work. Is that a crime?"

As in other weeks, however, entertainment TV's favorable portrayals of how free enterprise works and of businesses and businesspersons were far outnumbered by the unfavorable. Examples:

1. In NBC's "Sisters" and CBS's "Major Dad," families working together were depicted cynically. At times, of course, tensions rise and nerves fray in family-businesses. But this was never balanced by the vastly more important theme—that family businesses have served as the most typical means by which poor Americans and immigrants have become economically successful.
2. In ABC's "Civil Wars," thrift was ridiculed.
3. In ABC's "Billy," businessman Roger canceled a visit to his kids because he had to fly to Australia on business.
4. In Fox's "Vinnie & Bobby," a construction company cheated its customers.
5. In NBC' "Seinfeld," a doctor defrauded an insurance company.
6. In NBC's "Fresh Prince of Bel Air," a home shopping TV network sold cheap and worthless merchandise (such as a musical toilet seat and something called an abdominizer) to viewers addicted to shopping.
7. In CBS's "Davis Rules," Dan tripled his money by selling his failing clam business to a naive and trusting colleague.
8. In NBC's "L.A. Law," a businessman fraudulently sold high-calorie shakes as diet shakes.
9. In ABC's "Dinosaurs," a construction company (once again) cravenly chopped down a redwood forest to make room for a housing development.

Perhaps entertainment's most unfair portrayal of a businessman this week was by NBC's "Quantum Leap." It gradually transformed Phil from a small businessman widely respected in the community, who had paid all of his creditors even after declaring bankruptcy, into a drug dealer.

Some programs trivialized businessmen and women. NBC's movie *Roxanne: The Prize Pulitzer* never showed viewers the very wealthy and presumably very successful businessman working at his job. And though ABC's "Civil Wars" first painted a very appealing picture of Joy D'Amato, who had worked hard making a success of the employment agency she had founded, she evolved into an emotional cripple, dependent on her ne'er-do-well, guitar-playing husband.

GETTING THE FACTS WRONG

Among network TV's most serious mistakes this week in reporting economic-related facts and data were:

1. ABC reporter Forrest Sawyer's statement on "Nightline" June 1 that "the world is a vastly poorer place today than it was when you were born." He was wrong. By all evidence, the world is vastly richer than it was a half or quarter century ago, whether measured by life-expectancy, caloric intake, literacy, material living standards, sanitation and indoor plumbing, availability of affordable housing, or countless other factors. Sawyer should have said:

"The world is richer now than it was when you were born, largely because of economic growth. Developing countries must ponder this and try to maintain economic growth policies while addressing environmental concerns."

2. ABC "World News Tonight" Anchor Peter Jennings' statement June 2 that "government creates jobs" in urban Enterprise Zones. He was wrong. What Jennings should have said was:

"In Enterprise Zones, say advocates, investors will create jobs when government-made barriers are lowered or removed."

3. NBC Reporter Keith Morrison's statement on "Nightly News" June 2 that the airline fare wars are "a Darwinian process in which the consumer saves now and pays later." He was wrong. There is no evidence that the intense airline competition ultimately

leads to higher fares. To the contrary; since deregulation fares have fallen. Morrison should have said:

"The fare wars are a Darwinian process in which consumers win—and the most capable airlines survive."

4. Reporting as indisputable fact, by all networks on the Rio Earth Summit, that the world was teetering on the edge of environmental catastrophe, when, in fact, the extent of the environmental danger has been widely disputed. Only ABC science editor Michael Guillen on "Good Morning America" June 2 and Robert Bazell on NBC "Nightly News" June 4 challenged the doomsday assertions. Their prudent skepticism contrasted noticeably with Ed Rabel's hysteria on NBC "Nightly News" June 3; he warned that Rio "may be the last chance, they say, to save the planet."

5. CBS Economics and Business reporter Robert Krulwich's argument on "This Morning" June 4 that tough environmental regulations would be good for the economy because compliance with them would force businesses to buy new equipment. To which anchor Harry Smith added: "That all works in theory." Both were wrong; it works neither in theory nor in practice. To be sure, some new industries do sprout to provide products needed to satisfy government regulations; for example, seat belts and catalytic converters. Those special industries thus might benefit from regulations. But the economy would not benefit because the regulations merely would divert resources from one set of industries to another.

6. NBC reporter Mike Jensen's statement on "Nightly News" June 5 that jobs create economic growth. He had it backwards. He should have said:

"Unemployment figures are likely to stay high until the economy starts growing and only that, ultimately, will create jobs."

NEWSCASTS' MESSAGE

Messages conveyed by TV's economic coverage in this week were almost all unfriendly to a free enterprise economy. While the isolated facts might have been true in the specific cases, what was false was the implication, from TV's lack of offsetting examples, that the specific case typified the American economic system.

The messages heard and seen by viewers this week included:

1. Federal government aid was essential for rebuilding riot-damaged Los Angeles.
2. Businesses illegally disposed of toxic wastes, manufactured flawed jaw implants, misled consumers in labelling suntan lotion and fruit juices, and misled doctors in medical journal advertising.
3. A population explosion, which anchor Connie Chung, quoting Jacques Cousteau on CBS "Evening News" June 5, called "the genocide of population growth," threatened the environment. By contrast, reporter Sean Callebs on CNN "World News" June 5 noted that many experts say that population growth goes hand in hand with progress.

Most of the economic messages conveyed in the week were related to the Rio environmental conference. These included:

1. Only government action could prevent environmental catastrophe.
2. America was "Enemy #1" at Rio and the main obstacle to international cooperation to preserve the environment.
3. American officials "watered down" important environmental agreements.
4. America lagged behind other nations in programs to protect the environment.
5. Only scores of billions of dollars in extra aid from the West

would allow the Third World to develop economically in ways that would not endanger the environment.

6. Environmental experts all agreed that the world was facing ecological catastrophe and only massive government action could prevent it.

7. Poor peasants had no choice but to farm in ways that harmed "unique" rain forests and other valuable environmental areas.

8. Trade was destroying the Philippine forests.

Of the week's messages, the most confusing to viewers was probably that dealing with the May jump in unemployment. Depending upon the network, viewers were told that unemployment was up because the public was either more optimistic about the economy or more pessimistic about it.

No TV message was less informed on economic principles and how the free enterprise economy works than the ones dealing with Third World peasants. "Nightline" Don Kladstrup on June 1, for instance, seemed to think that Madagascar's peasants had no alternative but to pursue the slash-and-burn farming that was destroying their country's forests. There were, in fact, other alternatives. To alert the viewer to them Kladstrup should have said:

"Perhaps if the Madagascar economic system would give the peasants a stake in the land and a market on which to sell their crops for the best price, the peasants would have an incentive to preserve and improve their land—as have landowners throughout history. Then the peasants would half their slashing and burning."

Robert Krulwich on CBS "This Morning" June 2 repeated Kladstrup's error. Said Krulwich: "If you are poor, and there are going to be a lot more poor people living right along rain forests, you have a choice. You can knock down some trees, plant a crop, and feed your family. Or you can save the trees, protect some bugs, and starve. Now which would you do?" To Krulwich, the peasant had no choice. In fact, the peasant did.

Curiously, Krulwich hinted at an alternative when he alluded to the important role played by property rights. But then he ignored the obvious implication—that property rights and a market economy could broaden the choices of those peasants living by the rain forest. He did not explore whether property rights was a viable economic alternative to destroying the forest.

Krulwich could have done so by saying:

"Right now, if you are poor and live by a rain forest, you don't have much choice. But if you, or even your village, is given an ownership right to your land, you'll want to preserve and improve that land. Then you'll be able to eat, save the trees, and protect some bugs all at the same time. You might even have surplus crops to sell."

An important exception to the generally anti-free enterprise message in the reporting from Rio was the theme in several stories of the trade-off between tough environmental protection and economic growth. Though it was important that viewers were told of this trade-off, it would have been much better had the networks not ignored almost completely how free market approaches might make the trade-off less painful. Reporters could have alerted viewers, even if briefly, to the concept that the market could find ways to protect the environment at minimum cost to the economy. Instead, all the viewers heard and saw was that the environment could be saved only through enormous sacrifice.

What might have been the most valuable economic message in the week's network TV was the observation by CBS consumer reporter Hattie Kauffman on CBS "This Morning" June 3 that "everyday at the checkout stand we cast our votes. If we want our mascara clear or wine coolers clear, that's just what the manufacturers will give us." In saying this she reminded viewers of the enormous power of choice in the free enterprise system and how this unleashes the dynamics of competition. This was the simple, but valid, insight missing from most reporting on the economy.

LETTING OPPORTUNITIES SLIP AWAY

TV coverage in this week as in others missed opportunities to educate Americans on how their economy functions. Such squandered opportunities included:

1. Reporting by all networks on May's high unemployment figures. The unexpectedly sharp jump in joblessness could have been used as a peg to discuss how jobs are created.
2. Reporting by all networks on the possibility of an AT&T strike. Missed was the chance to describe the rapid changes in the telecommunications industry and how AT&T had become one of America's most globally competitive firms.
3. Reporting by all networks on the airline fare wars. Pegged to this could have been some discussion of how the consumer had been benefitting—with lower prices, more frequent service, frequent-flyer award benefits—from the fierce airline competition.
4. Bettina Gregory's ABC "World News Tonight" June 5 story on suntan lotion's inadequate protection against Ultraviolet A. In passing, Gregory mentioned that while the Federal Food and Drug Administration had been considering the Ultraviolet A matter for fourteen years, a private firm already had invented a badge to warn sunbathers when they risked overexposure. Gregory missed the opportunity to speculate why the private sector had responded faster than the federal bureaucracy to consumer needs.
5. Jeanne Meserve's CNN "Prime News" story May 31 about Chris Whittle's plans to set up a chain of for-profit schools. Though mainly an education story focusing on whether such schools would improve teaching, Meserve missed the chance to explore, even briefly, how the profit motive might create better schools.
6. Mark Litke's ABC "World News Tonight" profile May 31 of Namibia. The segment ended with Namibian official Chris

Brown saying that because Namibian peasants would share the profits of a new tourism industry, the peasants would ensure that the environment needed for tourism was maintained. This was a valid and very useful recognition of how economic forces, such as property rights and profits, could create incentives protecting the environment. This could have been the core point of the segment, with Litke analyzing whether similar economic forces could protect the environment in other developing lands.

7. ABC reporter Don Kladstrup's "Nightline" profile June 1 of Madagascar. Despite the considerable length of the segment, Kladstrup interviewed no economists or other experts who could have suggested ways for poor countries to save their environment without massive amounts of foreign aid or draconian regulations which smother economic growth. At the least, Kladstrup could have made and elaborated Mark Litke's point in the previous night's Namibia story on ABC: that economic forces could be marshalled for environmental protection.

The week's most seriously squandered opportunity was the Rio Summit coverage. Enormous time was devoted to it, yet there was almost no effort to give viewers new or different perspectives of the environment issue. Reporters could have pursued a number of story lines: whether nonconventional approaches could save the environment; whether it was valid for the Third World to claim that it could protect the environment only with hundreds of billions of dollars in new aid; whether new aid for the Third World would end up (as with much previous aid) in the pockets of corrupt officials rather than be used for the environment; and whether huge Rio-like global conferences ever accomplish anything.

CHAPTER THREE

A TYPICAL WEEK: SEPTEMBER 5-11

RIGHT ON DAY CARE, WRONG ON THE RECESSION

AS THE FALL season began, the news that dominated TV news in the week after Labor Day was the final stretch of the election. Clinton and Bush were pushing their economic plans and each was claiming to be this year's Harry Truman. Other big stories dealt with the Hurricane Andrew clean-up efforts, the hurricane relief aid bill before Congress, and baseball commissioner Fay Vincent's resignation.

In economic coverage, no one story dominated the news as had the Rio Summit in the May-June week. Instead, coverage generally was limited to the day on which a story broke: on Monday, a study was released claiming that white collar workers earned less; on Tuesday, Bush asked for a $7.6 billion aid bill for Hurricane Andrew relief; on Wednesday, GM unveiled its credit card; on Thursday, the Family Leave Bill was passed by Congress; on Friday, wholesale prices were up; and over the weekend, the GM strike ended.

Throughout this week, as in others, the networks continually garnished newscasts with dollops of economic statistics. Every morning viewers turning into CBS could find out whether the dollar, the Dow Jones stock market index, and the Tokyo stock exchange were up or down. From all networks viewers learned that manufacturing jobs had shrunk by 97,000, bank profits had soared, business and consumer confidence had dropped, wholesale prices had climbed, the average mortgage rate was 7.84 percent, capital investment was down, new unemployment claims were up, and a new, lower-priced Bentley auto had been introduced costing a mere 180,000 dollars.

Going a step beyond disjointed recitation of statistics, ABC's John McWethy on "World News Tonight" September 9 gave viewers the kind of useful background that was rare on TV. With it, viewers could evaluate the business confidence survey. He explained that for the survey, the Chamber of Commerce had asked five thousand businessmen and women across America to judge the nation's economic outlook, their own business sales, and hiring prospects. Most of these businesspersons, viewers were told, owned small stores and enterprises and thus were close to their customers. To put the survey's results in some perspective, McWethy explained what the trend line had been through the year.

GETTING IT RIGHT ON DAY CARE

Typically, when TV identified a problem, TV dwelt almost exclusively on how government could solve it. This was not the case, however, in network treatment this week of working mothers' need for child care. In covering this story, the networks were forced by events to report private sector efforts to solve the problem.

On September 10, ABC, CBS, and CNN reported that Amoco, Citibank, Exxon, IBM, Xerox, and more than one hundred other large firms had announced that they would spend about $25 million in forty-four cities on facilities and staff to care for the children of their employees. The firms also would offer their employees what is called elder care—care for aging parents.

According to ABC's Bob Jamieson on "World News Tonight" that day, the companies had said that the absence of government child care had prompted them, in their own self-interest, to establish child care facilities. Jamieson interviewed Barbara Katersky, vice-president of employee relations at American Express, who explained that child care would increase American Express productivity and make the company more competitive with foreign rivals that had taxpayer-funded child care.

From Jamieson's segment, viewers learned important characteristics of free enterprise:

1. If government does not address a genuine need, the private sector will.
2. What motivates private firms is at times altruism but mainly self-interest.
3. Such self-interested actions can benefit society.
4. Corporate investment in child care centers and elder care programs would increase productivity and competitiveness.

Jamieson's reporting demonstrated how even brief news reports can educate Americans about their economic system. With a bit more time, Jamieson could have improved his segment by explaining what Katersky had meant when she said that day care centers would boost productivity and competitiveness. Viewers also would have benefitted had Jamieson specifically pointed out that as soon as some companies offered day care, others would have to follow suit in order to attract qualified employees.

That, in fact, was the point made by family care analyst Dana Friedman on CBS "This Morning" September 11. She said that "with these giant corporations now financing family care, experts say, look for still more companies to do it if they want to attract and keep good workers."

On September 11, ABC returned to the day care story and again reported it in a way that told viewers something about free enterprise dynamics. On "Good Morning America," Mike Schneider said: "What is good for the family is apparently good for business." Reinforcing Jamieson's report the previous evening, this indicates that successful businesses must address their employees' needs and that they will do so without government mandates.

In contrast to Jamieson's report was Ray Brady's September 10 day care development commentary on CBS "Evening News." It not only gave viewers little insight on their economy but also probably misinformed them. Brady told viewers: "Don't look on all this as corporate charity. Most of the employees will be paying for the care. Yet, the companies feel it is crucial to provide these community services for their workers."

One problem with Brady's report was his statement about charity. To be sure, the corporate day care project was not charity; but Brady missed the point on why it was not. To him, apparently, the fact that workers would pay something prevented the day care centers from being charity. In truth, what did so was that the corporations would benefit from the day care centers—through higher productivity and competitiveness.

In failing to see this, as in much of his other commentary throughout 1992, Brady seemed unaware that in a free enterprise system a corporation need not give charity to do good; rather, good typically resulted from a corporation pursuing its interests in an open, competitive market. Firms committed millions of dollars to day care not because corporate executives became convinced that fairness required day care but because the executives concluded that their employees would be worried about their children less and be absent less and thus more productive if corporate day care facilities were available. To have been correct, Brady should have said:

"Don't look on this as corporate charity. As with most corporate actions, something done out of self-interest can also help others."

GETTING IT WRONG ON THE RECESSION

Presumably because the week began with Labor Day, the prolonged recession was the topic of six stories; this was more coverage on the subject than in the other sample weeks. CBS "This Morning" September 7 featured money editor John Stehr advising viewers on how to keep their jobs when the economy was in the dumps. CNN "World News" September 9 carried a short item that Hughes Aircraft would lay off four thousand workers from its missile division and that this would hit workers hard.

NBC "Nightly News" on two successive evenings looked at poverty. On September 5, Deborah Roberts cited a census report showing more people living below the poverty line than at any time since 1964. The following night, Jeff Madrick cited a report by the Economic Policy Institute which purported to find a rise in the number of "the working poor."

The Economic Policy Institute report also triggered a story on ABC's "Good Morning America" September 7. On it, Morton Dean declared that a survey was "catching up with what Americans already know: they are making less money." Then Sheilah Kast, citing what she described as a biannual report on the state of working Americans, said that white collar wages were dropping just as blue collar wages had dropped in the 1980s. The only specialist interviewed by Kast was the Economic Policy Institute's Lawrence Mishel.

One serious problem with Kast's report was her failure to tell viewers that the institute consistently had criticized and found fault with America's free enterprise economy. What was worse, Kast interviewed no one who disputed the report's statistics or its interpretation of them. Yet many economists, including those on Congress's Joint Economic Committee, had criticized the statistics, explaining that the only reason they seemed to show a drop in earnings was that they did not count all forms of compensation.

A second serious problem was Kast's failure to explain the weaknesses in the study's methodology. Had she done so, she would have told viewers that the study's source, the Bureau of Labor Statistics, had not included self-employed or supervisory workers in its data; this brought the numbers down. Avoiding this mistake were analysts at the Social Security Administration; when they included such workers, they found that the average wage increased during the 1980s. Neither Kast nor other reporters, moreover, noted that the study started in 1979. This meant that it included three years (1979–1981) during which the average wage fell precipitously—three years before it began to gain again in 1981 and to rise steadily throughout the 1980s. To have been accurate, Kast would have had to have said:

"Thanks to policies in the eighties, workers almost caught up to their 1979 level. With more of the same medicine, perhaps Clinton or Bush can revive that trend."

CBS "Evening News" September 7 offered the week's longest segment on the recession. In it, correspondent Bill Whitaker in Tokyo interviewed some of the several thousand Americans who had gone to Japan looking for work. According to Whitaker, Japanese companies were hiring American college grads who had found it tough getting entry-level jobs back home. The segment's message was summarized in Whitaker's punch line: "Many economists say that if the U.S. does not get its economic house in order, even more young Americans may come looking for work in Japan."

This misled viewers in several ways. For one thing, it implied that, unlike America, Japan was booming and had jobs aplenty. The opposite was true; Japan was suffering (and continued to suffer at least through late 1993) its most severe economic setback in nearly two decades. Not only were Japanese stock prices, property values, retail sales, business investment, and construction plunging sharply, but Japanese workers who had counted on lifetime jobs were being laid off. In almost every measurable respect, the Japanese recession was worse than the American.

For another thing, Whitaker misled viewers by failing to emphasize that Americans seeking jobs in Japan faced extraordinary obstacles (language among them) unless they had special skills and filled special slots. This implicitly, and perhaps inadvertently, was confirmed when Whitaker gave viewers only four examples of Americans landing jobs in Japan: dancer Steven Hanes who admitted that he had come to Japan because competition was too tough at home; Craig Swardout who was teaching English to Japanese business executives; and Frank Douglas and Stephan LaBrocke who were working at banks.

The obvious point that Whitaker should have made was that few unemployed Americans were dancers and not many more would qualify as English teachers. And while Whitaker noted that Swardout with his wife Rebecca were earning $72,000 in Japan, tripling their California salary where they had worked at a child abuse center, Whitaker did not point out that an influx of English teachers from America into Japan would drive down the rates that these Americans could charge the Japanese. Nor did the segment alert viewers to the very high cost of living in Japan.

TV's PORTRAIT OF BUSINESSES AND BUSINESSPERSONS

The networks this week aired twenty-six stories on business in addition to the five stories on corporations' plans for day care centers. In contrast to most other weeks, viewers were shown more than just the seamy side of business. The day care stories, for instance, gave viewers some understanding of how competitive pressures prompted businesses to address societal problems.

Similarly illuminating the creative aspect of businesses was Jeff Madrick's NBC "Nightly News" September 5 report on the spread of flexible and unconventional working hours. The story was marred only by anchor Deborah Roberts' introduction which told viewers that "even in these tough economic times companies are showing surprising flexibility." By saying "surprising," Roberts revealed her lack of understanding of how free enterprise functions. Flexibility has been one of its hallmarks, in sharp contrast to the rigidity of centrally planned and managed economies and of government bureaucracies. What Roberts should have told viewers was:

"In the face of trying times, American business is demonstrating typical flexibility."

In a business-related story, CNN "World News" on two successive nights carried short items on General Motors' announcement that it was issuing a GM credit card, the use of which could earn cardholders rebates on purchases of GM autos. ABC "World News

Tonight" reported this on September 9 with an analysis by Stephen Aug which touched most important bases. He asked, for example: "Who are the big losers?" The answer came from the president of RAM Research, Robert McKinley, who said that the big banks who were still clinging to high interest rates of 19.8 percent would lose big.

But Aug then seemed to suppress his journalistic inquisitiveness, failing to pose the obvious paired question: "Who are the big winners?" A discussion of this would have given viewers interesting information and some insight into how competitive forces operate. In this discussion, Aug could have pointed out that, as credit card competition heated up, the big winners would be consumers. This Aug did not say. Indeed, his only remark about consumers was that "some consumer advocates say all the advantages of the new cards may encourage consumers to spend too much." To Aug, the moral in this story was that consumers were always perilously close to danger in the free enterprise system and scarcely ever benefitted from it.

CBS "This Morning" September 11 looked at the rising costs of drugs. The segment was structured as a morality play in which good consumers battled evil corporations. Host Harry Smith set the tone when he told viewers they were going to hear about what "some call the nation's other drug crisis" and that "consumer groups [were] crying foul" at the rising costs. Then reporter Edie Magnus said: "The group, Families USA, accused the drug makers of greed, saying big drug companies are now making profits that far surpass other industries." CBS's lineup of Talking Heads confirmed the segment's tilt: two criticizing the drug firms (Ron Pollack of Families USA and Senator William Cohen of Maine) versus one defending them (Gerald Mossinghoff, president of the Pharmaceutical Manufacturers Association).

From Pollack, viewers heard that drug companies were "making those profits the old-fashioned way, by gouging consumers." This was echoed by Magnus in her kicker to the segment, framing the matter in terms of the people against big business. She said: "This wasn't the first time consumers cried foul. But with the administration squarely on the side of the pharmaceutical industry and heavy lobbying by the drug companies themselves, the votes in Congress to contain drug costs just aren't there—not yet anyway." To offset all of this, viewers were given only a Mossinghoff soundbite that drug firms had to remain economically healthy if they were to continue finding cures for diseases. Surely Mossinghoff said more in his interview.

What viewers did not hear was that the drug industry has been remarkably innovative. Charles Krauthammer pointed this out in his May 28, 1993, column in the *Washington Post*: "Indeed the supposedly damning statistic that 58 percent of new drugs are not really new means that an astonishing 42 percent are new, that is, constitute genuine therapeutic advances and make real contributions to human well-being. What other industry can say that?"

Twelve of the week's business stories dealt with businesses in trouble (TWA cutting jobs and the cities to which it flew) or with business frauds. Short items on NBC "Today" and CNN "World News" reported the indictment of a Silverado Savings and Loan executive. The "Today" item was followed by Garrick Utley's profile (repeated on "Nightly News") of disastrous investments made by a couple of S&Ls.

To Tom Brokaw of "Nightly News," who introduced Utley, the report was about "what some describe as the biggest bank robbery ever." Yet despite the segment's considerable length, all the viewer saw was a hodgepodge of disconnected factoids, soundbites, and scenes of a failed Florida real estate development. Utley could have been reporting on any failed investment. His segment told viewers almost nothing about either savings and loans or the savings and loan crisis.

Further reports of business misbehavior were on CNN "World News" September 8 (a New York meat company involved in laundering $82 million in food stamps), CBS "This Morning" September 11 (the dangers of tanning salons and misleading labels on food packages), and CBS "Evening News" September 11 (United Technologies pleading guilty to defense contract frauds).

Labor unrest was covered by six stories in the week. CNN "World News" and NBC "Nightly News" reported the end of a strike at a General Motors plant. CNN's David French called the strike a victory for the union and a defeat for GM. Viewers were not told why it was a victory for one and a defeat for the other. Striking Las Vegas hotel workers who stopped traffic outside the Frontier Hotel made it onto NBC "Nightly News" September 7.

ABC and CNN each carried a story on teachers' strikes. The message from CNN's Anne McDermott on "World News" September 7 was clear and direct: higher taxes alone could solve education problems. McDermott interviewed only striking teachers or those sympathetic to them. One after another, teacher Talking Heads painted a gruesome picture of education in California. Los Angeles teacher Lila Dawson-Weber even warned that "we have teachers who are going to lose homes, teachers who will have to file bankruptcy." No one was interviewed who offered an alternative (such as a variant of education choice proposals) or questioned whether money was the solution to education's problems. Viewers heard no one pointing out that many states that rank high in education performance rank low in per pupil expenditure.

The Other Stories

This week, viewers:

1. Heard Labor Secretary Lynn Martin on CBS "This Morning" September 7 make the correct point that most jobs in the 1990s were expected to be created by small- and medium-size businesses. As such, she warned against measures that would increase these businesses' tax and regulatory burdens.

2. Heard NBC's Irving R. Levine on "Nightly News" September 7 tell viewers that some companies were downsizing by offering workers early retirement. Levine's segment was generally informative, but he ended it by saying, "Whether workers jump or are pushed, it adds up to the same thing for the nation's economy— more people out of work." He failed to tell viewers about another implication for the economy: that inefficient companies, by down-

sizing, could become more competitive and ultimately fuel economic growth and then create more jobs. Levine should have said:

"Whether workers jump or are pushed makes a big difference to the worker. An early retirement option eases the pain of changes inherent in a dynamic, productive economy. And in the long run, the companies will be more competitive and this will lead to new jobs—either at that company or elsewhere."

3. Heard Peter Jennings on ABC "World News Tonight" September 8 say that fewer Americans had died in accidents in 1991 than in any year since 1924; even traffic fatalities were down.

4. Heard about Harlan, Iowa, a small town which, according to Fred Briggs on NBC "Nightly News" September 9, was bucking the trend of decline in rural America. Yet Briggs never told viewers just how or why Harlan was succeeding. Though Briggs interviewed plant manager Lonnie Miller who said that the town "did a good job of . . . convincing us that this was a good place to relocate," Briggs never asked Miller nor anyone else what that good job was or what had lured them back to Harlan. Instead, what viewers did learn from Briggs was merely that a town could revive if it hired a booster to promote it, held pep rallies, built a swimming pool, and spruced up its downtown.

5. Learned something very useful about the price of regulation and mandated benefits when John Gibson on NBC "Nightly News" September 11 described how workman's compensation payments in California were hurting business. Gibson interviewed Los Angeles restaurant owner Michael Stenison who told viewers that while he could survive riots and crime, "I can't survive worker's compensation insurance." Gibson helpfully explained that the cost of insurance for Stenison had jumped from $6,000 to $13,000 per month. Gibson then turned to clothing manufacturer Dennis Maroney who, said Gibson, would have to lay off sixty workers because of a 100 percent jump in his workmen's compensation bill. After Maroney told viewers that he would be leaving California, Gibson

said that "many otherwise flourishing businesses are leaving the state, or shutting down, or laying off workers, or not giving raises simply because of the cost of worker's compensation insurance."

6. Heard CBS's Robert Krulwich's analyze on "This Morning" September 8 why great numbers of women were entering the work force. From it Americans learned a number of valid and useful economic facts, including: (1) determination to keep up living standards in the face of rising prices was forcing wives out of the house onto the job market; (2) this began in 1973 with the extraordinarily sharp boost in oil prices; and (3) much of the drop in family income was the result of the recent recession.

Krulwich avoided the temptation, to which most reporters in 1992 succumbed, to lay just about every economic problem at the Reagan administration's doorstep. He did so by explicitly dating women's accelerated entry into the workforce from 1973 and by noting that family income had dropped primarily because of the recession.

A temptation to which Krulwich did succumb, as have most journalists, was to use data that ran from 1973 to 1992, thus diluting the significant gains of most of the 1980s. Key measures of the American economy had been in free-fall in the last half of the 1970s; they recovered dramatically in the 1980s. This recovery, however, is masked when data of the 1980s are thrown in with data of the late 1970s. It is masked further by the economic setbacks of the early 1990s resulting from Bush administration policy errors.

MANDATED LEAVE, PRODUCT LIABILITY, AND OTHER GOVERNMENT REMEDIES

In this week, fifteen stories dealt with regulation and other aspects of government involvement in the economy. CNN's Mark Leff on "World News" September 10, for example, reported on congressional efforts to reregulate cable TV. He said that "the number of subscribers and what they pay has gone up considerably since the

Reagan administration removed many federal rules." Leff perhaps meant this as a criticism of deregulation. Yet his data could lead to the opposite message: since the number of subscribers had increased, deregulation had succeeded in making cable available to more people. A further message could have been that great numbers of TV viewers would not have become new cable subscribers had the rates been as unaffordable as critics had charged.

The week's major story on government and the economy was congressional passage and the anticipated Bush veto of a bill to require businesses with more than fifty employees to allow those employees to take at least twelve weeks of unpaid leave to care for newborn and ill family members. This was known as the "family leave bill." The central issue was whether employee leave was a matter appropriate for the federal government to mandate or whether it should be left to businesses.

The networks mainly discussed the measure in stark political terms. This was understandable because the bill was a Democratic measure, backed by candidate Bill Clinton, which had landed on George Bush's desk just two months before the presidential election. The networks in these reports carefully balanced each Democratic Talking Head with a Republican Talking Head, mainly Labor Secretary Martin.

Less balanced was the reporting on the issue's substance, its economic aspect. The networks dwelled almost entirely on how such a law would help workers immediately. Almost nothing was said about what it would do to the economy and hence ultimately to workers. ABC, for example, ran two interviews with Laurel Stimper. Reporter Bill Greenwood on "Good Morning America" September 11 said that Stimper "might still be the vice-president of an Atlanta insurance firm if a family leave law had been on the books three years ago. But there wasn't. So while Stimper was on maternity leave, her boss decided to replace her." Stimper then told viewers that it was not right that she had been forced to choose between her career and her family.

Making the same point was another backer of the bill, Republican Congresswoman Marge Roukema of New Jersey. She told reporter Andrea Mitchell on NBC "Nightly News" September 9 that she had seen how important time off was when she had to care for her child who was dying of leukemia. Said Roukema: "I was free to stay home and take care of him. And I think of other working families. What do they do? Choose between their child and their job?"

Missing from almost all network coverage of mandated family leave was an analysis of how much it would cost the economy, how it might reduce efficiency and hence competitiveness, whether such programs in other countries created (as charged by the bill's critics) enormous problems, and how much mandated benefits prompted employers (in Germany, for example) to replace human workers with machines which obviously required no maternity leave, extra vacations, or similar benefits. Missing too was the prediction of many economists that mandated family leave would lead employers to discriminate against young women of child-bearing age. The only hint that mandated leave might carry costs was in Andrea Mitchell's report. She included a soundbite of Virginia businessman Phil Rosenthal saying that he could not operate if any of his sixty employees took long leaves.

The networks' slant on the issue was typified by Bob Schieffer on CBS "Evening News" September 10. To him it was a clearcut matter of the good guys versus the bad guys. He gave viewers the lineup: "Labor, women's groups, and senior citizens lobbies pushed for it. Big business said it was too costly and opposed it. And that's the line most Republicans took today." In truth, the major opponents of the bill were not big business but medium- and small-size businesses on which the bill would impose massive new regulatory burdens. Had Schieffer been accurate, he would have said:

"Special interest groups pushed for the bill; independent businesses, the economy's most productive sector, opposed it."

A week earlier Schieffer had been much more innovative in discussing the family leave bill. On CBS "Evening News" September 5, he told viewers how some businesses, without federal mandates, already were responding to employees' need for maternity leave. Viewers heard from a woman at a Maryland bank who was able to take off time to care for her ill father because the bank allowed employees to trade time off for a reduced salary. From this and other statements on Schieffer's segment, viewers could learn that the private sector could deal with employee problems. He interviewed labor specialist Ken Feltman, who told viewers: "Employers offer the [flexible time] plans obviously because of competitive pressures and financial reasons. Employees like the plans. They demand the plans increasingly."

The week's other major story on a regulatory matter dealt with the Senate's vote on a Bush administration proposal to change product liability laws. Bill-backers were arguing that permissive laws and sympathetic juries had been inflicting on American businesses huge costs that were unwarranted and vastly greater than those borne by America's overseas competitors. This was countered by bill-opponents who warned that the law would make it difficult for those injured by products to claim and win compensation.

At the core of the argument was an issue which, had it been addressed by the networks, could have taught viewers something important about their economy: The tension between a regulatory environment that attempts to ensure product safety and a market environment that encourages entrepreneurs to try new techniques and introduce new products. No network gave viewers the chance to learn this.

Of all coverage of product liability, the best was Robert Hager's on NBC "Nightly News" September 8. For one thing, he gave viewers useful details for understanding the issue: lawsuits in federal courts had jumped 1,100 percent since the 1970s and insurance companies were paying $2 billion annually in claims. For another, he noted that though the Bush administration had introduced the bill, it was backed by many Democrats. For Talking Heads, Hager looked beyond politicians and officials; he interviewed bill-opponent Ralph Nader and bill-backer Phyllis Eisen of the National Association of Manufacturers.

Quite different was Hattie Kauffman's approach on CBS "This Morning" September 7. From her, viewers heard that the bill was a clearcut face-off of consumers versus bill-supporters. "Consumers," obviously, is one of the American lexicon's warmest, friendliest, most endearing words; few would dare side against "consumers." Thus Kauffman stacked the deck against the bill when, in introducing her segment, she told viewers: "Consumers groups say the bill will make it more difficult for victims to sue the manufacturer. Supporters say we're a nation drowning in lawsuits."

What Kauffman concealed from viewers were the many experts who could have said that the bill would help, not hurt, consumers by bringing down insurance costs and making available a wider range of goods and services. Kauffman could also have interviewed economists who could have explained the high costs to the economy of the current product liability system.

Instead, CBS and Kauffman consistently framed the matter as the Bush administration against consumers. She said: "Consumer advocates say what the administration really wants to do is protect businesses, not the consumer." And for Talking Heads, Kauffman paired bill-backer Commerce Secretary Barbara Franklin against consumer "advocate" Linda Lipsen of Consumers Union and "victim" Jana Rousonno whose breast implant had leaked. From Lipsen viewers heard: "The bill should really be named 'the corporate wrongdoers protection act' or 'the corporate wrongdoers blame-the-victim act.' "

As bad as Kauffman's segment was, the week's worst product liability coverage was Bettina Gregory's report on ABC "Good Morning America" September 9. In a long segment, all of her interviews but one opposed the bill. There were "consumer advocate" Jill Claybrook, Joseph Sullivan who had "survived an accident with a defective ladder," and Democratic Senators Jay Rockefeller of West Virginia and Howard Metzenbaum of Ohio. Gregory's lone defender of the bill was George Bush whose words surely had less credibility with viewers than those of ostensibly nonpartisan "consumer advocates."

Invisible in the coverage of the product liability bill were those who had suffered under the current situation. While viewers heard from Sullivan about his defective ladder, from Rousonno about her leaking breast implant, and from a man about his two arms lost in a grain blower accident, they heard nothing from workers who had lost their jobs, businessmen who had closed their plants, and city officials who had seen their economic base shrink because of the huge costs imposed by the current system. Those claiming to be victims of flawed products should have been balanced with those claiming to be victims of a draconian product liability regime.

WHAT'S NEW ON THE MARKET

Reports of new products coming onto the market can give viewers some understanding of how the American economic system spurs creativity. In the week, ABC science Editor Michael Guillen on "Good Morning America" September 8 reported *Discover* magazine's awards for the year's best inventions. Viewers heard about private sector technological triumphs that would yield, among other things, safer automobile tires, video telephones, interactive compact disk recordings, and a method for making recycled plastic so pure that it could be used for soft drink bottles.

CBS "This Morning" September 9 reported that Canon Inc. planned to introduce a camera with a greatly advanced automatic focusing system. ABC "World News Tonight" September 10 reported that U S West Corporation would begin working with a French firm to devise the first-of-its kind electronic phone directory, what reporter Tom Foreman called "a sort of electronic Yellow Pages."

ENTERTAINMENT'S MESSAGE

This week, as throughout the year, entertainment TV's most honest portrayal of the business world appeared on NBC's "Sisters." Frankie, a vice-president in a corporation, was shown agonizing over the tough decision of whether and how to fire an associate. Viewers saw Frankie showing concern for the associate's feelings and for his financial predicament. But because the associate was not very competent, he eventually was fired. In the episode, Frankie was sympathetically portrayed, conveying to viewers something of the tough situations managers at times face.

Sympathetically depicted too was a pawn shop owner in NBC's "Fresh Prince of Bel Air." Though a rough woman, she was more than willing to make a deal to help her customers.

These two upbeat episodes involving business, however, were far outweighed in the week by others that, in one way or another, painted businesspersons unflatteringly—either as criminals, as bumblers, or simply as unpleasant. In the week, the criminal rogues gallery included:

1. A company, in Fox's "Married With Children," which was involved in a scam selling but not building time share condominiums.
2. A hotel owner, in CBS's "Murder She Wrote," who dealt in drugs and collected stolen art.
3. A business executive, in NBC's "Law & Order," who was indirectly responsible for his young son becoming a murderer.
4. A former accountant, in NBC's "Cheers," who used "white-out" on several balance sheets to stay, as he put it, out of prison.
5. A resort owner, in ABC's "Family Matters," who built all of his cabins at once and found that he had planned so poorly that he did not have enough money to finish any of them.
6. A repair shop owner, in ABC's "Going to Extremes," who did not keep his promise to have a blender fixed by the next day.
7. A restaurant owner, in CBS's "Northern Exposure," who yelled at his cook for no apparent reason.

This week's worst portrayal of business was on ABC's "Dinosaurs." A company manager and CEO plotted to ruin the reputation and invention of a teenage entrepreneur. The student had invented an energy efficient heating device which used a volcano as its energy source. Were it to be adopted, the invention would cut into what was called the company's "obscenely profitable" energy division. So instead of hiring the inventor or making its own product more efficient, the company bought the volcano used by the student's heating process and thus bottled up the invention.

Still Getting the Facts Wrong

Among network TV's most serious mistakes this week in reporting economic-related facts and data were:

1. Bill Whitaker on CBS "Evening News" September 7 implicitly calling on Americans, unhappy in their jobs or without jobs, to head for Japan where, he unambiguously implied, jobs were aplenty. He was wrong on two counts. First, it was extremely difficult, and long had been, for Americans speaking no Japanese to find work in Japan. Second, Japan for more than a year had been in worse economic straits than America. Whitaker should have said:

"With Japan's continuing economic problems, only Americans with special skills are likely to find more opportunity there than at home."

2. Anne McDermott on CNN "World News" September 7 offering but one solution to America's education problems: higher taxes for more education spending. To be sure, increased spending might correct some specific education shortcomings. Yet there has been no demonstrated correlation between spending more on education and improvement in education. In fact, North Dakota, Utah, and other states that have spent relatively little per pupil consistently have scored near the top in every measurable category of education performance. In 1992 state SAT score rankings, nine of the top ten states had per-pupil expenditures below the national average. To have been accurate, McDermott should have said:

"Rather than looking at the education problem only in monetary terms, some experts now urge officials to look at teaching

methods in states like Utah, where costs are low and test scores are high."

3. Bob Schieffer on CBS "Evening News" September 10 listing only big business and Republicans as opponents of the mandated family leave bill. He was wrong. The biggest group of opponents were small- and medium-size businesses. Had he mentioned this—and that such businesses were creating the vast majority of the nation's new jobs—he would have given viewers a balanced view of a complex issue. From that, viewers could have concluded that family leave legislation could impose significant costs on the economy.

NEWSCASTS' MESSAGE

From some of the networks' coverage in this week, viewers could have concluded that the free enterprise system functioned well. Among other things, viewers learned that private firms, to stay competitive and retain their employees, were planning to spend millions of dollars for day care centers. Private firms similarly were attempting to meet employee needs by offering flexible work hours and flexible leave. And viewers watching the CBS "This Morning" interview of Bush administration Labor Secretary Lynn Martin would have heard her explain, correctly, that most jobs have been created by small- and medium-size businesses.

Viewers also were given some glimpse of what government intrusion could do to the economy. From NBC "Nightly News" they learned that the high cost of California's worker compensation program was chasing businesses and jobs out of the state. And from CNN "World News" viewers learned (although this might not have been reporter Mark Leff's intent) that cable TV deregulation in the 1980s succeeded in making cable available to more Americans. This could have prompted viewers to conclude that the increased number of cable subscribers indicated that the price of cable TV perhaps was not as unreasonably high as critics had claimed. Purchases of cable TV, as purchases of any product, usually do not climb if the price is too high.

Generally, however, TV's message to viewers this week was that America's free enterprise system tended to stumble. NBC's Deborah Roberts, for example, told her audience that it was surprising that companies showed flexibility in tough times. ABC's Stephen Aug signalled that consumers always were perilously close to danger when Talking Heads in his segment said that GM's low-rate credit card might be bad because it could encourage people to spend too much. CBS's Bill Whitaker presumed that the American economy was malfunctioning and that Americans could find work easily in Japan.

As for American business, the message was that firms had bilked the U.S. government for $82 million in food stamp frauds, had cheated the Pentagon, and had put misleading labels on foods. Pharmaceutical companies, meanwhile, "make profits the old fashioned way—by gouging customers."

Occasionally, TV's message was simply silly. Example: Fred Brigg's NBC "Nightly News" profile of Harlan, Iowa, seemed to say that small towns could rejuvenate themselves by holding pep rallies, building swimming pools, and hiring a professional booster.

STILL LETTING OPPORTUNITIES SLIP AWAY

TV coverage this week, as in the other target weeks, missed what should have been obvious opportunities to educate Americans on how their economy functions. Such squandered opportunities included:

1. David French's CNN "World News" September 5 report that a "new study" on work place injuries had found that 139 teenagers in 1990 had died as a result of their jobs at fast food restaurants. One problem with the report was French's use of meaningless statistics. More teens could have been dying in fast food jobs, for example, not because the jobs were more dangerous than others

but simply because more teens were working in fast food restaurants than anywhere else. French should have used relative numbers.

But a much more serious problem with the segment was French's failure to tell viewers about the extraordinary role played by fast food chains in preparing huge numbers of inner-city teenagers for the working world by teaching them basic work discipline and skills. Rather than being dead-end, low-skilled employment for these teens, fast food outlets have become apprenticeship launching pads to better jobs. From French's stress on the "dangers" of fast food jobs for teens, viewers probably regarded such jobs with alarm, rather than with richly deserved admiration.

Had French sought to use rather than squander the opportunity, he could have said:

"Whatever the dangers of the job, poorly educated teenagers for decades have found fast food chains the first step up the ladder to better jobs. Ironically, where schools have been failing to educate inner-city youth for the workplace, McDonalds, Pizza Hut, Taco Bell, and others have been succeeding."

2. David French's CNN "World News" September 5 report that the settlement of the General Motors strike was a union victory and GM defeat. He might have been correct. Yet he did not ask (and then answer) why it was a victory for one and a setback for the other. Even a short explanation would have told the viewers something about the changing relationship between workers and management at large, aging companies. An attempt to explain, moreover, might have prompted French to note whether the terms of the strike settlement were a victory or defeat for car buyers and for American competitiveness.

3. Peter Jennings' ABC "World News Tonight" September 8 report that fewer Americans had died in accidents in 1991 than in any year since 1924. Viewers were not told why accidents were declining.

4. The reporting by ABC, CBS, and NBC on the Bush administration's proposal to reform product liability law (CNN did not cover the story). No reporter, including NBC's Robert Hager on September 8 in an otherwise informative segment, described how all consumers end up paying higher prices for goods or even find some goods disappearing from shelves because of the high cost to manufacturers of product liability lawsuits or product liability insurance. Reporters should have said:

> **"In this, as in almost all economic matters, there are complicated trade-offs. Thus what might initially appear as the sensible, even benevolent, solution of allowing high-award liability lawsuits is sure to have unwanted consequences. These may be costlier goods and even the disappearance of some products."**

5. Stephen Aug's ABC "World News Tonight" September 9 story on GM's new credit card asked only: "Who are the big losers in all this?" He did not ask the implicit companion question: "Who are the big winners?" Had he done so, he could have noted:

> **"The big winners from GM's entry into the credit card market will be consumers. They will benefit because fierce competition from GM will surely force down credit card interest rates."**

6. Bob Jamieson's ABC "World News Tonight" September 10 story on major corporations establishing day care centers. Though he touched most bases, Jamieson let down viewers by not pursuing the lead offered when American Express executive Barbara Katersky said that the day care centers would boost productivity. At that point, Jamieson could have explained:

> **"Productivity climbs when workers are not distracted by or absent because of worries about their children. This increased productivity can yield lower prices, higher salaries, increased competitiveness, and increased profits. This is an example, say economists, of how a free market economy's inherent dy-**

namics, without government mandates, can prompt sensible personnel practices."

7. Nearly all the reporting by the networks on the family leave bill pending in Congress. Reporters could have explained that all government mandates and regulations contained an inherent trade-off between the mandate's promised benefit and the mandate's cost to the economy. Reporters could have said:

> "Mandated leaves may have some benefits for workers. They also have potential down sides. These mandates will particularly be costly for small businesses. And that is where most new jobs are created. The added cost of mandate compliance could erode a small business's slim profit and thus force the business to close down or prevent the business from expanding and hiring new workers."

CHAPTER FOUR

A TYPICAL WEEK: DECEMBER 7-13

BAREBONES COVERAGE

THE TV NETWORK news coverage during the second week of December was overwhelmingly about the dispatch of U.S. Marines to Somalia. During the week the networks aired at least 344 stories about the military mission. This left little time for reports about much else—including business and economics.

In one respect, however, this week might have been typical. Since it was chosen for analysis by random sample, as were the three other 1992 target weeks, there is a statistical possibility that in one of every four weeks an event so dominates the news that Americans learn little about anything else during this time.

But reducing coverage of business and economic matters to the minimum might also have revealed the networks' attitudes towards such topics. Forced to pare to the bone what it gave viewers, network priorities apparently were: (1) a parade of mainly disjointed economic statistics; and (2) a litany of business troubles and transgressions. This in fact was the diet of the December week.

From the staccato statistical reports, viewers learned that: the national debt had reached $4.133 trillion; consumer confidence was climbing; a Federal Reserve study had found "no pick up in inflation, but the Fed's report has plenty of cautions"; inflation had increased very modestly; retail sales were up; and new claims for unemployment insurance had dropped 38,000.

NO BIG ECONOMIC STORIES

The week offered no big economic story. The longest report probably was NBC's "Today" segment by Mike Jensen of the difficulties small business had in obtaining bank loans. It demonstrated the potentials and shortcomings of the best and worst of TV's treatment of America's free enterprise economy, mixing some valid basic principles and useful information with information that simply was wrong.

From Jensen the TV audience heard correctly that "most new jobs these days do come from small business." He also conveyed some notion of the inexorable optimism and entrepreneurial spirit that drive the economy when he said that "people come in droves looking for loans, hoping to turn a small business into a bigger one." Jensen's many interviews, meantime, portrayed the small businessperson very favorably and sympathetically. Example: The camera caught Carmello Liberto, owner of a truck hauling firm, saying that if she could get a bank loan she would buy more trucks and hire more people.

Yet Jensen's reporting had serious problems. It seemed obliged, for instance, to balance the good-guy depiction of the small businessperson with a bad-guy, villainous depiction of banks and bankers. Jensen introduced one small businessman by saying that "the banks almost put him out of business." At another point, Jensen said: "Listen to this banker laying it on the line telling small business owners what the bank will do if they can't pay off their loans." The camera then turned on a banker who said: "If we have to rip a chair up, take a desk out, take light bulbs out, we're not going to get much money for that. If there's not enough business assets, and often times there's not, we'll look through the principal's personal assets."

To the viewer the message surely was unambiguous: banker nasti-
ness was what was preventing deserving small businessmen and
women from getting loans. From this the viewer could conclude
that bankers were in business mainly to deny loan applications. In
fact, banks love approving loans. That is how they make money.

There was a more serious problem with Jensen's reporting. It
failed to identify the real cause of the credit crunch suffered by
small business: the zealous enforcement of federal regulations in
the wake of the savings and loan banking problems. Such enforcement made banks extremely gun-shy of lending to any but the most
solid borrowers. Jensen obliquely touched on this when he interviewed computer hardware company owner Michael Hayward.
Hayward explained that "some banks are saying that they have
plenty of funds and they are loaning money, but the requirements
are so strict, so stiff, that money is being loaned to companies that
don't need it."

Such oblique treatment of the issue was unfair to the TV audience. Since Jensen and NBC apparently felt that the small business
credit crunch had merited the considerable block of time consumed
by the segment, the reporting should have explained the central
cause of the problem. It did not. Jensen should have said:

**"Government regulators are laying it on the line: No loans of
even the most minimal risk. That means no loans to small
businesses which produce almost all new jobs in the U.S.
economy."**

The week's only full-scale analysis of an economic issue was Ray
Brady's commentary on CBS "Evening News" December 11. In it he
woefully misinformed viewers by sketching an economic world in
which economic growth was just a matter of luck or whimsy.
Viewers heard Brady say that "if America's business leaders like
Mr. Clinton's economic policies, their own business policies could
bring on an expanding economy and, above all, more jobs." Clinton's economic success, Brady added, was a matter of "whether
Clinton will get much help on jobs from corporate America."

In the economic universe sketched for viewers by Brady, apparently, businesspersons' and investors' decisions were motivated not by a desire to boost sales, market share, or profits, but by a desire to "help" or not "help" Clinton because they "liked" or "disliked" his policies. From Brady, viewers had no inkling of the market forces that affect economic decisions and outcomes. Brady should have said:

"If Clinton's economic policies convince businesses that their cost of doing business will drop or their earnings climb, these businesses will make the investments and expand their operations in ways which will create jobs."

TV's PORTRAIT OF BUSINESSES AND BUSINESSPERSONS

During the week, network viewers heard almost nothing good or upbeat about businesses. The few exceptions were CBS newsbites on the "Evening News" that Lockheed Corporation was buying General Dynamics' jet fighter division for $1.2 billion, and on "This Morning" that Pepsi would introduce its clear, calorie-and-caffeine-free crystal soda at the Super Bowl and that McDonalds had begun selling vegetarian Big Macs abroad.

The sole positive story exceeding a soundbite about business was CNN's "Prime News" December 11 report that the public's growing concern about the environment had spawned stores catering to those who wanted to buy environmentally correct merchandise. But even this story had a cloud. Reporter Sean Callebs noted that mom and pop stores were suffering. He said: "Consumer interest in the environment has been the undoing of many mom and pop businesses. Stores like Seventh Generation no longer have the edge as environmental products move into major retail chains."

Viewers of network TV this December week mainly saw only the dark side of America's economy. Examples:

1. ABC and CNN stories discussed troubled Trans World Airlines, where employees and creditors were said to be ready to

take over the company and where Lee Iacocca was rumored to be about to assume control.

2. ABC and CBS stories told viewers that Campbell's soup company was recalling 400,000 cans of chicken soup because of glass particles in the rice. Only ABC's "Good Morning America" mentioned that Campbell's had recalled the cans voluntarily and had a toll-free phone number should worried consumers wish to contact the company.

3. ABC reported that federal authorities were investigating General Motors pick-up trucks that allegedly were prone to burst into flames when involved in crashes.

4. CBS updated a story about an Atlanta bank which allegedly had made illegal loans to Iraq. The main point of the update was that a special investigator had cleared the Bush administration of involvement in the matter.

5. CNN told viewers that New York City's WNEW, one of America's oldest radio stations, had broadcast its final program because, among other things, of "bad business decisions." CNN reporters Susan Rook and Brian Jenkins never told viewers what those bad decisions were.

6. NBC, in a newsbite, reported that engineers at Boeing Company were threatening to strike.

7. ABC and CBS carried the American Medical Association's warning to parents that baby-walkers could be dangerous. On ABC's "World News Tonight" brief item, viewers heard that the AMA had called the devices "a lethal form of transportation" because "they may allow babies to speed up quickly before you have a chance to stop them."

Reports for Consumers

This week's sole consumer affairs report was by ABC Consumer Editor Paula Lyons on "Good Morning America" December 8. She told viewers how to donate money to alleviate starving in Somalia.

The lone story on innovations and new products was a short CBS

"This Morning" December 11 item about new TV technology that would use high frequency radio signals for transmission. To host Harry Smith, this was a worrisome development. It would, he warned viewers, "pose a threat to the cable TV industry."

Smith's comment revealed a response frequently found on TV— that just about any economic development is bad. In his concern for the cable industry, Smith was identifying a set of victims of economic developments. To Smith and other reporters, such developments often were cast as threats; they create victims and never seem to benefit anyone.

ENTERTAINMENT'S MESSAGE

Even though much of this week's entertainment had a Christmas theme, there was still room to criminalize business. Examples:

1. In NBC's movie "Shadow of a Stranger," a lawyer was involved in forging contracts.
2. In CBS's "Hat Squad," a pizza parlor was a front for the "mob."
3. In NBC's "Law & Order," Phillip Marietta, owner of U.S.-based Nigerian Petroleum Company, paid African villagers to smuggle drugs into America by swallowing condoms stuffed with the drugs. Not only was Marietta a drug smuggler, he also was implicated in murder after a villager died of a drug overdose when a condom ruptured.
4. In NBC's "LA Law," movie mogul Ben Flicker cooked his studio's books.
5. In NBC's "Perry Mason," the part owner of a chain of fitness centers was a former mobster.

Even ABC's "Roseanne," which usually emphasizes hard work and positively portrays the entrepreneurial spirit, this week not only chronicled the imminent collapse of Roseanne and her husband Dan's motorcycle shop, but allowed Roseanne to snipe at the work ethic. Said she: "I knew we shouldn't have gone into business for ourselves. There's nobody to steal from."

Such dark depictions of business and businesspersons were offset only by a few business characters who, though not portrayed as very savvy in their businesses, at least seemed to be good folks. In ABC's "Commish," for instance, a tatoo parlor owner cooperated with a police investigation; in the ABC movie *To Grandmother's House We Go*, the manager of a minimart was a very attentive mother; and in NBC's "Out All Night," night club manager Chelsea Paige was kind to a pizza delivery boy who ultimately learned that being a business manager was not easy.

The week's only economics and business lesson on an entertainment program was conveyed by the dispute on ABC's "Civil Wars" between Sal and Madeline Labelle. Rightly endorsing the validity of contracts, the episode had a court order Madeline to honor her contract and return to work for her husband's perfume firm after she quit to work for a perfumer who was making a higher-quality product.

Newscasts' Message

Few economic messages were conveyed by network TV this week; those that were appeared in brief segments. Several of these incorrectly informed viewers about how the economy functioned. Erroneous, for example, were the messages that bankers were to blame for small business difficulties in getting loans and that new inventions mainly threatened existing businesses.

A handful of messages, however, though brief and often unexplained, did convey valid information about the economy. These included:

1. Bad business decisions could sink an enterprise even as venerable as New York City radio station WNEW.

2. Economic decisions typically involved trade-offs. The CNN

report on the environmentally correct merchandise, for example, not only stressed that new stores were opening to sell the product but also that the new competition was threatening the mom and pop environmental businesses.

3. The marketplace gave more valid signals than did market research. This point implicitly was made by CNN's Sean Callebs in the story about environmentally correct merchandise. He pointed out that though there was a great deal of research purporting to show that customers were willing to pay more for "green" products, when actually given an opportunity to do so, they were responding tepidly. As a result, said Callebs, some green companies had gone bust because "a lot of people took [the research] to heart and put products on the marketplace that were overpriced." The implicit but valid moral (learned painfully by, among many others, the inventors of the New Coke) was that no amount of research or planning by no amount of experts could predict what customers would buy or what the market would do.

4. Manufacturers and other businesses responded to market forces. In a segment cataloguing the vast spending power of older Americans, CBS's Hattie Kauffman said: "As those over 50 become the largest segment of the population, the entire product environment will have to change to satisfy them . . . The power that can change basic designs is the power of money." Such insight was seldom demonstrated by Kauffman in her other segments or by almost any of her fellow TV reporters.

MORE OPPORTUNITIES SLIP AWAY

Coverage this week that missed opportunities to inform and instruct viewers on how their economy functions included:

1. The CNN report on stores merchandising "green" goods. Though Sean Callebs correctly noted that "happy employees . . .

can't by themselves create a successful business," he squandered the opportunity to explain what did account for the success of such environmentally correct stores as Seventh Generation. And though the segment cited Seventh Generation CEO Jeffrey Hollander saying that a business "doing the right thing environmentally is not in conflict with making money," the segment never told viewers how Seventh Generation was making money or what kind of products it was selling.

2. The lengthy ABC profiles of Bill Clinton's incoming economic team. The reports were structured almost entirely along political lines—whether the appointees represented change, whether Congress would go along with Clinton's economic proposals, and how the appointees would get along with Congress. Reporter Charles Murphy, for instance, on "World News Tonight" December 10 said that Treasury Secretary-designate Lloyd Bentsen defended oil and gas tax breaks "with the fervor of a Reagan Republican." Missing from the report was the economic dimension of Clinton's economic team: what they were proposing for the economy and what the proposals would mean for the economy.

PART II

DISSECTING THE TARANTULA

HOW TV COVERS KEY ECONOMIC ISSUES

CHAPTER FIVE

REGULATIONS: TV'S ALL-PURPOSE RX

REGULATION HAS A friend in television. Network reporters seem to believe that government officials and bureaucrats have the information, ability, and tools to regulate economic matters effectively. Thus when network TV identifies a problem, network reporters generally turn to government for its solution. This was the message conveyed in the networks' 1992 reporting on regulation.

In 1992, American viewers had a 36 percent greater chance of seeing a story and hearing a commentary favorable to regulation than one critical of it. In this year, the four networks ran 1 hour, 41 minutes sympathetic to regulation compared to 1 hour, 11 minutes unsympathetic to it; an additional 14 hours, 54 minutes dealt with background on regulation.

Typical of TV's tilt toward regulatory solutions to problems was its coverage of one of 1992's main regulation issues: whether the federal government should reregulate the cable TV industry. Every reporter covering the issue accepted the notion that only the Federal Communications Commission could check the rapid climb in cable rates. Acceptance of this premise was explicit in the way that CNN's Carl Rochelle framed the issue for viewers of "World News" January 31; he told them that Congress was considering a bill "to regulate unreasonable price increases for special programming like

131

movie channels or sporting events, set standards for customers service, and promote competition by preventing local governments from keeping second cable distributors out of the market." For Rochelle, government regulations "promote competition."

Rochelle apparently was so committed to the regulatory approach to problems that he suspended the kind of healthy reportorial skepticism that should have prompted him to catch a key contradiction between the story's facts and his conclusion. Viewers were told, for instance, that after deregulation in the early 1980s, the number of cable subscribers had soared. This fact should have prompted Rochelle and other reporters to ask:

"If cable TV companies have been serving the public so poorly, why have so many households become new subscribers?"

The answer to that question would have allowed Rochelle and the others to continue to criticize cable TV companies. Yet it would also have prompted them to question, even if rhetorically, the need for reregulation. At the least, simply posing the question about the increased number of subscribers would have alerted TV viewers to a glaring inconsistency in the story. But the closest Rochelle came to this was his use of a soundbite by a National Cable Television Association official saying: "The 55 million people who subscribe to cable can't be all wrong."

The Message: Regulations Solve Problems

Throughout 1992, network TV's message about government regulation was that it solved economic problems. Examples:

☒ Competition was good, and regulation promoted competition. Coverage of the cable TV issue and other regulatory matters revealed that reporters had a strong and healthy belief in competition. Reporters seemed to know that monopolies were unhealthy for the economy, that they became inefficient, uncreative, and faced far fewer restraints on raising prices than did companies facing competition. The problem was that reporters also seemed to feel that regulations were needed to spur competition, as, for example, Carl Rochelle's statement that regulation would "promote competition."

☒ If greed was damaging the American economy, then government measures could curb greed—according to ABC's Sylvia Chase on "Prime Time Live" January 16.

☒ If cable TV prices were too high, government regulations could bring them down—according to Carl Rochelle when he told viewers during his January 31 story that regulation could prevent "unreasonable price increases."

☒ If individuals were harmed by companies, the federal government, not the American legal system and tort law, was the source of redress—according to ABC legal expert Arthur Miller on "Good Morning America" January 31 in his commentary on the accusations that breast implants had harmed women. Declared Miller: "It really is quite unrealistic to expect plaintiffs, who want to get as much money as they can by way of settlement, to act as sort of a public avenger. It is also unrealistic to expect the courts, who are just creaking and groaning under their work load, to act as sort of an information agency for the society at large . . . I think the real problem is to focus on the FDA [Food and Drug Administration] and FTC [Federal Trade Commission] to get the national administration and the state administration to do their jobs much more effectively than they have done it in the last six or eight years."

☒ If the workplace was unsafe, more federal inspectors and higher federal fines could make it safer—according to NBC's Jeff Madrick on "Nightly News" February 1.

Viewers also were told that regulators could ensure product safety. Examples:

☒ State laws were needed to make auto bumpers resist crashes at higher speeds—according to NBC's Betty Furness on "Today" January 8.

☒ Only government rules and inspectors could ensure quality housing construction—according to ABC's Sylvia Chase on "Prime Time Live" January 16.

☒ Only the government could force auto firms to make a seat that would protect passengers from rear-end crashes—according to CBS's Ed Bradley on "60 Minutes" February 16, when he told viewers, in his kicker to the segment: "If you can't talk to NHTSA [National Highway Traffic Safety Administration] about it, whom can you talk to? No one, I guess."

☒ Only the government could ensure fresh food—according to CNN's Brian Barger on "World News" August 12, when he told viewers that "inspectors for the FDA are in charge of making sure that the 13 billion pounds of domestic and imported fish consumed every year are safe to eat."

☒ Only the government could protect consumers who used drugs in ways for which the drugs were not intended—according to CBS's Rita Braver on "Evening News" November 22.

☒ Only the government could guarantee that products sold as "spring" water really came from springs—according to NBC's Fred Briggs on "Nightly News" November 23.

In covering regulatory matters, reporters at times got their facts wrong. The most egregious example was Bob Schieffer's CBS "Evening News" January 18 commentary. First he explicitly declared that "Suddenly, there's a lot of talk around Washington about the need for the government to take a more active role in helping industry." Then, to make his case, he said: "Government has worked with business for decades—mobilizing to fight World War II, building the first atomic bomb, landing on the moon and Star Wars."
Schieffer should have known that these examples were highly flawed. Each project cited was enormously inefficient and wasteful. What justified them was only their important contribution to national security in times of hot and cold war. In normal times, such waste would not have been acceptable. If Schieffer was determined to cite these projects, he should have done so to make the opposite

point: that even government projects considered successful had been extremely inefficient and wasteful.

Schieffer could have said:

> **"There seems to be a lot of talk about government taking a more active role in helping industry. Government, in fact, has worked with business for decades—in World War II, on the A-bomb, the moon project and, most recently, on Star Wars. The problem is that these were very costly, inefficient, and wasteful. This raises the question: can government help industry in a way that does not impose more cost than help to the economy?"**

Schieffer erred again the following month when, in his February 29 report on the airline industry, he rendered the verdict that airline deregulation had failed. He asked: "What ever happened to all those airlines, large and small, that used to fly Americans here, there, and everywhere around the globe? Fourteen years after deregulation, the industry is in a tailspin." But he contradicted this immediately when he told viewers that "air travel has doubled overall since deregulation, and when you figure in discounted tickets bought way in advance, prices have dropped nearly 30 percent." These figures, at the least, should have prompted Schieffer to say:

> **"Though deregulation may be causing some pain for the airlines as they adjust, it has been a boon for consumers—getting more Americans to fly and at very low prices."**

CBS's Ed Bradley in his "60 Minutes" segment on auto-seat safety also got it wrong. The explicit message of his kicker was that you could only "talk to" the federal government about greater safety. Yet consumers by the tens of thousands talk to the auto companies every day when they examine cars and kick tires in showrooms and make purchases. Just so, consumers who sought safer seats signalled their desires by buying cars that offered them.

A PRESCRIPTION WITH SIDE EFFECTS

Though regulation generally is TV's all-purpose prescription for economic ills, some reporters realized that the medicine had unpleasant side-effects, among these:

1. Regulation comes at a price.

CNN's Jeff Levine made it very clear on his "World News" July 5 segment that Food and Drug Administration plans to restrict use of real heart valves in transplants would make getting a transplant much more costly and difficult. And David French, in his CNN "World News" October 31 introduction to a story on proposed tougher federal rules for de-icing airplanes, said: "The regulations will make flying safer but may cause you some delays."

2. Regulations may not be the best solution to a problem.

This was the implied bottom line of ABC's Charles Gibson on his "Good Morning America" May 12 report on the debate in Portland, Maine, over whether it should restrict business activity on its waterfront. One Portland group was pushing for regulations to limit business activity to maritime-related firms; others wanted to allow shops, restaurants, apartments, and a wide variety of other economic activities. The segment's message was that the kind of tight restrictions sought by the first group could hurt the city's economy. The limitations of regulation also was the message of ABC's Paula Lyons in her May 28 "Good Morning America" story on playground safety. Stressing personal responsibility, she said: "Both sides would agree that neither guidelines nor laws provide the whole answer. Proper supervision of children at play and regular maintenance of the equipment they play on are also key." And she interviewed an expert who said that parents must be more aware of playground dangers.

3. Regulations are easily abused.

In a long "20/20" segment January 3, John Stossel described with unveiled outrage the widespread fraud of able-bodied workers exploiting workman's compensation laws. The segment showed viewers how ostensibly injured workers who were collecting fat compensation checks were really quite fit and were engaging in strenuous activity. Examples: a man who claimed to have a bad back was shown shaking a tree, a man with an ankle "injury" was shown jumping into a convertible, a man with "injuries" to his back, knee, wrist, and shoulder was shown jet skiing, and a man with a back "injury" was shown falling off a roof, getting up, and going back on the roof. Said an angry Stossel: "In these cases it's our business because it costs us money."

4. Regulators overreact.

ABC's "World News Tonight" January 15 described how regulators responded too harshly when they set tough new requirements on hospital waste disposal after some bloody syringes, vials, and other hospital refuse washed up on Long Island and New Jersey beaches in 1988 and triggered a public panic. Peter Jennings introduced the segment, saying: "Hospitals are now required to take extraordinary measures to dispose of their waste. It is costing hospitals millions of dollars—and may be a waste of money." Reporter James Walker then described how, after some medical objects washed ashore: "The public and the media went looking for culprits. They targeted local hospitals. Then came calls for government regulation." The result, said Walker: "Hospital disposal costs shot up 700 percent." Walker then asked viewers in his kicker: Since scientists say "that only 6 percent of waste requires special handling and with health care dollars scarce, should limited resources be spent to appease public misconceptions?"

GETTING IT RIGHT ON BREAST IMPLANTS

The year's biggest regulatory story was also its most balanced in reporting. It covered the mounting questions about and dispute over the long-term safety of silicone breast implants. Had TV newscasts handled other regulatory issues as they did breast implants, TV would have served Americans well by teaching them some economic basics—well-intended regulations could have very painful consequences, life was full of intelligent risk-taking, striving for a risk-free society inflicted an extraordinary price, and agonizing and complicated trade-offs were inherent in all economic decisions.

TV reported extensively on the breast implant matter. Most stories were carefully balanced, with experts on both sides of the issue and interviews with women who had received implants but who were on opposing sides of the controversy. In no other coverage of regulation—or perhaps any other economic issue of 1992— was the viewer treated so frequently to a "on the one hand . . . on the other hand" formula of reporting. If there was a tilt in coverage, in fact, it was slightly against the proregulation position.

Why was coverage of the implant controversy so uncharacteristically balanced?

The answer might be that reporters were pulled in opposite directions by two concepts to which they apparently have strong commitments: (1) that regulation is necessary and effective; and (2) that, as feminists insist, women have a right to control what happens to their bodies. Repeatedly, for instance, viewers heard from women who had been victims of breast cancer that breast implants had enabled them to carry on their lives with dignity. Their case was as powerful as that made by women charging that silicone implants had leaked into their bodies.

There is little doubt that the feminist argument was on reporters' minds. Katie Couric of "Today" was explicit about this when she declared in a January 7 story on breast implants: "The FDA announcement has renewed discussion not only of the safety of silicone implants but of the basic right of women to choose what happens to their body."

Equally explicit was ABC's Chris Wallace on "Prime Time Live" February 13 when he said that this was a "controversy that strikes at the core of women's health issues and corporate ethics." On NBC "Nightly News" February 20, reporter Robert Hager let viewers hear from Dr. Mary McGrath of George Washington University who said that the proposal to limit breast implants "is judgmental [and] paternalistic."

The feminist theme seemed to force reporters to look hard at the real consequences of a regulation that would ban silicone breast implants. Reporters had interviewed, and perhaps personally knew, women who insisted that they had the right to decide whether to risk a breast implant. A new regulation would deny these women that right.

A dramatic statement of this was Paula Zahn's January 21 CBS "This Morning" interview with Irma Partner who was about to receive a silicone breast implant.

ZAHN: "Irma, you are facing this surgery with those fears that are well founded among some women. Why do you feel so strongly about going ahead with the surgery in the face of the FDA moratorium?"

IRMA PARTNER: "Basically, for me, it's an issue of time. I need to get it done and get on with life."

ZAHN: "Are you concerned what might happen down the road if you were to have problems with your implants? Obviously the government has warned you that [a silicone implant] isn't a good idea to do at the moment."

Partner answered by making it clear that she wanted to be the person to decide whether the benefit outweighed the risk.

This too was the message of Marilyn Lloyd, a Tennessee congresswoman who told CNN's Jeff Levine in a June 17 interview: "How dare [bureaucrats] tell me what I can do with my life."

Because of their contact with Irma Partner, Marilyn Lloyd, and others like them, reporters did not look upon breast implant regulation as an abstract economic matter. Their real-life experience with it gave reporters a very valuable perspective on regulation. Perhaps for this reason—as well as the feminist angle—of all the year's regulation stories, the stories on breast implants were the least sympathetic to the regulatory argument. Similarly with their coverage of taxes—another issue about which reporters had personal experience rather than abstract knowledge. The tax issue was the only economic category in 1992 likely to get coverage that was favorable rather than unfavorable to the free enterprise argument.

The feminist theme implicit in the breast implant story also might have alerted reporters to the key economic concept of trade-offs: that every economic decision is a balancing act between the good and bad, the appealing and unappealing.

Reporters also seemed uncharacteristically aware that attempts to eliminate 100 percent of risk could be foolish and costly. Repeatedly viewers were reminded that the vast majority—sometimes put at 96 percent—of women who had implants had no trouble at all with them. Registered nurse Ceil Dempsey, interviewed on CBS "This Morning" January 7, said: The "Dow Corning court case— that is one isolated case. He [Food and Drug Administration chief David Kessler] is not listening to the 96 percent of women out there who are happy with their breast implants." This high success ratio was conveyed to viewers by the newscasts as an argument against a regulation that would impose enormous costs on almost all women for the benefit of relatively few.

Curiously, this understanding—that society cannot afford to guard itself against all risks and cannot afford to end all dangers— did not spill over to regulatory issues other than breast implants. When it came to reporting on auto safety or workplace accidents or food freshness or product labelling, to cite a few examples, reporters reflexively acted as though no matter what regulations cost, all risk, all danger should be eliminated. Viewers would have gained enormously had reporters learned enough from their coverage of the breast implant issue to ask: What cost is acceptable to society for eliminating all risk?

SUSPENDING JOURNALISTIC INSTINCTS

When TV reporters supported regulation as an appropriate government activity, except in the breast implant matter, they seemed to suspend some of their basic reportorial instincts. One is to search for examples to support points made in a story. Reporters would normally have cited successful regulations in stories sympathetic to calls for new regulations. Yet viewers were offered no examples of past or existing successes—possibly because few, if any, existed.

Another basic journalistic instinct is to search for examples that refute or qualify points made. In the case of stories on regulation, such a search should have led reporters to examples of deregulation. Had these been sought, reporters would have found deregulation successes in the telecommunications, airline, trucking, and energy industries. Yet these were all ignored.

Still another basic journalistic instinct is to grow cautious and inquisitive when encountering contradictions. Yet reporters ignored data refuting the case for regulation that at times crept into their reporting. An example of this was the segment by NBC's Jeff Madrick on "Nightly News" February 1. Making a strong case for tougher federal regulations to reduce the ten thousand estimated annual workplace deaths, Madrick cited a firm that had been on Michigan's worker-safety priority watch list every year since 1984. State officials, Madrick told viewers, had inspected the firm eighteen times and had fined it several times after finding 216 safety violations.

All of this was apparently true. If so, it contradicted the main theme of Madrick's report: That federal regulation as tough as Michigan's was needed. Madrick did not seem to realize that the example of the Michigan firm told viewers that even regulation and enforcement as strict as Michigan's could not prevent a determined violator from continuing to violate. This should have prompted Madrick to question whether regulations were the answer to problems like workplace safety in the first place.

The same question should have occurred to Sam Donaldson and

Jay Schadler on the ABC "Prime Time Live" January 9 segment dealing with widespread illnesses near a waste incinerator in Hudson, North Carolina. Schadler convincingly explained that something was amiss in Hudson because many townsfolk had fallen unaccountably ill. Schadler also convincingly explained, though he failed to realize it, that it was not a lack of regulations nor lax enforcement that had caused Hudson's problems.

According to Schadler, the company contaminating the area simply had ignored existing regulations. Viewers were told that toxic chloride emissions near the workplace were twenty times the legal limits. Viewers also were told that the company had been investigated three times by federal authorities. Yet the problem continued.

This should have prompted Donaldson and Schadler to ask speculatively: "Since regulations have not deterred the firm from polluting, what can?" Such a question might have led the two reporters to examine the free enterprise economy's powerful sanctions against those damaging the rights and property of others. Some of these sanctions are imposed by tort law. This might become the solution in Hudson where, according to the "Prime Time Live" report, twenty-two lawsuits had been filed against the company.

Donaldson and Schadler could have answered the question about ineffective regulations by saying:

> **"Where regulations have failed, the legal system may succeed. The twenty-two civil lawsuits pending against the company for damaging the rights and property of others may cost the company so much that it, at last, may mend its ways and stop polluting. And this may be a lesson for antipollution efforts elsewhere."**

Basic journalistic tenets also should dissuade reporters from labelling something a problem and identifying putative solutions to it but offering no evidence that the problem exists. Doing so violates what could be called a reporter's version of the *habeas corpus* dictum. Just as criminal law requires that a prosecutor "should have the body" before the prosecutor can declare that a crime has been committed, so too journalists should have evidence of the problem before producing the solution. Yet calls for a regulatory solution often proceeded without such as a *corpus*. Examples:

☒ NBC's Betty Furness, on "Today" January 8, explicitly advocated laws requiring that auto manufacturers make bumpers stronger. This, she said, would be good for the consumer. Yet Furness neither cited nor interviewed a single auto-buyer who had asked for stronger (and thus more costly) bumpers.

☒ NBC's Jeff Madrick, in his February 1 segment in "Nightly News" calling for tougher federal laws on workplace safety, offered no evidence that the cause of workplace accidents was lack of regulations. In fact, Madrick interviewed Joe Kinney of the National Safe Workplace Institute who said: "For any person getting up in the morning to go to work and rely on the government to protect them is foolhardy."

☒ CBS's Ed Bradley, in his February 16 "60 Minutes" segment on auto seat-back safety, made a strong case for federal regulations of seat-backs. Yet Bradley cited no increase of injuries resulting from ostensibly defective seat-backs.

☒ ABC's medical editor Dr. Timothy Johnson, on "World News Tonight" June 10, profiled Americans going to Italy and elsewhere abroad, where there were relatively few regulations, for drugs not approved for sale in America. The tone and message of Johnson's story were alarmist. In his kicker, he said: "As drug companies and politicians demand changes in how the FDA approves drugs, they might well look to countries like Italy as a reminder that the public can also lose if the drug regulators are not tough." The report never explained how the public or anyone else was losing in Italy. The closest that Johnson came was saying that "many [of the Italian drugs] don't work." But no one identified any Italians who had suffered from drugs that did not work.

☒ CNN's August 12 long segment in "World News" by Brian Barger made the case for increased federal inspection of fish; yet

Barger cited not one case of anyone having become ill from fish under the current inspection system.

☒ NBC reporter Fred Briggs' "Nightly News" November 23 story warned that bottled water labelled "spring" water might not have come from genuine springs. The report's entire tone suggested that there were questions concerning the actual source of the water and its purity. Yet the segment also said that 2.1 billion gallons of bottled water were sold in 1991, triple that of a decade earlier. With so much bottled water sold, if there were problems with the water surely some evidence of them would have surfaced. None was cited.

☒ ABC's "Good Morning America" December 3 segment looked at a new federal food labelling law. Host Joan Lunden rightly asked the question: "You have estimated that [new food labelling] could cost $2 billion in economic hard times. Is it worth it?" Neither she nor the report identified anyone suffering from the current labelling system. She also could have observed that if the consumer wanted more informative labels on food, the marketplace would undoubtedly deliver it.

If TV Wants to Improve . . .

To better the reporting on regulatory matters would require little extra expense or air time. The biggest improvement would be to inject into the stories some skepticism about the efficacy of regulations. Reporters could tell viewers, for example, that regulations often fail to achieve their intended results and almost always impose an unanticipated price.

It also would cost the networks nothing to skip those stories that call for regulations to solve problems when problems do not exist. Such a non-story was the toxic chemicals in fish on Brian Barger's CNN "World News" segment August 12. While he found traces of such elements in fish, he produced no evidence that anyone had been getting sick from fish tainted by the chemicals he was discussing. Indeed, an NBC "Today" January 16 story on contaminated fish had pointed out that "cooking kills contamination."

For only a bit more air time, the networks could teach viewers that marketplace competition typically is much more effective, and at much lower cost, in protecting the consumer than is regulation by government bureaucracies. CNN's Kathleen Koch, in her August 31 segment in "World News" on new rules for de-icing airplanes, could have noted that even without government regulations, airline companies had enormous incentives to de-ice as thoroughly as possible. She or a Talking Head could have explained to viewers that poor maintenance would result in airplane accidents which, in turn, would lose customers for airlines; this, in fact, already had driven airlines out of business.

NBC's Betty Furness, in her story on auto bumpers, similarly could have suggested that if consumers wanted stronger bumpers, the auto makers would produce them—just as consumer demand for airbags was forcing them increasingly to install them. And Brian Barger could have noted that it was not government inspectors but consumers, with their ability to switch rapidly from one seller to another, that had kept food quality high.

In relating the cable TV issue, all reporters spoke along the lines of CNN's Carl Rochelle—that regulation, of all things, could spur competition. In that story and others, reporters should have posed the challenging question: "What does increase competition?" and, "Have various federal and local regulations been responsible for creating and protecting the cable monopolies?"

Reporters could have pointed out the cumulative costs of regulations. Viewers could have learned that the costs of complying with regulations in just three areas (health care, environment, and legal fees) rose from 9.4 percent of gross domestic product in 1972 to 16 percent of GDP in 1990, according to economist Robert Samuelson. A reporter or economist then could have explained how this increase in the regulatory burden had affected economic growth, wage growth, and job creation.

In stories on specific regulations, reporters could have said:

"Although the effect on the economy of this one regulation

might seem small, critics argue that if you add up all the small regulations, you find a swamp of rules that cost the economy plenty."

THE YEAR'S BEST AND WORST COVERAGE

Viewers learned most about how regulations affected their free enterprise economy from:

1. ABC's John Stossel in his January 3 "20/20" look at workman compensation fraud in California. First he advised viewers that the fraud could cost $12 billion per year, implying that this would be an expensive unintended consequence of regulation. Then he pointed out that the compensation laws' high rates were driving businesses out of the state. He said: "This company, which makes metal doors, recently moved 125 jobs to Oklahoma to get away from California's Workman's Compensation. What really hurt was when California started to give out awards for stress." The cost of this, said Stossel, was "not just the companies raising prices. It's also that we pay more taxes for this . . . You want to be generous when people are really hurt. You want to help them. But the more generous you are, the less incentive there is to come back to work."

2. CNN's Ed Garsten in his "World News" March 18 story on a congressional bill dealing with auto and other replacement parts. The bill would have given original equipment manufacturers the exclusive right to sell and distribute replacement parts for up to ten years after production. Garsten clearly understood that market competition keeps prices low; as such, his report was a strong endorsement of competition. At one point in the segment, referring to the consumer's ability to choose where to buy replacement parts, Garsten told viewers: "A bill in Congress would make that choice almost impossible." Garsten also interviewed a trade association official who explained that the bill "will deter competition, [and] create a monopoly for vehicle manufacturers and their dealers. It is

unfair competition. And most importantly, the American consumer will suffer with higher prices and significantly poorer service."

3. ABC's Charles Gibson in his "Good Morning America" May 12 comments on the vote in Portland, Maine, on restricting water-front business activity to marine-related industry. Asked Gibson: "Why shouldn't the market determine what's on the waterfront?"

4. ABC's James Walker in his "World News Tonight" January 15 report on how, when medical flotsam started washing up on East Coast beaches in 1988, government regulators overreacted by imposing draconian new rules on hospital disposal of medical waste. Explained Walker: "Hospital disposal costs shot up as much as 700 percent." The reason for this, the segment explained to viewers, was that the tough new regulations scared hospitals workers to a degree where no one dared take a risk on disposal. As a result, almost all waste was thrown into the "red bags" that required special handling. Asked Walker: "With scientists maintaining that only 6 percent of hospital waste requires special handling and with health care dollars scarce, the question is, should limited resources be spent to appease popular misconceptions?" In this report, Walker made a number of points about regulation—that regulation imposed great costs, could result from misconception, and often ignored solid scientific evidence; and that resources were limited.

The year's best story on regulation was ABC's John Stossel in his "20/20" January 24 takeout on state governments that were trying to bar companies from imposing no-smoking and other health conditions on their employees during their non-work hours. Ostensibly the issue concerned states protecting the individual's right of privacy against the intrusiveness of employers.

Stossel, however, correctly saw it as a matter of states imposing regulations where none was needed. In paraphrasing those against these laws, Stossel told viewers: "Opponents of the new laws say all these lawsuits and new rules will just make it tougher for American companies to compete. And we don't need new laws, they say, because the competition of the market will prevent abuses. Employers with restrictive policies will have to pay more to hire their ideal worker. That will create opportunities for smokers and others." In closing, Stossel added: "I sympathize with the people who say the laws do more harm than good. How can American companies compete if every time they make a personnel decision they have to consult a labor lawyer to wade through the laws?"

Viewers had the worst chance of learning about regulation's affect on their economy from:

1. NBC's Betty Furness in her "Today" January 8 kicker to the story about California's laws requiring stronger auto bumpers. Though Furness could point to no consumer demand or desire for the stronger, and costlier, bumpers, she declared: "If other states follow California's lead and pass bumper disclosure laws, stronger bumpers may move up on the list of priorities for car buyers. New York and several other large states have considered this kind of legislation. We can hope the trend continues." She should have said:

"Critics of the laws say that if consumers really feel strongly about bumper strength, they will demand and get them from the auto makers."

2. CBS's Bob Schieffer in his "Evening News" January 18 commentary citing World War II, the moon program, A-bomb development, and "Star Wars" initiative as examples of how government could work successfully with business. More correctly, these should have been cited as examples of very costly and inefficient government projects that had been justified only by wartime conditions—both hot and cold.

3. CNN's Carl Rochelle in his "World News" January 31 report on passage of the Senate bill giving the Federal Communications Commission power to regulate cable TV prices. Rochelle accepted the premises of the regulators: that regulation would "promote

competition" and address "unreasonable price increases." Rochelle should have said:

"Defenders of the cable industry point to the millions of new subscribers as evidence that consumers obviously think they are getting their money's worth."

4. ABC's legal expert Arthur Miller in his "Good Morning America" January 31 commentary on the breast implant issue in which he just about dismissed the key role played by tort law to impose sanctions on those damaging others. Said Miller: "It really is quite unrealistic to expect plaintiffs, who want to get as much money as they can by way of settlement, to act as sort of a public avenger. It is also unrealistic to expect the courts, who are just creaking and groaning under their work load, to act as sort of an information agency for the society at large . . . I think the real problem is to focus on the FDA [Food and Drug Administration] and FTC [Federal Trade Commission] to get the national administration and the state administration to do their jobs much more effectively than they have done it in the last six or eight years." Miller was factually wrong on this. The truth is that plaintiffs have acted very effectively and efficiently as public avengers, while courts just as effectively and efficiently have served as information agency.

5. CNN's Brian Barger in his "World News" August 12 story on the nonexistent problem of toxic chemicals in fish. In his apparent determination to make the case that regulations must require more inspection of fish, he even faulted the Food and Drug Administration, one of the most intrusive and obsessive federal agencies. To prove that the FDA had been remiss, Barger sent samples of tuna to a Michigan State University pesticide research center which, said Barger, tested the tuna for more chemicals than did the FDA and looked for them at lower levels. The results, according to Barger: "By FDA standards, the tuna we tested would be considered clean and easily pass inspection. But we did find small traces of 18 toxic chemicals . . . We also found minute traces, 3 parts per trillion, of

dioxin." Later Barger told viewers: "Of the 100,000 chemical compounds used by industry today, the FDA has set health safety limits on only 14 of them in fish . . . Inspectors don't really know how many toxic chemicals are in the fish you eat." These numbers were probably staggering enough to terrify almost any viewer. Yet Barger never offered evidence that anyone was getting sick. In fact, the only time he referred to it at all was to say that "scientists still don't know how much exposure will cause [ill] effects in humans."

6. NBC's Bryant Gumbel in his "Today" December 3 commentary on food labelling regulations in which he implicitly called for regulation of advertising of food products. Said Gumbel: "One of the problems is, for example, Hellmann's mayonnaise won't be able to put 'lite,' if it doesn't meet your definition, on their label. They will still be able to advertise like that, right? They'll be able to use words in ads that they can't put on the label."

SYLVIA CHASE: WORST OF THE WORST

The year's worst reporting on regulation was by ABC's Sylvia Chase on "Prime Time Live" January 9. Her long segment, introduced by Diana Sawyer, described the ghoulish results of what are called truck underride accidents. These occur when cars plow into the rear of trucks and slip under them, whereupon the body of the truck crashes through the car's passenger compartment, at times beheading the passengers.

Chase's episode was a caricature of irresponsible reporting. Among her failings, she:

⊠ Alarmed viewers by not putting statistics into perspective. She said, for example, that two thousand persons had died in truck underride accidents in the past twenty years. While each traffic death, of course, was a tragedy, truck underride deaths scarcely deserves such attention; even if Chase's statistics were correct, they would account for about two-tenths of 1 percent of all traffic fatalities—which Chase did not tell the viewer.

☒ Failed to identify the bias of experts. In interviewing Byron Bloch, for example, Chase identified him only as a "safety expert" and an "ABC News consultant" who "testifies against vehicle manufacturers in trials." She did not tell viewers that for years Bloch has been a loud and frequent critic of the auto industry and has been paid to testify against it by trial lawyers.

☒ Used emotionally charged language and failed to put it in perspective. She said that at the "highest levels" of Republican administrations, "cost effectiveness has been put ahead of human life." Later she said that a government agency decided "that the lives saved would not be commensurate with the cost of implementing the proposed standards." Chase then cut to Bloch who indignantly asked: "We're going to cost out the value of American citizens? Toss them away?" What Sawyer and Chase did not say was that "cost-effectiveness" routinely has been put ahead of human life by government and, indeed, by all Americans as individuals. This is a trade-off encountered at every turn in life. Example: reducing the speed limit to 5 miles per hour probably would save more than forty thousand lives per year; America, however, could not afford the cost that such a measure would impose on business, commerce, and mobility. Chase gave the viewer no help in framing a perspective within which the emotional language could be evaluated.

☒ Interviewed only critics of the trucking industry and only critics of the federal decision to reject the change in truck design advocated by Bloch, Chase herself, and the others. In addition to Bloch, among those interviewed by Chase were: a man whose brother had been killed in an underride accident; the mother of Rhona Miller who had become a quadriplegic at age fifteen when her car crashed under a truck; Brian O'Neill of the Insurance Institute for Highway Safety; and former Carter administration official Joan Claybrook, a longtime opponent of American auto companies. To offset the many critics, Chase gave viewers only 15 seconds of Steve Campbell, safety director of the American Trucking Association. Ostensibly he was interviewed to explain why American trucks were designed as they were. Yet in the few seconds in which he appeared—perhaps a distorted extract of Campbell's full interview with him—Chase was depicted as evasive and confused.

CHAPTER SIX

FEDERAL SPENDING AND THE BUDGET: PEP TALKS AND MISSING ECONOMISTS

WHEN IT CAME to covering federal spending and budget matters in 1992, the network TV style sheet seemed written to tilt the argument against free market approaches and solutions. Network reports on spending were 24 percent more likely to cite government programs than the market as an answer to problems. In reports on the budget, the tilt was a 16 percent advantage for government solutions.

For all of 1992, the four network newscasts gave viewers only 24 minutes coverage of government budget matters in which a free enterprise approach was credible versus 28 minutes which were critical of the concepts necessary to a free enterprise system; some 5 hours, 16 minutes of budget coverage were background information. On government spending issues, 69 newscast minutes supported a free market approach, while 84 minutes did not; 10 hours, 24 minutes were background.

This meant that viewers were likely to hear and see, first, that government spending was good and, second, that when spending was cut Americans would suffer. The only area of spending in which the message was at all ambiguous was welfare, about which viewers got a picture of a system out of control, costing great sums, and, above all, failing to help those in need.

The Message: Programs Solve Problems

The notion that government solves problems better than the private sector is as complex as it is contentious. Most political experts of almost all political stripes would agree that the answer, at the least, is mixed. Conservatives who deeply distrust government, for instance, concede that government action is needed to defend the nation from enemies and to defend individuals and property from criminals, but dispute that government intrusion in general is salutary rather than baleful.

Viewers, however, who watched network TV's reporting of spending and budget matters in 1992, got little sense that the role of government was a matter of some dispute. To the contrary. In discussions of spending and the budget, as well as of other matters, viewers generally were told that, on the whole, government had the answers.

That was explicit in Bryant Gumbel's remark on "Today" January 21. Commenting on a demand by an official of the National Urban League for a Marshall Plan-size federal program for America's cities, Gumbel said: "That's a wonderful plan. I'm sure nobody could disagree with any element of it. Except for one major problem, how do you pay for it? Particularly with time and money so tight." In fact, many would disagree; there was enormous dispute about how much and what government could do to reverse inner-city decline.

Gumbel's endorsement of government action was similar to the message viewers had received a few weeks earlier from CBS's Giselle Fernandez. Her January 3 "Evening News" story on rapid transit costs was a brief for increased government subsidies. The underlying assumption was that public transit need never pay its own way. Thus, although Fernandez said, "without the tax subsidies to make up on the shortfall, it's now up to the commuter alone to pick up the tab," she left no doubt that commuters would not and should not pay more.

All of Fernandez's interviews reinforced the argument against higher fares. In her kicker, emphasizing that transit was a matter for government, Fernandez said: "There just may be light, though, at the end of the tunnel. Congress has just approved a multibillion dollar budget that over the next six years may help get America's mass transit system back on track. Until then, commuters feel like they're just being taken for a ride."

What Fernandez ignored were the studies that found ridership on public transit systems declining steadily over the years. Had she taken these into account, Fernandez could have said:

"As long as more and more federal dollars go to a system that serves less and less of the public, taxpayers will feel like they're just being taken for a ride."

The reporting on the Los Angeles riots also assumed that the only response to urban distress was increased government spending. This was the unambiguous message from ABC's Beth Nissen on her "World News Tonight" segment May 12. Viewers saw several successful L.A. residents praising government programs for helping them get started on their careers.

When reporters went beyond Los Angeles to discuss urban issues, the pep talk for federal spending continued. Thus when ABC "Good Morning America" anchor Joan Lunden visited Portland, Maine, viewers saw and heard the city's current and former mayors calling for more federal help for cities.

Missing completely from Lunden's interviews was anyone suggesting that perhaps the cities and states should try to get by on their own resources. Such views also were missing from just about all of the extensive reporting on California's budget crisis. Typical was NBC's Diana Koricke on "Nightly News" July 19. She explicitly assumed that only increased federal aid or higher taxes could solve the state's problem. When California spending cuts were discussed, they were depicted almost entirely in terms of the pain that they would impose. No mention was made that spending could be cut without diminishing the quality of service.

When government spending was portrayed as a problem, the problem's cause almost always was identified as something other than the spending itself. One cause frequently cited was the recession, which, the report maintained, was reducing the tax revenues needed to pay for government programs.

Tax collections, of course, do dip in a recession. And journalists should report that. But to stop there, as almost all TV newscasters did, was to ignore the equally important other half of the story: that government programs had been growing at a staggering pace. Reporters could have asked (but did not) whether the problem was not the result of falling tax collections coupled with overspending by government. But reporters seldom even hinted that spending might have been out of control, or why.

Typical of network coverage of the issue was Brian Rooney's story on ABC "World News Tonight" September 2. Commenting on the California budget problem, he said: "The state budget crisis was brought on by a two-year recession that caused state revenues to fall. Meanwhile, a huge influx of needy immigrants came into the state while more and more of the taxpayers were moving out . . . The crisis was a result of bad times." Rooney would have served viewers better had he said:

"Out-of-control state spending, coupled with a two-year recession that caused state revenues to fall, brought on the current budget crisis. A huge influx of needy immigrants only aggravated the crisis."

BUDGET CUTS: "OUR KIDS ARE AT RISK"

When cutting government programs was discussed, much of the reporting consisted of emotional interviews with the potential victims—those who would be affected directly by the cuts. In her

July 17 story, for instance, NBC's Koricke told viewers: "Students in kindergarten to college will suffer." NBC's George Lewis on "Nightly News" August 31, who also reported on California's budget problems, said: "The disabled and health care workers have been among those urging officials to get off the dime. They say essential services will be disrupted unless some real money is forthcoming." Later in his segment, Lewis interviewed a Los Angeles hospital official who told viewers: "If the budget isn't done in a short period of time, we'll have to consider layoffs and cutbacks in services to medical patients."

Two days later, Lewis took "Nightly News" viewers to a "clinic in North Hollywood, slated to be closed because of cutbacks. The workers say children, especially poor kids, are being victimized in the process. They contend that lower health care standards will help spread communicable diseases such as tuberculosis." Lewis interviewed nurse Carla Angela who warned viewers: "TB is up 800 percent in this county. [If] these kids . . . aren't treated they'll be going to school with our children, [so] our kids are at risk. We're at risk."

Meanwhile, on ABC that evening, Brian Rooney said that California "welfare recipient Tracy Martinez-Robinson and her daughter were already cut to $535 a month and that will drop to $504 by November." Martinez-Robinson then told the TV audience: "I anticipate if there is another cut, that we will have barely enough to pay the rent and have a dollar left over for the month—so we're looking at bordering homelessness."

Viewers heard of more woes from CNN's Don Knapp on "World News" August 27. He reported: "Despite cerebral palsy, Candy Hernandez is fiercely independent, thanks in part to life in this group home. But the home Candy shares with five disabled housemates is about to be closed, its residents shipped out to state hospitals." Several weeks later, CNN's Greg Lefevre on "World News" September 2 told viewers a "thirty-year-old quadriplegic was among the hundreds of homecare residents kicked out when [California] cut off checks, forcing the homes to shut down." Lefevre then interviewed nurse Elena Soto who predicted: "You'll have an increase in TB cases. . . people will be going without medical care."

Ignored by these reporters was the other side. They could have pointed to those paying for the government programs and said:

"These programs have their own victims, though: people who are thrown out of work or can't find a job because of the higher taxes and budget deficits needed to sustain such government spending."

WELFARE: "MORALLY BANKRUPT"

The only government program to which TV reporters brought basic journalistic standards of inquiry and even curiosity was welfare. Thus when welfare advocate David Liederman adamantly opposed a welfare reform plan on "Today" January 22, host Katie Couric would not let him get away with it. She demanded: "You admit that the welfare system is morally bankrupt and in desperate need of an overhaul. How would you try to rehabilitate it?"

In a similar vein, CBS "This Morning" host Paula Zahn, on January 15, was gentle with New Jersey Governor James Florio when he was describing his tough approach to reforming his state's welfare system. Zahn was near-nodding agreement when Florio told viewers: "The welfare system is not working . . . What we're talking about is everyone taking some responsibility . . . taking individual responsibility for the course of your own actions." Tough-talking on welfare by Wisconsin governor Tommy Thompson also got a friendly hearing from Zahn on "This Morning" May 15. NBC "Nightly News" anchor Tom Brokaw was equally sympathetic in his February 3 interview with Michigan governor John Engler, who described his efforts to force welfare cutbacks.

Newscasters also criticized welfare, at least implicitly, in stories exposing those who had taken advantage of government programs. Example: ABC's Diane Sawyer and Chris Wallace were indignant in the October 22 *Prime Time Live* story about a former Tennessee Valley Authority worker who fraudulently had received $150,000 tax free in government disability checks, a former Louisiana letter carrier who undeservedly was receiving $1,700 a month in disability pay, and others. Introducing the segment, Diane Sawyer told viewers: "Your money may be going to people who cheat the system, people who claim they can't work but in fact they can."

Wallace, in interviewing one of the accused cheaters, snapped: "You've made a pretty good living off a bad knee. . . . You've been convicted of filing a false statement, defrauding the system, and yet the government still pays you full benefits." Later Wallace asked a Labor Department official: "How do you think the average person watching tonight feels about paying a person $20–25,000 a year, tax free, who has already been convicted of defrauding the system?"

THE DEFICIT: WHERE WERE THE ECONOMISTS?

Congressional consideration of the Balanced Budget Amendment in June 1992 gave the networks the opportunity to discuss the federal deficit. They did so relatively extensively. The problem was that almost all the focus was on the political horse race aspect of the problem: Which party's bill would win? Which party would gain electoral advantage? And so on.

Ignored in the coverage was the substance of the matter—the deficit. Reporters did not explain the deficit problem; they did not tell viewers what a mounting deficit might be doing to the economy, nor what a deficit might mean to employers and employees, savings, investment, and economic growth.

In stressing the deficit as a political problem, reporters gave viewers interviews only with politicians. Missing were economists. The typical segment on the deficit began with a recitation of how huge the deficit had become and how it was contributing to an already monumental federal debt. Then the story shifted to Americans whose suffering would be alleviated, viewers were told, by new or expanded federal programs that, sadly, the government no longer could afford because of the deficit. At this point, the typical segment introduced the politicians, balanced between Republican and Democrat.

Bob Schieffer on the June 10 CBS "This Morning," for example, interviewed House Speaker Tom Foley, a Democrat, and Senator Strom Thurmond, a Republican, and then ran a George Bush soundbite. That same day, CNN's Bob Franken on "World News" interviewed Democratic House Members John Dingell, John Lewis, and Leon Panetta and GOP House leader Robert Michel and ran a Bush soundbite. Viewers heard them assess whether the balanced budget amendment would pass Congress. Viewers heard nothing about what a balanced budget would mean.

IF TV WANTS TO IMPROVE . . .

Coverage of federal budget and spending matters could improve if newscasts would:

1. Give viewers some notion that problems are not necessarily solved by more government spending. The network's stories on California's budget crisis, for instance, almost all assumed that only more spending could correct problems. They also assumed that spending cuts would impose great and unavoidable pain. These stories denied viewers the chance to see and hear those who contend that spending could be cut without harm to the services.

2. Give viewers a chance to hear from free market exponents. Rarely were they interviewed in 1992. Typical was Charles Gibson's analysis, on ABC "Good Morning America" January 29, of the Bush State of the Union speech. Gibson's two guests were Jonathan Kozol and James Fallows. Both were well-known advocates of government solutions to problems. Indeed, at one point in the interview, Kozol complained that the Bush prescriptions for the nation offered "no new money, no new plans." Gibson's segment would have served viewers better had he balanced Kozol and Fallows by giving a free market advocate a chance to analyze the Bush speech. Viewers then might have learned that some problems could be addressed without the "new money" or "new plans" urged by Kozol.

3. Give viewers a chance to hear how private charities address problems that government spending programs fail to solve. Viewers rarely heard about groups like the Red Cross, the Salvation Army, Teach for America, or numerous church-related, inner-city programs that dealt with social problems much more efficiently that did government. Nor did viewers hear about studies that have shown that when government spending and tax rates decreased, private charitable contributions soared.

4. Tell viewers how government spending in other countries had arrested economic growth. This most dramatically has been the case in the European Community where a wide range of government-mandated benefits and generous unemployment compensation prevented the creation of more than 13 million new jobs between 1965 and 1991. In stories on government spending programs, reporters could caution:

"Critics wonder if such spending would not add to the deficit and slow economic growth, thus harming more than helping the population."

THE YEAR'S BEST AND WORST COVERAGE

Viewers had the best chance of learning that government programs seldom solve problems from stories dealing with waste, fraud, and corruption. Reporters rarely criticized government spending on any other matter. Examples:

1. Mike Wallace's interview with economist and GOP Congressman Richard Armey on the June 28 CBS "60 Minutes" expose of the Federal Farms Subsidy Program. From Armey, viewers had a chance to learn that government subsidies were extremely wasteful and hurt the economy.

2. Steve Kroft's introduction to the CBS "60 Minutes" July 5

segment on the Rural Electrification Administration. He said: "Once a government project gets started, it is nearly impossible to shut it down—even if its mission has been accomplished—even if it's run hopelessly amuck. Take the REA, the Rural Electrification Administration, by all accounts one of the most successful projects . . . [It is] now welfare for the wealthy."

3. Harry Smith's August 14 interview on CBS "This Morning" with Martin Gross, author of *The Government Racket: Washington Waste from A to Z*. Not only did the interview allow Gross to give viewers infuriating examples of government waste, but Smith endorsed Gross's observations by saying: "These kinds of numbers are the sort of stuff that make people want to just stand and scream" and, "If you want to see some numbers that will just really knock your socks off, this is the book where they are all located."

4. Greg Lefevre's kicker to his CNN "World News" September 2 story on California's budget problem. Explaining the state of mind necessary for responsible government, he said: "The budget crisis introduces an entirely new state of mind. For decades Californians asked the state for money and the government spent it. That was called case-load driven. Now the state spending is revenue driven, spending only what it takes in."

Viewers had the poorest chance of learning how government spending and budget matters affect the economy from:

1. Bob Schieffer's false dichotomy in his remarks on CBS "Evening News" May 9 when he said: "President [Bush] seems to favor new emphasis on programs he has talked about before—to use tax breaks to help inner-city poor to own their own homes and start up businesses. Others in Washington want more emphasis on putting people back to work." What viewers heard from Schieffer was a dichotomy: on one side tax breaks, on the opposite side putting people back to work. But, in fact, many economists explain that the kind of tax breaks proposed by Bush would have spurred the

investment that would have created the jobs needed to put people back to work. Schieffer should have said:

"President Bush's approach to putting people back to work emphasizes tax breaks and incentives."

2. Beth Nissen's comments on ABC "World News Tonight" May 12 on the CETA job training program that had been killed in the mid–1980s by the Reagan administration. Nissen told viewers: "The CETA programs gave 4,500,000 poor people like Cynthia a first chance, a way out. But the program was considered wasteful and badly managed. CETA was phased out by the Reagan administration in 1982." Nissen misinformed ABC's audience. CETA mainly was abolished because it had failed as a training program; a study had found that few of its graduates were able to keep their jobs for the long term. Nissen should have said:

"CETA was abolished because, unlike private part-time jobs, it was unable to teach young people the skills and habits to prepare them for the future."

3. Bryant Gumbel's questioning of a guest in a NBC "Today" December 16 discussion of the Clinton economic summit. Asked Gumbel: "Based on what you heard coming out of Little Rock . . . what is your best guess as to Clinton's economic priorities at this point: cutting the deficit or creating jobs?" This was another false dichotomy. Gumbel was telling the "Today" audience that cutting the deficit and creating jobs were mutually exclusive. In truth, if the deficit were cut by trimming government spending and reducing the government's share of the gross domestic product, the economy would have more resources with which to create jobs. Gumbel should have asked:

"How will Clinton try to cut the deficit, with spending cuts or with tax increases that some say could destroy jobs?"

CHAPTER SEVEN

THE ENVIRONMENT: PANIC AND PRESSURE

CONCERN ABOUT THE environment, for many good reasons, has been the late twentieth-century's apple pie issue. Huge majorities of Americans consistently tell pollsters that the environment ranks at or near the top of the nation's chief problems. Intense interest in the environment is reflected by TV's broad coverage of it. During 1992, newscasts in the aggregate devoted nine hours to environment stories. To be sure, a good portion of this was the extensive reporting from the United Nations environment conference in Rio de Janeiro. Yet even without the Rio Summit, as it popularly was known, TV coverage of the environment would have been considerable—ranking higher than taxes and health care and almost as high as federal spending and the budget.

Yet for all the TV reporting, American viewers received a lopsided message about the state of the environment and what could be done to preserve or improve it. For one thing, much of the coverage (as was true in reporting on regulation and government spending cuts) was a litany of horror stories about the dismal, near apocalyptic state of one or another aspect of the issue.

For another thing, coverage almost always endorsed solving environmental problems through tough government regulatory

164

measures rather than through market mechanisms and other means consistent with a free enterprise economy.

This tilt is confirmed by the numbers. Throughout 1992, American TV viewers were 30 percent more likely to be told by network newscasts that government, rather than the private sector, effectively could address their environmental concerns. The networks during the year ran 56 minutes of news favorable to government solutions to environmental problems versus 43 minutes critical of government solutions. CNN was the network most enamored of government action; its viewers had a three times greater chance of hearing that bigger government was needed to solve environmental problems than of hearing those critical of government regulation.

THE MESSAGE: A WORLD POISONED AND DEVOURED

The year's main network TV message on the environment was its dire state. Said ABC's Barry Dunsmore on "World News Tonight" May 31: "With the world headed toward environmental catastrophe, they [environmentalists] charge the U.S. has been watering down and blocking the conference planners' attempts to achieve some modest international agreements." The following day on "Nightline," ABC's Forrest Sawyer declared that the world was being "poisoned and devoured by ravenous billions of us. And there is no end in sight."

Offered as evidence of the world's bleak ecological plight was an inventory of disappearing assets. From CNN's Greg Lefevre, viewers learned on January 3 that: "The Labrador duck is no more. Extinct. So too the Carolina parakeet, and the ivory billed woodpecker." To this list, CNN's Deborah Potter added on January 11: "The forests are shrinking . . . species are vanishing day by day." On February 12, CNN added the Chesapeake Bay to the list, telling viewers that 99 percent of the oyster beds were gone, acres of underwater grass were diminishing, and fish and ducks were becoming scarce. Vanishing too, according to ABC's "Good Morning America" May 13, were whales. As was the ozone layer, per ABC

"World News Tonight" February 13 and CBS "This Morning" February 27. Warned CBS's Harry Smith gravely: "Droughts, storms, floods, even extinction of some species, could be the result [of global warming]."

Not everything, of course, was disappearing. CNN's Deborah Potter pointed out that the desert was expanding. As were other things. According to Michael Oppenheimer of the Environmental Defense Fund on NBC "Nightly News" June 4: "The world is facing the potential for record heat, record drought, forests going up in flames, sea levels rising, creating an unprecedented refugee problem."

Expanding most dangerously, apparently, was population. Repeatedly viewers were told that growing population was the main cause of the world's environmental problem. On June 5 viewers could see and hear this on CNN "World News" and on CBS "Evening News." CBS's Connie Chung quoted Jacques Cousteau on the need to halt the "genocide of population growth." While almost every economic theory and school views people as valuable assets, TV environmental coverage portrayed them as horrifying liabilities. Without any challenge or even a raised eyebrow from anchor Charles Gibson, John Prescott, director of the New England Aquarium in Boston, told viewers of ABC's "Good Morning America" May 13: "The real pollution problem, I think we all have to basically admit, is people."

While the abstract notion of "overpopulation" was the general culprit in the battle for environmental purity, the key adversary identified by network TV was business, what TV called "economic interests." This assumption pervaded most of the reporting on the environment. At times, it was absolutely explicit, as in the crisp dichotomy presented by Greg Lefevre's January 3 segment. For the one side he invited experts who recited a list of species about to be extinct. For the other was Interior Secretary Manuel Lujan whom Lefevre did not even introduce as a representative of the Bush administration but as "on the side of industry." The story, for Lefevre, was a struggle between environmentalism and industry/business.

So too for NBC "Today" host Bryant Gumbel on June 8 when he said: "Isn't President [Bush] sending a message that says that environmental concerns are secondary to business interests?" Lefevre and Gumbel both ignored the obvious—that Americans, as job-holders, job-seekers, and consumers, might have legitimate objections to some environmentalist demands. It would have been more accurate for Gumbel to have said:

> **"Isn't Bush saying that there is a trade-off—even tension—between environmental concerns and those of an economy that must create jobs?"**

GOVERNMENT IS THE ANSWER

When it came to solutions for environmental problems, network TV informed that the solutions would come from government. On ABC "World News Tonight" February 13, reporter Barry Serafin approvingly cited those making such statements as that "more federal funds are needed for monitoring and research" of the "red tides" problem. ABC's Charles Gibson on "Good Morning America" May 13 even prodded his guest by asking: "How do you attack the problem, John? Is it government money?"

The case for vastly expanded government action on environmental matters as against free market approaches became an insistent drumbeat during the networks' extensive coverage of the Rio Summit. In report after report, the bottom line was that only massive government action and spending could save the world from what was described as certain ecological apocalypse. One message, for example, repeated again and again that the developed nations should pay some $150 billion annually to undeveloped countries so that they could industrialize without adding to the globe's pollution. Almost no counterarguments to the strong progovernment message were seen or heard by viewers. There was almost no one on the American TV screen to suggest that the environment could be protected by innovative ways that did not involve costly government activity.

Indeed, in the first full week of the Rio conference's coverage, the network newscasts interviewed thirty environmental experts who were not government officials. Of these, twenty-eight represented environmental groups advocating increased government action; only two suggested nongovernment alternatives.[1]

A RARE UNDERSTANDING OF TRADE-OFFS

The sole environmental area in which the networks offered viewers balanced reporting was on the potentially high cost of measures to protect the environment. In spotlighting the cost, TV introduced viewers to the important economic concept of trade-offs: that every economic action imposes some price or cost, direct or indirect, visible or hidden. This is the profound truth behind Milton Friedman's famous quip about "no free lunch."

That message—that environmental protection would not be a free lunch—was generally received by viewers from much of TV. Two ABC broadcasts, for example, looked at environmentalism's cost to jobs. On "World News Tonight" February 28, anchor Peter Jennings introduced a segment on dolphins by saying: "Saving the dolphins could drive some of the tuna fishermen out of business." Reporter Gary Shepard went on to explain that using nets that occasionally snagged a dolphin "is the only commercially viable way to fish for tuna."

Earlier that month, the February 4 edition of "Nightline" looked at what is called the Wise Use Movement. Introducing it, host Ted Koppel said that it was a "growing movement that says it's the environmentalists who are wrecking the country." ABC science editor Michael Guillen started by telling viewers: "For a lot of people in this country, the environmental movement has gone too far. Wide open spaces like these, they say, are crowding out their rights as Americans." And in his kicker, Guillen concluded: "Now the Wise Use Movement wants to defend man against the assaults of an environmental movement they claim has lost sight of one very important reality. This country, they say, can no longer afford to save the earth at all costs."

Reports on the Rio environmental conference also cited the trade-offs, explaining that slower economic growth and fewer new jobs might be the result of tough regulations to reduce pollution, protect animal species, and otherwise solve what were described as environmental problems. As NBC's Tom Brokaw explained on the "Nightly News" June 1: the task of the Rio summit was "how to save the earth and not go broke in the process."

The cost to consumers was the theme of the CNN "Prime News" November 1 report on an expensive new additive mandated for gasoline to reduce carbon monoxide emissions. Reporter Carl Rochelle carefully balanced his man-in-the-street soundbites: the two people who said that anything was worth helping the environment were countered by two saying that there was "no reason why we, the gas-buying public, we should be socked again" by higher gasoline prices. Rochelle then added that "there may be a slight decrease in engine performance" from the mandated gasoline.

For CBS "Evening News" March 2, the cost of environmentalism was its potential infringement of property rights. This was the theme of reporter Rita Braver's segment on the Supreme Court's case about a South Carolina couple, the Lucases, who had bought beach-front property and then were banned from building a house on it when the state suddenly passed an environmental beach-front conservation law. Said Braver: "The dream became a nightmare." Through Braver's interviews, viewers heard David Lucas say: "Can they [the government] take my property and not pay for it? The Constitution says—No."

IF TV WANTS TO IMPROVE ...

Viewers could learn more about the economic implications of environmental measures were the networks to:

☒ Balance the frequent appearances of scientists and other experts strongly advocating only a government solution to environmental problems with scientists and experts suggesting other possible solutions. The viewer, for example, was poorly served by the Rio conference coverage which pitted twenty-eight government-solution advocates against only two proposing non-government alternatives. The viewer was no better served by a CNN "World News" January 11 segment which offset extensive proregulation arguments by the World Watch Institute's Lester Brown, UN Environmental Program Chairman Maurice Strong, and German Environment Minister Klaus Topfer with a lone, short soundbite from Kent Jeffreys of the Washington, D.C.-based Competitive Enterprise Institute. To make matters worse, the Jeffreys quote used by CNN addressed the decline of socialism and said nothing about the environment. TV networks easily could find experts who could suggest nongovernment ways of protecting the environment by seeking interviews, among other places, at the National Wilderness Institute in Washington, D.C., and the Political Economy Research Center in Bozeman, Montana.

⊠   Question the alarmist claims made by environmentalists. Network reporters almost never gave viewers a chance to learn that there was enormous disagreement in the scientific community about the extent to which the world's ecology is threatened. Thus while CNN's Greg Lefevre, in his "Prime News" January 3 segment, gave viewers useful examples of how the Endangered Species Act might be imposing high economic costs, he accepted unquestioningly all the scientific claims upon which the act was based and gave viewers comments only from such environmental alarmists as Stanford's Paul Ehrlich and Jacques Cousteau. Yet years of exaggerated claims by the alarmists, according to a series of *New York Times* articles in March 1993, have panicked the public and lawmakers into enacting very costly but unwarranted environmental laws. Rather than continue to feed this panic, network coverage of environmental issues could begin to stress the questionable and even flimsy scientific base for many of these alarmist statements. A major exception to this was the reporting by ABC science editor Michael Guillen. On "Good Morning America" June 2, he pointed out that scientists could not make up their minds about global warming. He noted also that some experts said that burning the rain forests might be good because it created a cloud cover that slowed global warming.

☒   Balance the statements on the putative problem of overpopulation. The networks could give viewers a chance to hear from those who argue that a growing population, rather than being a liability, could become an asset if the economic setting created incentives that mobilize talent. In such a setting, these experts could explain, extra population contributes to society rather than drains it. Only CNN "World News" on a June 5 segment noted that "many say population growth simply goes hand in hand with progress and development. They say the world can sustain more people and mankind's genius can cope if problems or shortages crop up."

☒   Explain that America and other advanced countries pollute less than do countries whose economies are undeveloped.

☒   Offer stories explaining private sector efforts and actions that protect the environment. Completely missing from the 1992 news was any glimpse at the vast, and growing, private sector initiatives that protect the environment. The nonprofit Nature Conservancy, for example, has bought 2.8 million acres of land containing rare or endangered plants and animals.

TV even missed stories of companies whose profit motive prompts them to protect the environment. The International Paper Company, for instance, has disallowed timbering in large portions of its Southern Pine Forests. The company employs wildlife biologists to maintain animal habitats on tracts of land that, in the aggregate, are bigger than Yellowstone National Park. The fees charged by International Paper for hunting, camping, and hiking on the land constitute nearly a quarter of the company's profits.

These projects are by no means uncommon. According to Donald R. Leal of the Political Economy Research Center: "As demand for environmental amenities and outdoor recreation has grown during the past two decades, private landowners in both the profit-making and nonprofit sectors have become a virtual army of environmental protectors." This army is still invisible to network reporters.

☒ Offer stories illustrating free market or quasi-free market policies for environmental protection. In the year's stories on the problems of fisheries being overfished, reporters typically first interviewed fishermen, who complained about government regulations, and then interviewed scientists who explained that the fishing industry would be destroyed without massive government action to limit fishing.

Had reporters interviewed free market environmentalists, viewers could have learned about such alternatives as Individual Transferable Quotas (ITQs). Instead of the policy that set a limit for the entire industry, which led fishermen to catch all their fish early and flood the market, this policy would be similar to pollution trading. ITQs would grant to fishermen quotas that they could use or sell at any time of the year, thereby eliminating the need to rush and assuring a fresh supply of fish to consumers all year. The policy has worked well in a number of states and countries, but, as with most free market environmental policies, was ignored by TV.

☒ Report on the unintended environmental consequences of government programs. Some government programs not only are economically unsound, they also harm the environment. Reporters could inform viewers, for example, about how tax-supported agriculture programs create perverse incentives for farmers to drain wetlands and destroy animal habitat to maximize their federal subsidy.

THE YEAR'S BEST AND WORST COVERAGE

Viewers had the best chance in 1992 to learn something about the relationship between measures to protect the environment and a healthy economy from:

☒ CNN's Greg Lefevre on "Prime News" January 3 who said: "Growth means jobs and places for people to live and food for them to eat, electricity for our standard of living. Does the Endangered Species Act place animal survival over man's?"

⊠   CBS's "Evening News" June 1 segment of "Eye on the Earth" in which Paula Zahn pointed out that while most Americans said that they were "concerned abut what's happening to the planet we share . . . not many are willing to share the sacrifice to clean it up." Added reporter Wyatt Andrews: "Few are willing to give up the worst polluter of all—the automobile. And even fewer make any tough sacrifices for the environment." The segment also reported the high costs of environmental regulations. Viewers saw how the Clean Air Act's restrictions on oil refineries were forcing Chevron to fire 650 people. Said Andrews: "In Port Arthur [Texas] the recession, the decline of big oil, and the drive to save the planet have helped wreck the town."

Viewers had the worst chance to see the relationship between environmental measures and a healthy economy from:

⊠   The bulk of coverage from the Rio conference. Overall, network reporters suspended their journalistic standards and in-quisitive instincts when they accepted, almost without challenge, the dire assessments and draconian prescriptions offered by environmental extremists. And seldom was a tough question put to them. Seldom also did any network offer a Talking Head to counter or temper the views of the extremists.

⊠   A series of special reports hosted by Christiane Amanpour for CNN during the Rio conference. She and other reporters used unsubstantiated alarmist language to describe environmental problems and focused entirely on government measures to solve them. Although they had a great amount of air time, not once did they mention any free market environmentalist ideas for reform.

⊠   Don Kladstrup's report for ABC "Nightline" June 1 about the environmental problems of Madagascar. Kladstrup and those he interviewed gave viewers the impression that population growth was the key environmental problem in Madagascar and that peo-ple were destroying the island's environment. Kladstrup did not interview any free market environmentalists who could have told viewers that with less restrictive economic policies, Madagascar's residents could raise the crops to feed their families and, at the same time, conserve their environment.

☒   Richard Blystone's report for CNN "World News" June 11 about Norway's environmental policies. Christiane Amanpour opened the segment saying: "Money is the main sticking point to a greener future." Then Blystone introduced viewers to Norway's intrusive environmental policies. Norwegians, for instance, were paying $5 a gallon for gasoline, of which almost two-thirds was taxes. Blyston only saw the bright side: "It is an encouragement to take the trolley, or ride a bike, which is healthy, too." While he did note that the measures made Norway less competitive, his answer was not that Norway make free market environmental reforms, but that the rest of the world follow Norway's economically painful path.

NOTES

1. For more analysis of TV's Rio Summit reporting see Chapter II.

CHAPTER EIGHT

HEALTH CARE: TV'S BEST KEPT SECRET

AMERICA HAS THE world's finest health care system. But Americans would not know it from network TV's 1992 health issues coverage. One after another, TV stories were a litany of health catastrophes and a catalogue of the culprits causing them. The only truly upbeat health care stories were those advocating government action. Typifying this, and unusual only for succinctly stating its inherent message, was the closing statement by ABC's Nancy Snyderman on "Good Morning America" July 15. After telling viewers that America's health care system was in dire straits, she said: "There is hope. There are now more than twenty health care bills before Congress."

So negative was TV's reporting on health matters and so skewed its balance that in a random flipping of the dial an American would be more than twice as likely to find a report advocating government approaches to health issues than nongovernment, free market approaches. In fact, viewers had less chance of seeing a balanced story on health than on taxes, regulations, the environment, or any other economic subject. During the year, of all TV network reporting on health, only 19 minutes were favorable to a free market approach to health issues, while 43 minutes were opposed; 4 hours, 4 minutes covered background.

HEALTH CARE COVERAGE

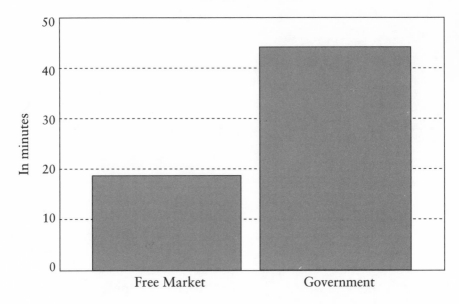

Time devoted to arguments on health care reform

THE MESSAGE:
A Choice Between Medication and Food

The Catastrophes

What Americans learned from TV about their nation's health care was that the system was failing. At no time in 1992 did network TV report on the hordes of foreigners who continually were flocking to America for health treatment, nor on the American medical schools which were packed with foreign students—both evidence of how highly the world regards American health care. Unreported by TV too was how nearly every American has a broader choice than anyone else in the world of doctors, health practitioners, treatments, safe medicines, hospitals, and clinics and a higher certainty of quality treatment. The strengths and advantages of America's health system was probably network TV's best kept secret.

Instead, what viewers heard and saw from CBS's Richard Threl-keld, for instance, on the "Evening News" January 2 was a profile of the clearly anguished McKinney family in New Hampshire. Denise McKinney had multiple sclerosis, viewers learned, and the family could not afford doctors. The family only could hope that it would get through the winter without colds.

On NBC, a Robert Bazell "Nightly News" segment January 15 reported on a St. Paul, Minnesota, man who was paying off $10,000 in medical bills and a Minneapolis couple who had to forgo doctor visits because they could afford only hospitalization insurance. From Sarah Massey, the Minneapolis wife, viewers heard: "We only go [to doctors] if we're on our deathbed." Bazell repeated this message in an October 21 interview with an eighty-two-year-old woman on a fixed income who said: "Either you have to cut down on medication or you have to cut down on food."

Others at NBC had the same message. On "Nightly News" June 30, viewers heard about "David and Melissa Dwyer who have two children, a rented house with a view, and no health insurance." David Dwyer told reporter Fred Briggs: "We'd be in a big fix if something did happen [to our health]."

On ABC, a Tim Johnson "World News Tonight" February 3 segment featured a North Carolina woman with cancer. CNN's Brooks Jackson on "World News" February 6 gave viewers a look at a woman with lupus who had no health insurance and thus had to go without medicine. "We had a choice one time to make," she told viewers, "whether to buy food, groceries, or to buy prescriptions."

Echoing this message was Connie Chung on CBS "Evening News" May 24; she gave viewers a Vermont woman who said that raising children without health insurance was "a matter of feeding them or getting them healthy. It's not an easy choice." CNN's Andrew Holtz on "Prime News" December 31 told viewers about a Colorado man who "is happy to have a job, even if it doesn't offer any health coverage. And though medicine alone to treat the effects of diabetes and cancer costs him more than $4,000 a year, he says the cost of his care prompted his former employer to fire him. He had to sell his home."

THE CULPRIT

To TV networks, the cause of America's faltering health care system was easy to define: the dual culprits were drug companies and insurance companies. On "World News Tonight" February 4, for instance, viewers heard reporter George Strait say: "Many hospitals express anger and frustration at what they call the drug industry's arrogant refusal to moderate price increases." To make his point, Strait interviewed one critic of drug companies after another: Senator David Pryor, the Arkansas Democrat, has denounced the pharmaceutical industry repeatedly; a pharmacist who advised hospitals on how to pay less for drugs; an official of a health maintenance group; and hospital pharmacist Harry Demanico who said that he and drug companies "are usually at odds. They are trying to sell me something I don't want to buy. And they'll use every method at their disposal to make sure they win and that I lose."

Strait countered his series of interviews hostile to drug companies with only two very short soundbites from Gerald Mossinghoff, president of the Pharmaceutical Manufacturers Association. One of the soundbites seemed carefully framed by Strait to make it seem that Mossinghoff was saying that drug companies would "avoid" congressionally imposed price restraints. To give viewers a balanced story, Strait and other reporters should have said:

> **"Defenders of the drug industry point out that American drug companies set world standards for product innovation. They fear strict regulations might shut down this engine of progress."**

Perhaps even more culpable than the drug companies, in TV's eyes, was the insurance industry. In reporter Fred Briggs's NBC "Nightly News" June 30 long look at Vermont's efforts to control health care costs, the sole insurance company cited was Aetna which, said Briggs, "had been increasing premiums 25 percent a year" and then "pulled out of Vermont" when controls were imposed. The prospect of tougher controls, said Briggs, "has a lot of other companies ready to leave Vermont."

Bryant Gumbel on "Today" December 4 ostensibly offered viewers a balanced look at the debate over insurance companies; Gumbel first interviewed Carl Schramm, president of the Health Insurance Association, and then offset this by interviewing Dr. David Himmelstein of Physicians for a National Health Program. But the interviews were scarcely balanced.

At one point Gumbel cynically asked Schramm whether the insurance industry proposal was really "some magnanimous change of heart," or just an attempt to stay ahead of "what seems inevitable." Later, when Schramm explained an aspect of the industry proposal, Gumbel retorted: "That begs the question . . . why does the government need the insurance industry?" Gumbel pushed for price controls by government and more government involvement by consistently questioning the very necessity of an insurance industry.

By contrast, Gumbel allowed Himmelstein to dodge questions, never forcing an issue. First Gumbel tossed Himmelstein softball questions like: "What do you think of these new [insurance industry] proposals from the Health Insurance Association?" Later he gave Himmelstein free rein to bash the insurance industry.

The Gumbel\Himmelstein exchange:

GUMBEL: "Dr. Himmelstein. Using this plan as a starting point, how would you like to see it adjusted to more aggressively go after the soaring costs of health care?"

HIMMELSTEIN: "Well, we think the insurance companies are the problems in health care and what we'd like to see adjusted in this plan is we'd like to see the insurance companies taken out of the health care system. They don't do anything useful . . ."

GUMBEL: "So, you don't want them in it at all?"

HIMMELSTEIN: ". . . they cost us billions of dollars."

GUMBEL: "You don't want them in it at all?"

HIMMELSTEIN: "No. We don't want them in it at all."

GUMBEL: "Is that realistic?"
HIMMELSTEIN: "We think it's realistic. It's what the American people want."

This was the same message delivered by CNN's Susan Rook and Andrew Holtz on the "Prime News" December 31 segment about a Colorado proposal called Colorado Care. Rook opened CNN's favorable coverage of the plan by saying: "Part of the plan involves forcing out most insurance companies." Explaining that the state would decide which insurance companies could offer what kind of coverage, Holtz cited Colorado's governor who strongly endorsed the plan: "Governor Romer says Colorado Care would wipe out insurance discrimination and create a new playing field where [insurance companies] compete to offer the best quality and service." In his kicker, Holtz called the plan "a more honest way of financing things," adding that "the current health care system doesn't work." Holtz interviewed and cited advocates of the plan, but never interviewed opponents nor even mentioned or paraphrased criticism of the plan.

When TV did profile a health insurance company, the message was that insurers were con artists. This was the theme of John Camp's CNN "World News" March 12 segment describing an insurance fraud that had left policyholders with worthless health coverage. Camp told viewers: "But even more cruel than not having health insurance, is believing you and your family are protected, only to discover too late your insurance is worthless. And that's just what's happening to an alarming number of people because of a regulatory loophole."

At no time in the year did TV profile the thriving, honest insurance companies and brokers. Short of such a profile, a reporter could have said:

"Yes, insurance rates are climbing. But defenders of the insurance industry point out that much of this is because of government-imposed burdens that insurance companies must pass on to consumers."

THE PRESCRIPTION:
Again, Government

If high insurance costs and lack of coverage were the health care problems identified by TV in 1992, and pharmaceutical manufacturers and insurance firms were TV's culprits, TV's unanimous remedy for this was government.

ABC's George Strait on February 5 told viewers that he clearly favored what he called "a national plan." Tim Johnson, a physician who reported on medicine for ABC, said on February 6: "We will have to have some kind of national budget process that does put a cap on expenditures for health." And in the kicker for Brooks Jackson's long February 6 segment, the CNN "World News" camera turned to a woman, suffering from lupus and unable to afford health insurance or medicine, who asked: "Why can't the government help out?"

Government as solution was also the message of TV's treatment of how rising insurance costs were hurting American business. CNN's David French, in a "World News" story February 5, told viewers: "[Auto] industry leaders want their own kind of health care reform. U.S. automakers in particular complain high medical costs are putting the brakes on their ability to compete."

The following day, CNN's Brooks Jackson explained that health care costs could add $700 to each car made by an American automaker. Then Jackson implied that the solution to this was government by saying that for "Canadians and Japanese, who have government health insurance, the costs amount to less that $250 per vehicle." In this segment, Jackson gave viewers a very sympathetic businesswoman who explained how rising health care costs were making it difficult for her to stay in business. Then they heard Jackson say that, to seek relief, this businesswoman "went to Washington, lobbied Congress for change—and got nowhere."

Network TV's apparent preference for government health plans was reflected in its treatment of the conflicting proposals tabled early in the year by the Bush administration and by congressional Democratic leaders. Though reporters correctly alerted viewers to the fact that the Bush plan was mainly an election-year political gambit, they failed to post a similar warning on the Democrats' plans which surely were equally politically motivated. A more serious imbalance was TV's scant coverage of the private sector substance of Bush's plan compared with its detailed coverage of the Democrats' government plan, which included interviews with Senators Edward Kennedy and Jay Rockefeller and House Majority Leader Richard Gephardt—all Democrats.

Emphasis on government also characterized the stories about how states were addressing health care problems. These included:

• NBC's June 30 "Nightly News" profile of Vermont's efforts in which reporter Fred Briggs left no doubt that he believed that the state government's health plan would solve the problems of those whom he had interviewed.

• CNN's Andrew Holtz reporting on a development in Oregon for "World News" August 8 and on Colorado Care for "Prime News" December 31.

• NBC's Tom Brokaw on "Nightly News" October 26, endorsing Hawaii's state-mandated health care system "as a model for the rest of the country." Curiously, reporter George Lewis later in the story added, seemingly with approval, that Hawaii's system "dates back to the plantation days when the large sugar and pineapple growers set up their own clinics and hired doctors to take care of workers."

• The least balanced profile of a state's approach to health care appeared on NBC "Nightly News" January 15. Anchor Tom Brokaw introduced it saying: "Minnesota is one of the states leading the way to help those with no insurance and to help those with skyrocketing premiums." Throughout the segment, reporter Robert Bazell described the ostensible benefits of the state-run health care plan in dramatic and sympathetic terms, ignoring almost completely the possibility of a private sector solution. The lone voice questioning the state-run system was Minnesota Republican Governor Arne Carlson. Viewers were given Carlson in two doses. The first was a very short soundbite in which he said that the plan "just didn't fit Minnesota that well." In the second he warned: "The last thing we should do is create an enormous bureaucratic structure, because once you put a bureaucracy on line, it's the hardest thing in the world to get rid of."

Against Carlson, Bazell lined up a phalanx of victims: a man with cancer who had no insurance; a family unable to afford to go to doctors because they only had hospitalization insurance; and a family with children and no insurance. Then Bazell introduced Democratic State Representative Paul Ogren who pushed a bill for a government program by telling viewers that "it's entirely possible that health care is the one instance where government can actually do a better job than the private sector."

IF TV WANTS TO IMPROVE . . .

Network TV newscasts need not invest great resources nor consume significantly greater amounts of air time to improve health issue coverage. Newscasts simply could:

1. Give viewers some notion of the enormous strengths of the American health care system. This NBC anchor Tom Brokaw did on February 6 by explicitly saying that "American medical care is world class." But the problem was that at no time did he or his network return to this. The other networks never mentioned it at all. He and his colleagues could have done so by adding a phrase that said, for instance:

"For all of its problems, the American health care delivery system still ranks at the top of the world. Now, the country must try to get the cost under control."

They could also have said:

"For all of its problems, the American health care delivery system must have a lot going for it. Foreigners flock here for treatment and aspiring physicians and other medical specialists struggle to get into American med schools."

2. Broadcast a report on America's huge export earnings from health-related products and services.

3. Give viewers some notion that government health plans had various problems. Reporters routinely looked abroad for models of health care systems for America to follow. Yet the reporting, by and large, ignored the problems in those foreign systems. In the year, for instance, no one reported on the catastrophic condition of Britain's nationalized health care nor the serious problems creeping up in the routinely praised Canadian, German, and Scandinavian systems. Some evidence of problems in government health plans should have hit reporters in the eye. Example: In his report on Vermont's attempt to control health care costs, NBC's Fred Briggs said that many insurance companies were ready to leave the state. That should have prompted him to observe that one result of the Vermont plan could be the elimination of the private insurance industry in Vermont.

4. Describe through a sentence or an occasional story how some government regulations and actions were creating health care problems. Viewers could have been told, for example, that unwarranted caution and a maze of red tape have kept the Food and Drug Administration from approving the marketing of effective new drugs, and that income tax laws exempting employee health benefits from taxation have created the third-party payer system that has eliminated most consumer pressure to keep health care costs low.

5. Give viewers some indication that there might have been market-based ways to reduce health care costs and expand coverage.

6. Introduce to the public more advocates of private sector solutions. These were almost invisible on TV in 1992 except for the appearance on CNN of Patrick Roony, chairman of Golden Rule Insurance Company, and the several appearances by Bush administration Secretary of Health and Human Services Louis Sullivan. Sullivan told CBS "This Morning" viewers February 6 that the "private sector has been a vibrant source of creativity, innovation, and competition. . . . Our health care system is the most advanced system in the world." Yet after Sullivan had stated this and described the Bush proposal for using the private sector, host Harry Smith said that: "It [was] hard not to be cynical" about it. Smith never expressed cynicism about health care proposals that relied on government.

7. Dig a little deeper into the statistics given. Canadian health care consultant Jacques Krasny has pointed out, for instance, that U.S. health care costs are higher than Canada's because a larger share of the American population consists of the elderly and Vietnam veterans. This is no small matter; the elderly, 12 percent of the American population, account for more than half of American health care costs. No reporter mentioned this. Also ignored were misleading aspects of Canadian statistics. Canadians hide the cost of government-built hospitals and of health insurance for health care workers and do not count the cost of Canadians who come to America for state of the art technology.

THE YEAR'S BEST AND WORST COVERAGE

Viewers had the best chance of learning about America's high quality private sector health care system from:

1. CBS's Steve Kroft's observation on the March 1 "60 Minutes" that "roughly 80 percent of the people in the state of Oregon have at least some health insurance." From this, viewers received at least a hint that America's existing health insurance system, which is mainly private sector, covered the vast majority of Americans.

2. ABC's George Strait on the January 15 "World News To-night" when he explained that when hospitals act like informed consumers and shop around for drugs, they push down drug prices.

3. CNN's Jamie McIntyre on "World News" April 14, in what was the year's best health care reporting. McIntyre interviewed Patrick Roony, chairman of the Lawrenceville, Illinois-based Golden Rule Insurance Company, who explained his proposal for a medical care savings account. McIntyre then told viewers: "The idea is to get people to shop for minor medical services the way they shop for groceries. Imagine if employers paid 80 percent of the grocery bill. How many consumers would bother to check prices and compare before buying?"

Viewers had the poorest chance of learning how America's health care system functioned from:

1. CNN's Andrew Holtz in his barely comprehensible "World News" report on Minnesota's proposed "Healthright System." Holtz neither explained what the system was nor how it was supposed to cut costs. The segment merely spliced together inter-views.

2. CBS's Robert Krulwich in his "This Morning" commentary June 23 which accepted the premise, without citing any evidence, that government was more efficient than the private sector. Krul-wich very favorably reported the claim by "Consumer Reports" that a government-run, single-payer health insurance system would save $70 billion in administrative costs annually. Krulwich neither questioned this number nor noted that in no other area of activity was the government more efficient than the private sector. Krulwich also accepted without question an expert's assertion that America should follow the model of other nations. Nor did he tell viewers that those nations had begun encountering severe prob-lems in their government-run health insurance programs.

3. ABC's Jack Smith in a "World News Tonight" report Febru-

ary 1. Smith said in his kicker: "If there were not just one form, but just one insurance provider, the savings would be even greater—$100 billion—enough to make health insurance coverage affordable to everyone." Smith's story did not offer any other views on health care reform, nor did he explain in the least his very questionable kicker. Had he balanced his story, Smith would have said:

"Although some believe a single-payer system will save money, others contend that health care costs are out of control because the health care industry is shielded from competition. A single-payer system would reduce competition even more, say some. And they stress that history offers no examples of a monopoly like a single-payer system reducing costs."

4. ABC "Nightline," in a February 6 National Town Meeting. This lengthy show should have given ABC a chance to air various points of view. Yet the "Nightline" panel was stacked with those opposing free enterprise solutions. It was not until two hours into the show that a small businessman in the audience finally challenged the one-sided discussion. He noted such free enterprise solutions to health care problems as medical savings accounts and licensing reform. But the panel shrugged off his ideas, even after he argued that medical savings accounts would provide incentives to avoid costly, unnecessary procedures, about which the panel earlier had expressed concerns.

CHAPTER NINE

TAXES:
THE VIRTUE OF A
REALITY CHECK

TV REPORTERS CLEARLY understand something about taxes. Of all the economic topics they covered in 1992, only their reporting on taxes presented data and arguments more favorable than unfavorable to the elements essential for a thriving free enterprise economy. To be sure the tilt was slight—35 minutes of favorable to 30 minutes of unfavorable treatment. And the vast bulk of the reporting—4 hours, 50 minutes—was simply background.

Still, there was a tilt. Thus viewers watching reports on tax issues, in contrast to those about all other economic topics, had a better than even chance of learning something about how their free enterprise economy functioned and how the tax structure affected it.

Why were reporters more likely to get it right on taxes than on any other topic in 1992? Perhaps because taxes were the only economic topic with which journalists had direct and personal—rather than merely theoretical—experience. Regulations, federal spending, tariffs, the deficit, and other economic matters probably were abstractions. About them journalists had no reality check with which to verify what they were told.

Taxes were a different matter. Journalists, after all, pay taxes. More than that. They have seen that taxes prompt them to alter their own behavior and spending patterns. This might explain why almost no story on taxes that year even hinted that taxes did good. On the contrary, the presumption that taxes would impose pain on individuals and the economy was universal. Thus reporter Jim Stewart matter-of-factly told viewers on CBS "This Morning" March 20 that "Republicans say more taxes of any kind only hurt the nation's ailing economy." He did not question the premise— nor did any other TV journalist. Nor was economist Arthur Laffer disputed when he declared on ABC's "Good Morning America" December 29 that "I've never seen a tax yet that taxes an economy into prosperity."

What journalists did question, of course, was just how much pain would be imposed and whether the pain would be a fair trade-off for such things as an ostensible deficit reduction or expanded government programs. Yet there was no question that taxes were painful and should be kept as low as possible.

This understanding was made pointedly clear when reporter Mike Schneider became exasperated questioning World Watch Institute Vice-President Christopher Flavin on ABC's "Good Morning America" December 29. In response to Flavin's statement that a gasoline tax would be relatively painless, Schneider asked almost indignantly:

"How can you say less painful for the low income people? Because this is a tax that doesn't distinguish between how much money you make. If they are going to raise it ultimately, say like Mr. Perot had wanted 50 cents per gallon, low income people are going to have to pay it. People who live in the West who don't have mass transit as much as the people in the East are going to have to pay it. People who drive more to work are going to have to pay it. It doesn't seem to be particularly progressive, does it?"

Flavin tried to recover by arguing that drivers in other countries paid gasoline taxes much higher than America's. To which Schneider said:

"One of the great things about this country has been our sense of freedom. And the automobile in many ways seems to have personified that. Why do we have to take that sense of freedom away and match the other countries that don't have the same freedom of mobility?"

Still undeterred, Flavin suggested that perhaps it would not be so bad if Americans would drive less. To which Schneider snapped: "You're talking, in some cases, what sounds almost like social engineering."

It was rare in 1992 to find a TV reporter so tenacious in his or her efforts to refute the claims of an advocate of government interference in the marketplace.

REPORTING THE POLITICAL HORSE RACE

Taxing is one of the few government actions that can affect economic activity directly and enormously. A sensible tax policy can set an environment in which the economy grows, creates jobs, and boosts living standards. Tax policy even can create incentives to save and invest. Conversely, tax policy can inflict great damage on an economy, penalizing investment and risk-taking and hence strangling growth.

While the public can do little about some of the key factors that affect the economy, the public wields considerable power over taxation by holding legislators accountable and penalizing them for raising taxes.

But what the public understands about taxes depends to a great extent on what the public learns from TV. In 1992, the four networks devoted nearly 6 hours to discussing tax matters. The trouble was that even though coverage tilted slightly towards stories that expanded public understanding of free enterprise, many stories focused mainly on the political horse race aspect of the tax issue: which party's measure was gaining or how a tax measure would help or hurt a party and its candidates.

On February 27, for instance, Bob Franken on CNN "World

News" told viewers that the passage in the House of Representatives of the Democratic tax bill was a "victory for the Democratic leadership" and that the measure "infuriates Republicans." He was right on both counts. But the bill also would have economic consequences for the nation. Of this, Franken said nothing.

Politics was also the central theme in the March 20 newscasts. This date was the deadline set by George Bush for congressional action on an economic package. Marching across the screen that day to discuss the various economic options before Congress were Bush, Democratic Senators George Mitchell and Lloyd Bentsen, and Republican Senator Bob Dole.

Conspicuously absent were any economists or others who could have discussed the bill's economic impact. Typical of the network approach to the matter was Andrea Mitchell's report on NBC's "Nightly News." She let stand completely unchallenged the numbers offered by Democratic House Ways and Means Committee Chairman Dan Rostenkowski when he said that the Bush proposals would increase the deficit by $27 billion over six years. Mitchell called on no economist to interpret or question what was a very disputed figure.

Nor did Bryant Gumbel on that morning's "Today." Instead he confined himself to a long interview with George Mitchell who, predictably, trashed the Bush proposals and pushed the Democratic package. No TV analyst or economist told viewers what the two packages could mean for the economy. What CNN's Charles Bierbauer said about a Bush statement that day typified the reporting on March 20: It was "more politics than policy."

THE MESSAGE:
Pain and Problems

When the economic aspects, rather than the politics, of taxes were addressed by TV reporters, viewers at last were given a chance to learn that taxes imposed economic pain and caused economic problems.

This was clear in two ABC segments. On January 26, "World News Tonight" told viewers that the luxury tax of 1990 "has not worked the way it was planned." Reporter Steve Shepard explained how that tax had discouraged purchases of pleasure boats and how this, in turn, had forced boat and yacht builders to lay off workers. A lengthy "Good Morning America" segment September 24 showed how soaring property taxes in Michigan and other states were driving poor Americans out of their homes. Viewers were taken to an auction where houses were being put on the block for unpaid taxes.

Making the point that tax cuts created incentives that could boost economic growth was financial columnist Andrew Tobias on CBS "This Morning" January 17. He told viewers that an investment tax credit would speed investments by companies. Brooks Jackson on CNN "World News" April 14 described how tax deductions sought by the real estate industry would put plumbers, carpenters, and other construction workers back on the job and give the industry a chance to recover from the losses caused by the 1980s' glut of office building construction. CNN's Mike Capps on "World News" January 29 told viewers that Bush's call for a tax credit for first-time home buyers would spur housing sales. And that same day, ABC's Charles Gibson told "Good Morning America" viewers that changing the withholding schedules as proposed by Bush would put more money in people's pockets and thus increase economic activity.

LETTING OPPORTUNITIES SLIP AWAY

For all the air time given to taxes, TV ignored tax aspects that would have advanced the economic understanding of viewers. Missing, by and large, were economists; it was mainly politicians who were asked to comment on and explain taxes.

Of the few economist who appeared, CBS seemed to have had the most. The network's Talking Heads included Martin Feldstein, Paul Craig Roberts, Charles Schultze, and Lester Thurow. When

CBS "This Morning" April 15 paired economist Roberts with Robert Reich, later Bill Clinton's labor secretary, Roberts quickly—and correctly—pointed out that Reich was no economist. (He is a political scientist.)

Even when economists appeared, however, they were not always able to give the viewer any economic insight. When CNN interviewed Nobel Laureate Economist Robert Solow on November 25, for example, he was asked mostly about Bush's economic forecasting record, the trends of consumer confidence, and the prospects for the Christmas shopping season. Reporter Frank Sesno asked Solow few questions that would have expanded viewer understanding of how the economy functioned.

Missing too from the year's tax coverage was the notion that the free enterprise economy was "dynamic" rather than "static." A "dynamic" economy routinely adapts rapidly to changes. Example: Increasing the tax on an activity will prompt people to avoid that activity. Were the economy a "static" mechanism, people could not change an activity if it were taxed.

That the American economy is dynamic was a point that Brooks Jackson could have made in his CNN "World News" April 14 story on the consequences of the 1980s' commercial building boom. But to Jackson, the story was simply about the painful hangover of overbuilding. His long segment focused solely on the continuing high vacancy rates and the lobbyists' attempts to win tax deductions from Congress to help the real estate industry. On this, Jackson's reporting was nicely balanced.

What Jackson missed was the equally dramatic theme that in a dynamic, free enterprise economy, offsetting compensations quickly emerge. He could have noted that while builders and real estate companies might have been suffering from the office-tower glut, tenants were benefitting enormously from lower rents. This, Jackson could have told viewers, was making the tenants' businesses much more competitive, and enabling many businesses to expand and others to get launched. These businesses would not have been able to do this if they had had to pay high rents. As a kicker to such a story, Jackson could have said:

"While the building glut is bad news for the real estate industry, it's good news for tenants."

Another common omission by TV journalists was their failure generally to probe beneath the statistics they reported. They thus neglected to create a context or perspective for their statistics. ABC's Sheilah Kast, for example, in her "World News Tonight" story January 31, accepted without question the criticism that the Bush proposal for an additional $500 income tax deduction per child would mainly benefit the wealthy. She told viewers that for those in the 15 percent tax bracket, "the Bush proposal would . . . save $75, but [for] families with incomes above $60,000 . . . that same $500 exemption would save $140 per child. And [for] those in the highest bracket, with incomes over $120,000 a year, it would save $155."

These figures were accurate as far as they went; and the figures were spread widely by opponents of the Bush proposal who were charging that Bush mainly was helping the wealthy. But the figures were also misleading. Kast, as a reporter, should have put them in perspective by going beyond the simple numbers and explaining to viewers that the sole reason the wealthy would save more in dollar terms from a specific tax break was because the wealthy were paying so much more in taxes—and would continue to pay much more.

Kast could have illustrated this point by talking about two hypothetical families: the first in the 15 percent tax bracket; the second in the 31 percent bracket. She could have explained that the first family currently was keeping $4,250 of the last $5,000 that it was making and that under the Bush proposal (assuming a deduction for one child), it would keep $4,325. The second family currently was keeping only $3,450 of the last $5,000 earned; under the Bush proposal, it would keep $3,605. With the Bush proposal, the first family would still be paying considerably less in taxes than the second family in dollar terms and in percentage terms.

Another failure in perspective was TV's discussion of the tax on capital gains. Though it was one of the key issues of 1992, reporters never quite explained what a "capital gain" was. The only thing that viewers learned from Harry Smith on CBS "This Morning"

January 29, for example, was that cutting capital gains taxes "was the great bogeyman of the last five or six years." And the one bit of economic information about capital gains conveyed on the segment by Smith, by CBS's Connie Chung, and by reporters on other segments was flawed: the assertion by opponents of capital gains tax cuts that the wealthy would mostly benefit from cuts. No TV reporter questioned this. Had they done so, they would have found that the main beneficiary of capital gains tax cuts would be the middle class.

Missing too from the year's TV reporting was an attempt to differentiate between the "wealthy" and "business." The two generally were viewed as synonymous. A typical TV news phrase was: "A tax break that benefits the rich and business." While some businessmen and women are wealthy, others are not. Widely ignored by TV reporters were small business and the small businessman and woman. A tax measure good for the wealthy, therefore, would not necessarily be good for small business. Since most new jobs result from small business expansion, a more useful TV news phrase would have been: "A tax break that benefits job creators."

IF TV WANTS TO IMPROVE . . .

To improve coverage of tax issues would have been neither difficult nor have required much extra air time. In the CNN story about attempts to get a tax break to alleviate the office building glut, for instance, Brooks Jackson needed only to add a sentence on the benefits of lower rents. His segment was long enough, moreover, for him to have interviewed a company that had expanded its operations because of the cheap rent. This would have taught viewers that a free economy is dynamic and can exploit opportunities as they emerge.

In the many stories on March 20 about the economic package, reporters could also have allowed viewers to hear from economists as well as politicians.

In discussing how the tax burden was distributed, reporters

could have explained to viewers that, according to the IRS, the wealthiest 1 percent's share of all taxes rose from 19 percent in 1980 to 27.5 percent in 1988. The wealthiest 10 percent's share rose from 49 percent to 57 percent during the same period. Since reporters showed they understood that tax policy influences behavior, they could have explained that when tax rates dropped, the wealthy shifted their money from unproductive tax avoidance shelters to the wealth-creating market. This, among other things, produced higher tax revenues from the wealthy.

Reporters also could have shown how Social Security and other payroll taxes impeded job creation. Since reporters seemed to understand that taxes influence the behavior of individuals, reporters should have realized that taxes influence the behavior of businesses as well. Taxes that drive up the cost of labor, the reporters could have said, could block job creation. As a source, reporters could have cited economist Robert Samuelson's explanation that "companies won't hire new workers—especially the young and unskilled—if they have to be paid more than they're worth."

THE YEAR'S BEST AND WORST COVERAGE

Viewers had the best chance to learn in 1992 how taxes were affecting their free enterprise economy from:

1. CBS "This Morning" April 15 in its interview with economist Paul Craig Roberts. He explained how reducing the marginal tax rates on capital would "[lead] to more investment, higher productivity, while simultaneously shifting the average tax burden from labor to capital."

2. ABC's Charles Gibson, when he asked White House chief-of-staff Samuel Skinner on "Good Morning America" January 29 whether changing the withholding schedules would not require the government, in the short term, to borrow $25 billion more. This perceptive question alerted viewers that there was a cost to money.

Implicitly, moreover, it told viewers that by paying extra withholding taxes, Americans had been giving the Treasury an interest-free loan of a gigantic size.

3. CNN and CBS in covering Democratic presidential nominee contender Jerry Brown's proposal for a flat tax. This informed viewers of the high cost to the economy of America's complicated income tax system. CNN's Brooks Jackson, for example, on March 26 told viewers that "most economists say a flat tax would be simple, efficient, and great for business." Jackson interviewed an expert who said: "The cost of capital is going to be down, it's going to be better for investing in this country." To the claim by one Talking Head that a flat tax would shift the tax burden from the rich to the poor, Jackson even offered a rejoinder: "There are ways to modify the flat tax so it falls less harshly on lower income people."

4. ABC's Mike Schneider in questioning Christopher Flavin and highlighting the costs and inequities of a gasoline tax.

5. ABC's Steve Shepard on how the disincentives created by the 1990 luxury tax sent "the boating industry . . . into a tailspin. Builders have gone broke. Yards have closed. And boating industry workers have been laid off." From Shepard's interview with Bush chief-of-staff Samuel Skinner viewers learned that if the luxury tax were eliminated, "we will get more revenue from [boat builders] productivity than we are getting from the yacht tax when there are no yachts being built."

6. ABC's Paula Lyons on how high property taxes were driving poor Americans out of their homes.

Viewers received the worst information about their economy from:

1. ABC's Sheilah Kast in discussing how a $500 extra tax deduction for child dependents would affect different income brackets.

2. CBS's Connie Chung in her "This Morning" January 29 interview of House Majority Leader Richard Gephardt. He argued that a capital gains tax cut would help only the richest Americans and that Bush's State of the Union proposals were just more "trickle down" that would fail. Not only did Chung not challenge him, she prompted him to go further in his attack by asking if Bush's tax cuts would make the deficit larger. At the least she should have paired that question with a question of whether Democratic spending programs would make the deficit worse.

3. NBC's Bryant Gumbel in his "Today" April 23 interview of John Kenneth Galbraith. Gumbel did not challenge Galbraith's assertion that voting Americans kept the rest of America down by keeping taxes low.

PART III

THE EXPERTS

CHAPTER TEN

THE BUSINESS AND ECONOMIC REPORTERS: AUG, BRADY, AND LEVINE

THE BUSINESS AND ECONOMIC REPORTERS are network newscasting's designated hitters. They are the specialty squad sent onto the field specifically to tell viewers more about their economy than the typical newscast does. From the economic reporters, viewers can expect to receive the most direct, concentrated, and pure information about the economy.

Who were these reporters in 1992?

On NBC, Irving R. Levine was chief economics correspondent, a veteran of more than thirty-five years with the network. With his signature bow tie and scholarly glasses, he appeared as TV's professor emeritus, an image reinforced by a voice that droned on in the style favored by academics in their lecture halls. A reporter of the Old School, Levine began in print journalism, writing for the *Providence Journal-Bulletin* and the International News Service. At NBC, he covered the Korean War and reported from London,

Moscow, Rome, and Tokyo. In some ways, Levine launched a genre, in 1971 becoming TV's first full-time economics reporter.

On ABC, Stephen Aug has been covering economics and business since 1981 and wears the title Business Editor. He began reporting in 1961 when he joined the Associated Press. Seven years later, he moved to the now-defunct *Washington Star* as a business reporter and ultimately took charge of the paper's business section. What Aug's readers surely could not know but what Aug's viewers quickly discovered were his entertaining facial expressions, bizarre ties, and determined effort to end his stories with a joke or pun. Example: After a story on Coca Cola's well-being and its increasing executive pay, a grinning Aug said: "Sales have been rising Spritely so the pay went up as well."

On CBS, Ray Brady had TV's most impressive business and economics credentials: former editor of *Dun's Review*, assistant managing editor of *Forbes,* and associate editor of *Barron's*. He joined CBS in 1977. At first look, viewers might think the white-haired Brady a kindly grandfather. But this cuddly image would be punctured immediately by Brady's whining voice and his chronically dismal, negative view of the economy and just about everything else.

Although CNN had several business and economic shows, for example Lou Dobb's "Moneyline," the network did not have a designated business or economic reporter for its regular news shows during 1992.

These business reporters have vastly differing styles. Aug appeared most frequently in 1992, but much of what he said was straight reporting on the government's release of economic statistics, announcements of corporate earnings, and similar matters. He took delight, in his morning appearances, in ending with a pun, turning a phrase, or injecting an off-beat item. This might have amused viewers and been a welcome way to start a day. Yet viewers might also have wondered whether the puns and trivia advanced their understanding of the economy (or of anything else). Yet overall, viewers did come out ahead listening to Aug. He gave them a relatively good sense of how the American economy functioned.

By contrast, Brady probably wasted viewers' time. Not only was he unnecessarily gloomy, he also erred on matters of fact more than any other reporter, drew conclusions unwarranted by the facts, and rode a single hobby horse—that the only cure to the economy's many ills was government action (and even then Brady was not sure that the ills could be cured).

STEPHEN AUG:
Good News for Viewers

Viewers probably saw more of Aug in 1992 than any other TV economic reporter, for he appeared regularly on ABC's "Good Morning America" and its "World News Tonight." During the year, he was on the air 164 times.

Such frequency was good news for ABC's viewers. He conveyed a better grasp than his counterparts of how a free market functioned, of the complexity of market dynamics, of what arcane economic terms meant, and of how lower taxes and lower trade barriers benefitted Americans. Unlike the chronic, if not terminal, negativism of Ray Brady and, to some extent, Levine, Aug found reasons to be upbeat. In his June 17 profile of a Georgia firm, for instance, he told viewers: "Business has been great . . . Business is so good that they have hired five more people. That's 20 percent of the work force and then they even have to work ten to twelve hours a day, seven days a week to get the work out." And, he concluded cheerfully in his kicker: "Lagging sectors like retail and service should look better by the end of the year."

Much of the time viewers heard and saw Aug rattling off straightforward business and economic news, unvarnished, and with little interpretation or analysis. Usually, this was very useful for viewers. At times, though, Aug pushed this formula too far, becoming a mere bulletin board of items whose importance and relevance was uncertain and unapparent. Example: His January 10 "Good Morning America" segment ran only 86 seconds, but he squeezed four items into it: mortgage refinancing, falling wholesale prices, the Postal Service's plans for the Elvis stamp, and news about the Louis Harris polling firm. A 95 second segment on May 29 also covered four items: rising auto production, Northwest Airlines' request for employee wage concessions, the electronic show's opening, and an increase in Kellogg's cereal prices. To much of this catalogue of disconnected items, the viewer surely could have asked: "What's the point?"

Much more valuable for the viewer was Aug's occasional insertion of a phrase to highlight some fundamental economic principle or insight. Viewers learned on February 7, for instance, that "employers do not usually begin rehiring until well after business picks up"; on March 27 that rising long-term interest rates "could choke off or at least slow down an economic recovery"; on April 9 that the hysterical warnings that Wall Street would be roiled were the Japanese to start selling their American stocks probably were wrong because the "Japanese have been largely out of the U.S. stock markets for the past three years so any sales of the remainder should have little effect"; on September 4 that federal job programs created only temporary jobs; and on December 18 that regulations had cost banks 14 cents of every dollar banks spent.

Unlike almost all other commentators, Aug occasionally helpfully defined economic terms and phenomena for viewers. Example: On August 21, he explained that "the national debt is the amount of money the government has borrowed to finance years of annual budget deficits." By contrast, other reporters and commentators typically and incorrectly have used the terms "budget deficit" and "national debt" almost interchangeably.

Aug routinely demonstrated understanding of issues that his counterparts on other networks seemed to find baffling. On the matter of the capital gains tax, Aug on January 21 told viewers that when the tax increased, "fewer people are willing to invest" and that some economists believed that lowering the tax "would encourage people to invest in new business." This lesson in basic economics could help viewers understand the importance of the capital gains tax issue. Aug then interviewed Norman Ture, one of America's leading free market economists. In fact, it was one of the rare appearances of a free market economist on any network newscast all year.

On trade, Aug repeatedly stressed the advantages of lowering trade barriers and, on July 6, told viewers that "if the trade talks ultimately collapse, the fear is that each country will try to protect its own industries. That could be the worse thing that happens."

On Bush administration proposals to give businesses a tax credit for buying new equipment (the investment tax credit), Aug on January 22 not only lucidly explained both sides of this complicated matter, but revealed that he understood that the dynamic nature of a free market allowed tax revenues to climb when tax rates were cut. "The government," Aug said, "would be collecting taxes on the profits generated by all the new manufacturing."

During the year, Aug slipped only a few times. One was conveying to viewers as hard fact statistics that still were controversial. In his May 14 report, for instance, he cited a study's findings that American workers' inflation-adjusted wages had fallen 6 percent since 1987. Not only did he fail to tell viewers that the group that had released the study was being funded by organized labor (which had an interest in portraying American workers as underpaid), but also that many economists were criticizing the study as very unreliable.

More troubling was Aug's implicit premise in several commentaries that government was the main engine of economic growth. In his September 11 report, he said that unemployment could be lowered only through "higher spending" by government.

But overall, viewers in 1992 were probably wise to tune into Aug over any other economic commentator. The main pain viewers might have suffered was from his grating attempt to conclude his "Good Morning America" segments with what he apparently thought was a cute tidbit. These included such messages as that the Fuller Brush-man was not selling door-to-door much anymore, that Listerine was offering mouthwash in a new flavor for the first time in its 113-year history, that a Denver firm was offering gold-plated braces for teeth, that Frito Lay was changing its Dorito's recipe, that advertising space in Moscow's Red Square was for sale for May Day, that the cost of attending the Senior Prom was up, and that Elsie the cow was returning to Borden, Inc. ads.

RAY BRADY:
The Return of Joe Btfsplk

Probably least well served were viewers watching CBS "Evening News." They received their economic analysis from Ray Brady who, in his ninety-three stories and commentaries throughout 1992, almost never found an upbeat, cheerful, positive, or even constructive thing to say about the economy or business. Like the character Joe Btfsplk in the "L'il Abner" comic strip, Brady dragged a threateningly dark rain cloud wherever he went. Examples:

• When Brady analyzed the auto industry (as he did on January 6), the story was all gloom, with him warning that "it's not just Detroit that's worried about the future. It's also . . . as many as 13 million workers who count on the American auto industry for their livelihood."

• When he looked at retailing (January 14), again all was gloom, with him predicting more bankruptcies, "less competition, and higher prices for consumers."

• When he found (on January 22) good news for home buyers because of "low prices and slow [housing] sales," he quickly found that this meant "bad news for the economy."

• When he reported on Macy's filing for bankruptcy (January 27), he speculated that if Macy's problems should "bring down other stores it will mean further delay in the return of good times for Macy's and the American economy."

• When he reported (April 3) that poor job prospects for college graduates were prompting many Americans to go abroad to work, he warned that this was "a new trend for this country: a kind of brain drain, American-style." Returning to this theme in a report from Prague (July 7), he informed viewers that "young

[Americans are] finding here one thing their homeland can't give them—jobs . . . For some, this is the land of opportunity that the U.S. once was . . . So they stay in this fairy tale city of enchanted castles and storybook scenes, dreaming of a homeland that—for now—seems to have little for them."

• When he reported (April 24) on the airline price wars that were slashing fares and offering what probably was history's cheapest air travel to millions of Americans, he concluded that this would drive small carriers out of business. He warned viewers: "Everyone knows what happens when you have fewer companies in an industry: prices go up. So the moral might be: Fly now, you might pay more later on."

• When he reported from the Berlin Air Show (July 6), he ignored all the overwhelming signs of disarray and discord in the European Community and the fact that America was ringing up a huge trade surplus with Europe. Instead he saw only problems for America from what he called a "new spirit of Europe, a new Europe; one determined to compete with the U.S. not only for business, but above all for jobs . . . Europe's forming itself into a giant common market . . . For years Americans have worried about Japanese competition, but now many economists say a united Europe will be a fierce new competitor—not just for now, but through all the rest of the 1990s."

• When he reported August's slight dip in the unemployment rate (September 4), he stressed not only all the persisting negative indicators but ended by saying: "Finally, adding to the nation's economic and job woes, another blow. Hurricane Andrew could mean still more Americans on the unemployment rolls when the jobless figures come out next month."

Brady was more than the purveyor of Btfsplkian gloom. He was also master of the snicker and the snide aside. From him CBS viewers could conclude only that the economy was a miasmic swamp holding nothing but predatory dangers for the average American. In such a nasty environment, the best counsel that Brady seemed to have for viewers was that they should "watch out for Number One"—as he advised on February 17 and again on October 26.

Brady also emphasized that the American free enterprise economy was dangerous to consumers in segments that were, in effect, consumer reports. Some of these contained straightforward consumer advice, as when he explained which personal expenses were tax deductible (March 23) and how the best mortgage rate could be found (April 27).

Most of Brady's consumer reports, however, were explicit warnings of the hazards lurking in the marketplace. On January 23, he said that thousands of Americans were "suffocating under bills." On February 4, the danger was the rising number of health care cases where "insurance companies refuse to pay." On February 19, it was con artist scams against the unemployed. On May 11 to May 15, in a series on "The Financial Side of Marriage," it was couples who failed to negotiate financial prenuptial agreements which could "avert a costly breakup"; he paired this with advice on how to pick a divorce attorney and an admonition always to "know where the money is." On November 17, it was mail frauds promising phony prizes.

Brady's economic world was permanently rigged against the average American. It was populated by a huge cast of villains. On February 20 the villain was job stress, on April 24 it was airline deregulation, on June 22 it was mortgage companies that were stalling on home refinancings in hopes that interest rates would rise, on June 26 it was insurance companies, on November 6 it was "Big Business," and on December 12 it was "Corporate America."

Banks, in particular, were singled out as dangerous to consumers. On March 11 Brady warned viewers that "the real robbers are inside the banks" because of the fees bankers were charging for services. On April 6 he warned that bank credit cards were "financial time bombs" and on November 24 that "credit card companies . . . [were] ripping off" consumers.

Though Brady's list was long on villains, heroes and champions were almost nonexistent. The broad American public, meanwhile, was depicted typically as long-suffering rubes, ready to be fleeced by swarms of unethical businesses.

When a hero did make it onto a Brady commentary, it was likely to be the federal government. For Brady, federal policies and programs were the prescription that kept at bay the danger of the marketplace. He was most explicit about this in his open endorsement of Bill Clinton's calls for increased federal intervention in the economy. Commenting on Clinton's election victory, Brady on November 5 told viewers that "if the Clinton plans work, people could start spending again." The following day Brady quoted economists saying that "Clinton's proposed construction program could get America back to work."

Even in his straight reporting, Brady did not serve viewers well. In too many instances he got his facts wrong or drew obviously erroneous conclusions from facts. Examples:

• In a January 14 report on retail bankruptcies, Brady concluded by saying: "Down the road, stores could be like the airline industry. The fewer of them around, the less the competition—and the higher prices go for consumers." While the general point about competition was correct, Brady erred in citing the airline industry as an example of the potential dangers consumers faced in retailing. In fact, Brady was off by 180 degrees. Since airline deregulation, air fares have plummeted, the number of passengers has soared, and the frequency of service to cities has multiplied dramatically. He should have said:

"Just as smaller retailers brought big stores down with lower prices, the smaller retailers must continue delivering the goods at low prices or the market will discipline them too."

• On February 28, again reporting erroneously on air fares, Brady said: "There are bargains out there, bargains galore. Trouble is the airlines don't always publicize them." In fact, the extensive advertizing of discount air fares was what triggered the air fare wars and brought about the lowest inflation-adjusted air fares in history.

• In a September 16 report on the dollar's fall on world currency markets, Brady said that "the cheap dollar also drives up the price of foreign products in this country. And these days that's everything from petroleum to bananas and from automobiles to clothing." While Brady's general point was correct, his examples revealed considerable ignorance of U.S. trade. In fact: (1) since world petroleum was priced in dollars, dollar fluctuations would have no effect on America's cost of imported petroleum; (2) since bananas came mainly from Central America where the dollar remained strong, bananas would not increase in price; and (3) since much of America's imported clothing came from China via Hong Kong, and the Hong Kong dollar was pegged to the U.S. dollar, such clothing would not be affected by dollar fluctuations.

• In an October 26 report on the changing needs of the Baby Boom generation, Brady described the Boomers as "76 million of them, most of them now in their thirties and forties. And they've had it all—homes, cars, luxury vacations and, above all, well-paying jobs." Here Brady confused the Boomers with the Yuppies who comprised no more than a tiny slice of the Boom generation. The living standards of the vast majority of Baby Boomers have been similar to those of the vast majority of other Americans.

• In a December 11 commentary on the Clinton "economic summit" in Little Rock, Brady said that "whether President-elect Clinton will get much help on jobs from Corporate America is questionable. While some of the executives say they'll be hiring, more than half say lean and mean remains the order of business." Brady here assumed that Corporate America, the biggest firms, created jobs. In fact, almost all of the 19 million new jobs created in America in the 1980s were created by small businesses. The Fortune 500 as a group failed to create any new jobs on net. Brady should have said:

"What matters for job-seekers is what effect Clinton's policies will have on small businesses, which create most of the jobs in our economy."

IRVING R. LEVINE:
Accentuating the Negative

On camera only thirty-seven times in 1992, much less frequently than his counterparts on the other networks, Levine was deployed mainly to add depth to selected stories. He taught viewers some useful basic information. On February 5, viewers heard what was probably the year's best explanation of why certain statistics have been used to indicate the economy's direction. Levine described how climbing paperboard output, sales at fast food restaurants, and purchases of recreational vehicles could signal an expanding economy.

Three days later, he gave viewers another basic lesson: that the typical entrepreneur raised money from his or her own savings and from family members. Levine noted too that small businesses had added great numbers of jobs to the economy. And he did better than his counterparts in giving viewers a balanced account of the controversial cable TV reregulation legislation.

On August 12, Levine displayed what, for network TV, was a rare respect for the common sense of consumers. First he reported that critics of the oil industry wanted new government regulations to alert drivers that costly high octane gasoline was, in the opinion of the critics, no extra benefit for cars. But then Levine implicitly rejected the notion of such new regulations, suggesting that the "easiest way" for drivers to figure out what octane they should use would be "to look in your owner's manual—if you can remember where it is."

Where Levine failed viewers was when he shared with them his cosmic view of how the economy functioned and what measures could make it function better. Like Brady, Levine apparently found it nearly impossible to paint the economy in anything but grim, Btfsplkian tones. From Levine a viewer easily could conclude that the economy could hardly be in worse shape.

Typical of this was Levine's March 23 report on bankruptcy, using as an example the effort of the Sassafras company, a retail chain, to reorganize financially. As Levine reported it, bankruptcy had left the Sassafras' owners "heavily in debt to relatives, [while] Sassafras suppliers and the bank have lost money, and most of the 150 laid off workers are still looking for jobs." As far as that went, Levine was accurate. Yet these observations distorted enormously the useful role played by the bankruptcy process.

Viewers would have learned much more had Levine said:

"While 150 of the laid-off workers are still looking for jobs, bankruptcy protection is giving Sassafras a chance to claw its way out from under its huge problems and to stay open for business. This keeps three hundred employees on the payroll and gives the owners, suppliers, and banks a chance to recoup some investment. The alternative would be much worse— shutting the doors altogether, throwing all 450 out of work, and losing everything."

A similar stress on the negative marked other Levine stories. On March 27, he warned viewers that foreign investment in America "is running dry." This was ominous, said Levine, because Japan was "the main foreign lender to the U.S." and thus Japanese and other foreign retreats from American credit markets would help "push up interest rates." Not only was this unnecessarily gloomy (interest rates, in fact, were down sharply by year's end), but inaccurate. Levine was telling viewers that America depended heavily on foreigners to finance the federal debt. But in fact, "the main U.S. lender," to use Levine's phrase, has been America itself— individuals, banks, pension funds, insurance companies, and so forth. Only a tiny one-eighth of the federal debt has been funded by foreigners, whose actions thus have had only marginal effect on American interest rates.

On May 25, Levine spread more gloom by using discredited statistics to predict that tough times would continue. While there were many valid reasons why tough times would (and did) continue, these were not the reasons cited by Levine. The problem, he told viewers, was that America was losing high-paying jobs and thus "even when the economy turns up fully from the recession, the trend towards low-pay jobs won't end." The truth was (and is), the trend in America has not been toward low-end jobs but in the opposite direction—towards well-paying skilled jobs. This trend, in fact, is what has prompted the concern about whether enough Americans were being trained adequately for these skilled jobs.

Perhaps the disappearing jobs about which Levine was talking were in manufacturing. Had he said so, he would have been correct. But then he would have had to add that manufacturing jobs had been disappearing for decades as increases in industrial productivity allowed factories to produce more goods with fewer workers. And this shrinking of the manufacturing work force, Levine could have noted, was occurring not only in America, but in every other advanced industrial nation.

When Levine did share some good news with viewers, he muted it. Reporting on international economic issues on September 20, for example, he worried that America's trade surplus with Europe would drop $4 billion in 1992, to $12 billion. The real news to viewers probably was the revelation that America had any surplus at all with industrially advanced and fiercely competitive Europe. After all, Americans had heard TV commentators almost unrelentingly deplore America's international competitiveness and highlight America's trade problems.

Levine would have served viewers better had he said:

"America continues to beat Europe in Europe's own backyard, posting this year what is expected to be a significant $12 billion surplus with the highly industrialized Europeans. This is down from last year's $16 billion—but probably only because stagnant European economies are importing less."

Even reports of very brisk Christmas shopping could not lift Levine's despair. After interviewing, on his December 22 broadcast, four merchants who all said that business was great, Levine ended the segment by pointing to California's soft economy and Sears Roebuck's announcement of layoffs. Said Levine: "That means layoffs in the new year for thousands of more workers."

Often Levine's portrait of national gloom was followed by a

prescription for improvement: government action and programs.
Examples:

• On January 6 Levine said that the American auto industry was
in trouble. What the industry needed, he explained, was an ambi-
tious program of federal tax credits, federally subsidized low interest loans, and federal pressure to cut auto executives' salaries.

• On January 10 Levine said that American workers must learn
new skills and their teacher should be the federal government. But
"as for government retraining programs," he added, the troubled
was that "some have been cut as much as 40 percent. That leaves
many of the unemployed without the skills to take a job even when
the recession ends." For Levine, job retraining was a matter for
government. He ignored, in this broadcast, the vast and successful
job retraining programs run by private firms. Levine somewhat
modified his stress on government retraining programs when, on
March 21, he interviewed workers who were improving their own
skills, without government programs.

• On December 13, Levine said that economists were wrong to
think that a tax cut would create jobs. To make his point, he
interviewed a couple who said that a $200 tax cut "wouldn't do
absolutely anything for us. I would use $200 . . . for the gas back
and forth, pay tolls—that's about it." Levine ended the segment
saying: "There is no sure way to create jobs through tax changes."
In the context of Levine's report, the message was that jobs were
created mainly by the government.

In the year, Levine's best segment was his February 8 story that
"a growing number of laid-off Americans, who can raise the
money, are investing in their own businesses." What viewers
learned from this was that small businesses typically start with
funds neither from banks nor federal agencies but from personal
savings and help from family members.

Levine's worst segment was his January 16 report that the Persian Gulf War had kept "oil prices down." As evidence for this, he

told viewers that oil was "$17 a barrel" when the war began and "is now at about $19 a barrel because Desert Storm kept the oil pipelines open." Levine's arithmetic apparently failed him. His figures showed a 12 percent price jump, hardly evidence that oil prices had been kept down. Later in the segment, Levine said that "the shock of the invasion [of Kuwait] tipped the U.S. economy into recession." This too was wrong. The recession had begun one month earlier; few economists, in fact, blamed the recession on the war. The main causes of the recession were the significant hikes in federal taxes and regulation costs beginning in 1990.

Squandering Valuable Opportunities

As TV's designated hitters for economics and business affairs, Aug, Brady, and Levine had a special responsibility to viewers. Their charter was to sweep more broadly and delve more deeply than did the general-assignment newscasters and anchors. Yet, too often, they disappointed and failed the viewer—by getting facts wrong, reflexively calling for government action, using examples and metaphors that were inappropriate.

Most seriously, perhaps, the economics reporters failed in their special responsibility when they squandered valuable opportunities to give viewers some insight, or extra perspective, or new information, about the American economic system. This happened often in the year. Examples:

☒ Aug's January 3 kicker to his review of the economy stated that "last year about 14,000 retailers went out of business. This year it could be closer to 16,000." By stopping there, Aug squandered the chance to help viewers understand the economy. Aug could have taught the lesson by adding:

"But entrepreneurial optimism, apparently, keeps blooming because last year hundreds of thousands of new businesses opened their doors—their eager owners obviously confident

that they could avoid the mistakes and potholes that doomed the others."

☒   Levine's long January 10 commentary focused on government-funded job retraining programs. In his kicker, Levine said: "Some government retraining programs have been cut by 40 percent, leaving many without skills to take a job even when the recession ends." Viewers would have benefitted by hearing about the massive and continual retraining efforts by private American businesses. These probably accounted for almost all retraining in the country, were more efficient, and less costly than government programs, and retrained specifically for jobs requiring new skills. A profile of private sector retraining would have been a more valid subject for Levine's takeout than his discussion of a federal program. At the least, Levine owed it to viewers to say in his kicker:

"While some government retraining programs have been cut by 40 percent, the good news is that private companies continue to retrain most American workers. They do it because they can compete better and make more money only if their workers have the latest skills."

☒   Brady's January 14 story about how the recession was forcing hard-hit retailers out of business concluded: "All these stores going out of business have meant bargains and big sales for the customers. But down the road, stores could be like the airline industry: the fewer of them around, the less the competition—and the higher prices go for consumers." This was clearly repudiated by the facts. While some stores had closed their doors, others like Wal-Mart, The Limited, Toys R Us, Woolworths, and a whole new generation of discounters were expanding vigorously—ensuring competition and lower prices. (In fact, Aug had reported this on January 3.) Brady's kicker would have been better and more accurate had he said:

"All these stores going out of business have meant bargains for the customers. Other stores, meanwhile, especially discounters, have expanded. This all means that in today's cutthroat

market, bargains for customers will continue—at least for a while."

☒ Brady's January 27 story about Macy's bankruptcy filing, like stories by the other reporters on Macy's and other bankruptcies, dwelt exclusively on the grim news—legendary businesses shutting their doors, veteran employees tearfully leaving what they had regarded as families rather than jobs, loyal customers losing their favorite stores, and so forth. Viewers were told almost nothing about why bankruptcy was a useful device for the economy. To their commentary, Brady and the other reporters could have added:

"For all the grim aspects of a bankruptcy, it gives a business a chance to catch its breath and, in many cases, to try again. And it gives creditors an orderly way to get paid at least some of what they are owed. The spectacle of bankruptcy, moreover, reminds us all that even big companies pay for the mistakes they make."

☒ Levine's April 11 story and those on other days by the other economic reporters ticked off the evidence that the economy was crawling out of recession, while at the same time citing signs that the recovery had stalled. Viewers would have appreciated some explanation of the contradictory evidence.

☒ Aug's May 7 commentary on the economy noted that despite the recession, the largest black-owned businesses were growing. This was one of the year's very rare mentions of African-American businesses by any TV newscaster or commentator. Similarly rare was any mention of Hispanic, or women's businesses. Yet the number of African-American, Hispanic, and women's businesses grew faster in the 1980s than those of any other group. In the context of a report on minority business, reporters could have explained:

"Although it may seem counterintuitive, tax cuts help minorities and others at the bottom of the economic ladder by stimulating growth and, therefore, opportunities."

☒ Aug's May 13 story explained that the Federal Deposit Insurance Corporation might base its "insurance premiums on the safety of each bank." This was accurate as far as it went, which was not far enough. Aug did not explain why such a move would help banks or the economy or consumers. Viewers would have learned something extra had Aug added:

> **"Just as the threat of higher auto insurance premiums may prompt some drivers to drive more safely, so too higher premiums may prompt bankers to act more prudently. Under today's system, reckless and careful bankers alike pay the FDIC the same rate. So what's their incentive to be careful with depositors' money? There is none."**

☒ Levine's July 7 story about the high subsidies received by the politically powerful French farmers (covered also in Aug's November 5 story) told viewers that American farmers faced very unfair competition from foreigners. The only counterpoint to this was a very brief soundbite from a French farmer saying that American farm subsidies were "quite high." At the least, Levine should have added:

> **"The French farmer has a point. American farmers receive billions in taxpayer subsidies every year."**

He also should have pointed out that farm price supports keep food prices artificially high for consumers.

☒ Aug on November 20 analyzed U.S. trade negotiations. Though throughout his commentary he correctly emphasized the advantages of lower trade barriers, his kicker was curiously unbalanced and missed an opportunity to inform the viewer. In the kicker he said: "To [the steel and textile industries] a free trade agreement could mean a flood of lower-priced imports. And, to those industries, that means less business and fewer jobs." To that he should have added:

> **"But to other industries, it means expansion, more jobs, and new markets. And to consumers it means lower prices."**

MISSING THE BIGGEST STORIES

In two of the year's major economic stories—continuing jobless-ness and troubles at IBM—the economics reporters woefully missed opportunities to educate viewers.

Repeatedly and accurately, reporters noted that despite some signs of a recovering economy, job growth remained very slow. Typical was Aug's February 7 report in which he said that "service industries, especially retailers, are losing jobs much faster than the government figured they would. Factories also continued to lose jobs." Levine on April 11 told viewers that "while the recovery from the recession appears underway, the missing ingredient is an in-crease in jobs. . . . [Many companies] while not firing people are still finding ways to trim workers." And on November 13, Levine said, "What is most troubling is that there is no letup in layoffs." Ray Brady, in his September 4 commentary, pointed out that unem-ployment figures "show a huge job loss; 83,000 jobs gone last month."

All of that was correct and of interest to viewers. What was missing was an attempt to explain why jobs were still evaporating even though the economy had begun climbing out of the recession. Ray Brady was given a perfect chance to address this when econo-mist David Jones said on Brady's September 4 segment: "It's un-heard of in a recovery to see employment as weak as it was signalled today." But Brady ignored Jones's comment. As a result, viewers of that broadcast and of all others throughout the year were left to assume that what was happening was some quirk.

Viewers would have been much better served had Brady and his counterparts interviewed the many economists who could have suggested that the higher federal taxes and increased regulations imposed after 1990 had been discouraging businesses from ex-panding payrolls. This same thing, the economists could have added, had been happening in Western Europe for more than a decade and was a main reason why there had been vast automation but almost no new jobs there.

Where economic reporters most failed viewers was in covering IBM's grave problems. In each of the year's twenty-one segments about IBM, reporters talked about the company's troubles in ways that made them paradigmatic of disturbing trends in the America economy. "There goes IBM," viewers in essence were told by gloomy reporters, "another American one-time economic super-star sinking into ruin."

Typical was Brady's December 15 segment on IBM's announcing a 25,000 cut in its work force. Brady, like commentators on the other networks, rightly was troubled by the announcement and about the soon-to-be-dismissed workers and the future of IBM. Brady and his counterparts exuded appropriate sympathy and sadness. From IBM's travails, Brady concluded his story saying: "There will be a lot more slashing of payrolls by American com-panies. And the jobs that are going are jobs that are not coming back."

The problem with Brady's conclusion, and with those of almost all other reporting on IBM, was that it was wrong. The "jobs" that Brady said "aren't coming back" in fact already were back—not at IBM, of course, but at dozens of other American computer industry firms. The story Brady and other reporters completely missed was one of the year's most exciting and illuminating business developments—the triumph of American upstart computer com-panies over giant IBM. What none of the commentators noted was that the American computer business in 1992 was booming and driving foreign competitors (particularly the Japanese) to the wall.

Brady and his colleagues should have told viewers in exultant tones that IBM's troubles, though a tragedy for that firm, in effect were a morality play dramatizing the extraordinary dynamism of the American economy. Brady and the others could have said:

"IBM was not brought low by the Japanese or other foreign competitors. Not at all. Rather IBM has been wounded gravely by small American entrepreneurial firms that have moved quickly to take advantage of market opportunities. Giant IBM did not. These small American firms—some have become giants like Dell—not only are causing great problems

for IBM, but also for the Japanese and German computer industries which once seemed poised to threaten America."

Yet the economic reporters saw only the dark side of the story—IBM's troubles. Blinded perhaps by their penchant for negativism, the reporters did not note, and thus failed to tell viewers, that the American economy was so dynamic and offered so many opportunities for new entrepreneurs (in contrast to Western Europe and Japan's rigidity) that even a giant like IBM was vulnerable.

Brady's kicker should have been:

"All in all, there will be a lot more slashing of payrolls at IBM. That's the price paid for getting stodgy. At other U.S. computer companies, however, business is booming and payrolls are expanding. Perhaps IBM should take a lesson from them."

CHAPTER ELEVEN

THE CONSUMER AFFAIRS REPORTERS

IF ECONOMIC REPORTERS are network newscasting's designated hitters, then consumer reporters are the third base coaches. They relay important signals to consumers about new products, possible physical and material dangers, and ways to save money. From consumer reporters, viewers acquire real world information that they can take with them into stores.

Who, in 1992, were these reporters?

On CBS, Hattie Kauffman reported on consumer affairs for "This Morning," having joined the show in March 1990. She started her broadcasting career on Minneapolis radio and then moved on to Seattle's KING-TV in 1981. There, as a reporter and weekend anchor, Kauffman won four Emmy awards. From 1987 to 1990, she reported for ABC's "Good Morning America."

On ABC, Paula Lyons reported on consumer affairs for "Good Morning America," having joined the show in 1989. Before becoming a reporter in 1979, Lyons taught in the American School of Buenos Aires and was a youth and family program developer at the John F. Kennedy Family Center. She then entered Democratic politics as press secretary, assistant director of communications, and ultimately deputy director of federal relations for Boston Mayor Kevin H. White. Democratic politics also drew her to work in a

California gubernatorial campaign and a Boston campaign in 1973 and 1974. From 1979 to 1989, she was a consumer reporter for WCVB-TV in Boston.

NBC divided consumer reporting duties in 1992 among Betty Furness, Michele Gillen, Andy Pargh, and Lea Thompson.

CNN had no designated consumer reporters, relying on general assignment reporters to cover consumer stories.

HATTIE KAUFFMAN:
Mission Unaccomplished

Viewers of CBS "This Morning" in 1992 knew Kauffman as the show's correspondent for the "Consumer Guide" segment which usually aired once a week. On it she addressed a number of areas: saving money on bills; new products; dealing with salesmen and agents; consumer legal rights; and con artist scams. Though Kauffman apparently kept up with market trends to inform consumers, she seemed to have another mission: advising consumers about how government intervention in the economy would affect them. In doing this, she occasionally saw the problems of government intervention; but mainly she did not.

In her April 13 report, Kauffman questioned why consumer products carried so many warning labels. To make her point that many such warnings were silly, she told viewers that one brand of sun shades for car front windows warned that the car should not be driven with the shade on the window. To her question, What caused such absurd advisories? she answered that frivolous lawsuits had been forcing guiltless companies to demean the intelligence of consumers. She interviewed communications expert Gerald Goldhaber and asked the fundamental consumer's question: "But even if you do have a warning that should be there, are consumers really listening, or are we just getting flooded by so many warnings that we're just tuning out?" Goldhaber agreed that people were becoming so inundated with warnings that they were ignoring them all, even the useful ones.

Kauffman's June 12 report touched upon another aspect of government intervention by giving consumers an idea of the power they wielded. She described how high costs had made it increasingly difficult for communities to recycle such products as newsprint. The low-tech, labor intensive process kept costs high, she explained, while a glut in the market kept profits from newsprint sales low. She went on to tell viewers about a New Jersey law requiring the use of some recycled products. But, she explained in conclusion, government action like that by New Jersey would be "futile unless more companies are willing to use recycled materials and more consumers are willing to buy the products." Kauffman's message: If consumers really want recycled products and refuse to buy anything else, they will get them.

Typically, however, Kauffman underestimated free enterprise. On January 21, responding to a *Consumer Reports* study, she addressed the issue of bacteria in tuna. She acknowledged that "during canning, tuna is cooked at such high temperatures, any bacteria in the contaminants will probably be killed. So eating canned tuna does not pose a health hazard." An attentive viewer then might have asked: "So what's the story?"

For Kauffman, apparently, the story was the need for tougher government regulation, even though no health hazard existed. This was clear from her segment's kicker: "The Food & Drug Administration is responsible for inspecting canned tuna, but since the *Consumer Reports* study won't be released until later today, the FDA has not seen it and so would not comment." To this the puzzled viewer could have asked further: "Why should the FDA be concerned about food that is obviously not dangerous?"

This question Kauffman ignored. In so doing she violated the *habeas corpus* dictum of reporting: for a reporter to declare that a problem exists, the reporter must first produce evidence of a problem. Yet Kauffman had identified no one who had become ill from eating the fish, nor relayed any complaint by any consumer about the fish.

On September 7 Kauffman tackled product liability, pegged to the Bush administration's Product Liability Fairness Act. She interviewed Commerce Secretary Barbara Franklin and Linda Lipson of the Consumers Union. Kauffman allowed Franklin to make the case for the bill: mainly, that unless the law were changed, companies would continue to fear marketing new products because a frivolous lawsuit could bankrupt them. Lipson then argued against the bill, saying that America needed its existing generous liability laws because the Food and Drug Administration was not powerful enough to protect consumers.

Kauffman was hardly neutral in this debate. Most of the air time went to opponents of the bill, including a heart-wrenching interview with a woman whose faulty breast implants had disrupted her life. The woman warned that had the bill been law when she began to have problems, the amount of punitive damages for which she could sue would have been limited. Though Kauffman had time for that lengthy observation, she had none for what could have been a similarly heart-wrenching story about how the attorney fees from frivolous lawsuits were forcing small businesses to fire their workers or even go out of business. Kauffman gave the segment's kicker to Lipson who said: "There may be some manufacturers out there who are afraid of lawsuits. But if you look into why they're afraid, their products are generally dangerous and they probably should be afraid. That shows that the system works."

Kauffman also committed a common reporting error: She apparently assumed that interviewing both an administration official and a "consumer advocate" created balance. But the latter, of course, would have far more credibility than any official. True credibility balance would have been achieved had Kauffman interviewed advocates of litigation reform outside the administration, such as the Manhattan Institute's Walter Olson.

On September 30, Kauffman told viewers about proposed changes to the Employee Retirement Income Security Act, generally known as ERISA, which limited the liability of group health insurance funds when they refused to cover certain treatments. Again Kauffman devoted a great amount of time to an emotional story supporting one side of the issue. She interviewed a woman who had lost her baby because, said the woman, her insurance company would not pay for 24-hour hospital care for her high-risk pregnancy. The unreformed ERISA, she said, had prevented her from suing for damages.

Kauffman then gave an opponent of ERISA changes a chance to tell viewers that the increased number of lawsuits that would result from the changes would raise health care costs. To which Kauffman responded: "Still, consumer groups say benefit plans must be held accountable for the decisions they make." But were that the case, Kauffman should have told viewers about free market reform proposals that would make benefit plans more accountable by giving consumers choices among many insurance companies.

Truck safety was Kauffman's issue on October 2. She told viewers that in 1991 some three thousand people had died in accidents involving trucks. Though current regulations limited truck drivers to no more than 70 hours on the road in an eight-day period, she explained, many ignored the rules. She then grilled John Landis of the federal Department of Transportation about the department's proposal to allow drivers to restart their hour count at zero whenever they had a 24-hour break.

Seemingly incredulous, Kauffman asked: "How can you propose increasing the amount of hours that a driver can be behind the wheel?" Instead of questioning the need for less obtrusive regulations, Kauffman should have asked whether regulations did any good. After all, she had already told viewers that current regulations were being ignored. Kauffman overlooked how tort law, a free enterprise mechanism, could be the solution. Kauffman also failed to give viewers any evidence that truck accidents were caused by tired drivers.

Kauffman's most misleading story concerned meat imported from Canada. She devoted her May 11 and May 12 reports to it, with a follow-up story July 15. Kauffman's report questioned whether Canadian meat sold in the U.S. was healthy. She implied strongly that the answer was no, and then identified a villain: a provision of the U.S. free trade agreement with Canada. "The Canadians ship us more than 700 million pounds [of meat] a year," Kauffman said. "Because of the free trade agreement we have with Canada, the U.S. Department of Agriculture has a special system for inspecting Canadian meat. Critics say it's a system full of loopholes compromising consumer safety."

Kauffman reported how, under the free trade agreement, most Canadian meat was not inspected by American inspectors. She talked to Congressman Pat Williams of Montana, Department of Agriculture meat inspector Bill Lehman, and John Harmon of the General Accounting Office. They all said that the inspection system was flawed and did not protect American consumers. Warned Williams: "I frankly think it jeopardizes Americans' health." Kauffman then told viewers that 1 to 2 percent of American meat was rejected by American inspectors, while 6 to 8 percent of Canadian meat was rejected.

The only person interviewed who favored the existing system of inspection was Mark Manis of the Department of Agriculture. He pointed out that the Canadian meat rejection rate seemed high because Americans only inspected meat from Canadian inspectors who had records of allowing bad meat to pass. Ignoring this point, Kauffman closed her report by cautioning viewers about the meat they were eating. Then, despite her April 13 report about how frivolous labels could be desensitizing Americans to real risks, she lamented that "there's no requirement that meat be labelled."

Kauffman's critical faculties escaped her during this report. She again violated the *habeas corpus* dictum; in short, lack of evidence that a problem exists. Had there truly been a problem with Canadian meat, Americans would have become ill. Yet Kauffman gave viewers no evidence that any American was suffering any discomfort from eating Canadian meat. As a curious reporter, moreover, Kauffman could have questioned the motives of Williams, who represented Montana cattle ranchers, a constituency that surely has been affected by rising imports of meat from Canada since the free trade agreement.

Kauffman seemed to assume that government inspections were the best, or even the only, way to protect consumers. The fact that Canadian meat had not increased health problems in the United States should have dashed that assumption. Kauffman could have improved her story by noting Williams' and others' objections, and then pointing out:

"Though there are complaints about increased meat ship-
ments from Canada, no consumer has been hurt or even
complained. If Americans are buying greater quantities of
Canadian meat, there must be a reason."

PAULA LYONS:
Big Faith in Big Government

During 1992 Lyons informed "Good Morning America" viewers
about such topics as selective binding by magazines (which allows
publishers to target their editorial product to specific audiences);
radon dangers in their homes; how to shop for mattresses; and the
perils of mail fraud. Several of Lyons' segments focused on businesspersons. On May 11 she talked to two New England inn-
keepers about running a bed and breakfast.

In her segments, Lyons (like Kauffman) conveyed some information to consumers about how the free market functioned. The
problem was that Lyons showed even more faith in government
control of the economy than did Kauffman.

Like most other network reporters (see Chapter IX), Lyons
showed the best understanding of free enterprise when the issue
was taxes. Her September 24 broadcast from Michigan profiled
some elderly Americans who were losing their homes. The culprit:
property taxes. These taxes, Lyons explained, went up as property
values rose, but retired people on fixed incomes could not keep up
with the rising rate. As a result, reported Lyons, they sometimes
were evicted from the homes which they had worked a lifetime to
acquire.

On May 28, Lyons alerted parents to dangers in the playground.
She told them to avoid playgrounds with old swings and those
lacking wood chips or other cushioning materials around slides.
She talked to two women from the Consumer Federation of America who wanted the federal government to set standards for playground equipment manufacturers, but also spoke to a Consumer

Product Safety Commission representative who said that voluntary guidelines should be the remedy. Staying above the fray, Lyons was realistic about the efficacy of government involvement: "Both sides would agree that neither guidelines nor laws provide the whole answer. Proper supervision of children at play and regular maintenance of the equipment they play on are also key."

Too often, though, Lyons regarded government action as helpful for consumers and usually she neglected to mention the costs. On January 16 she brought the *Consumer Reports* study on fresh fish to viewers' attention. Beginning well, she explained how fish, which had a shelf life of seven to twelve days, often lost their freshness before they reached the store. Lyons explained that even fish that did arrive at the store fresh could lose this freshness if display cases were not kept cool enough. She pointed out that the issue was not health, for contaminants were killed during cooking, but quality. With her coverage of these points, Lyons was informing consumers about quality concerns regarding a staple of most diets. Then she moved on to possible solutions.

Lyons allowed Trudy Lieberman of *Consumer Reports* to give viewers the free enterprise option: "I think that as people become better able to choose quality and reject those products that are not good quality, maybe retailers will pay more attention." But this did not seem to satisfy Lyons. When listing things consumers could do to get fresh fish, she said, "and finally, you might want to speak up about it." To her, this meant speaking up to government. This became clear when she interviewed Edward Goth, also of *Consumer Reports*, who told viewers: "We think the responsible government agencies at the local level, at the state level, and at the federal level ought to hear from consumers that fish quality isn't what it should be."

Lyons' message in this segment was that government should monitor not just the safety of products but also the quality. Like Kauffman, Lyons also failed the *habeas corpus* test: she gave no evidence of anyone harmed by fish. Lyons ended by saying: "You're not getting what you pay for, that's the issue." Viewers would have learned more had Lyons said:

"If buyers feel they're not getting what they pay for, in a free market they can do something about it. As Trudy Lieberman said, they can start demanding better fish from stores."

Concerning another product, twice during 1992, Lyons took the auto industry to task for alleged safety defects. On April 9, she focused on heater coil failures in several BMW, Isuzu, Renault, and Volkswagen vehicles. She told viewers that since 1986 there had been seventy injuries and one fatality caused by such failures. But throughout her entire six-minute story, she did not interview any car company representative. She did spend considerable time with Sean Kane of the Center for Auto Safety and Doug Chisolm of the Institute for Safety Analysis, groups that frequently had sought increased government regulation of the economy. She did not identify these as groups long hostile to the auto industry.

On October 15, Lyons' target was GM trucks. This time she told viewers that because of the placement of the gas tank on certain models, there had been "more than 300 fiery deaths." Again, Lyons went to what she identified as "public interest groups" for interviews, this time talking to Debra Barclay at the Center for Auto Safety, Joan Claybrook of Public Citizen, and "safety expert" Byron Bloch.

In both of her stories Lyons failed to put into perspective the statistics that she used. Had she done so for the GM truck report, for instance, she would have told viewers that federal statistics revealed virtually no statistical difference between the fatal crash rates of Ford and GM trucks. This was true even in side-impact crashes, those allegedly causing the GM gas tanks to explode. But Lyons relied completely on observers that were far from neutral. The Center for Auto Safety, Public Citizen, the Institute for Safety Analysis, and Byron Bloch were all well funded by trial lawyers, who had an interest in making car companies look bad.

Lyons' most misleading story was on July 9. That day she reported on the Federal WIC (Women, Infants, and Children) program which gave coupons to low income families to use at special farmers' markets. "The beauty of the program," Lyons began, "is it can be adapted to meet an individual community's needs." She then interviewed only those who supported the coupon program, including two WIC program coordinators, two Boston WIC recipients, and two farmers. Hugh Joseph, one of the program coordinators, told viewers: "Three million dollars this year is going to help 500,000 households and 2,500 to 3,000 farmers."

Sandra Robertson, another WIC program coordinator, said: "I can't imagine who would be against such a program." Responded Lyons: "Who indeed?" She then cast the Bush administration as the culprit for targeting the program for cuts. She gave the kicker to Robertson who said: "It would be a great loss if this program is not funded. Every state in the union should have this program because it's a good program and it meets the needs of a lot of people." Nancy Snyderman, cohosting "Good Morning America" that day, ended the segment saying: "What a wonderful program. And something that works."

WIC may indeed be a useful program. Even so, there were legitimate concerns about it, all of which Lyons ignored. She also ignored such issues as requiring recipients to work, even though those issues were at the forefront of most debates about WIC. And while noting her concern about low income Americans having enough money for food, Lyons could have mentioned that government was driving up food prices through farm price supports. Lyons left consumers in the dark about this.

NBC:
Flouting Free Enterprise

NBC was the network least likely to give viewers accurate information about free enterprise during its consumer reports. Only "Gadget Guru" Andy Pargh, appearing occasionally on NBC "Today" to tell viewers about new products, did not fundamentally misrepresent free enterprise during 1992.

Lea Thompson was the most frequent consumer reporter for "Today." One rare instance when she did not mislead viewers about their economy was on July 1. That day she warned viewers about unscrupulous repairmen who used the new Clean Air Act as an excuse to overcharge for fixing air conditioners. She outlined the phony reasons that they might give for higher charges, but also pointed out that there were legitimate reasons why repairmen might have to charge more. She interviewed a repairman who explained the complicated new process which the law forced him to follow. "Bottom line, though," Thompson finished, "you are going to have to pay quite a bit more when you get your air conditioning serviced because companies have to pay for all that new equipment and it will take them a lot longer to recover the freon and check for leaks."

Although Thompson did not question the wisdom of the new regulations, the July 1 story was one of the few consumer reports on any network in 1992 to show viewers in detail the cost of a regulation.

In most of Thompson's segments, though, viewers were mis-informed about free enterprise. On January 16 Thompson told viewers (as Lyons did on ABC) about the *Consumer Reports* article questioning the freshness of store-bought fish. After detailing the contaminants, Thompson said: "The fishing industry . . . thinks cooking kills bacteria, so you shouldn't stop eating fish." This implied strongly that only the fishing industry "thought" that cooked fish were harmless; in fact, *Consumer Reports* also not only thought so but declared unequivocally that it was so. Thompson then told viewers about the possibly toxic pollutants found in the fish without explaining what levels scientists considered harmful.

Thompson ended the segment with Ellen Haas of Public Voice saying: "Congress must act to prevent further deaths and further sickness from eating contaminated fish." Yet neither Thompson nor Haas gave any health statistics citing any deaths or any sickness from the fish. In fact, in the program's next segment, *Consumer Reports'* Trudy Lieberman told Bryant Gumbel that there was no health problem, as Thompson's report had led viewers to believe. The only difficulty, said Lieberman, was that "the high levels [of bacteria] we found might indicate that you won't get the tastiest meal."

On April 1, Thompson reported on the alleged flaw in the heater coils of some foreign-made cars; Paula Lyons would report on this eight days later. Thompson gave injury numbers without putting them in any context or comparing them with any other cars. (Thompson reported sixty injuries from coil explosions, Lyons later reported seventy.) Thompson interviewed no one from any of the automobile companies, spending nearly the entire segment attacking them, as would Lyons at a later date. Thompson also relied on the Center for Auto Safety, interviewing the center's Clarence Ditlow, who was not an engineer.

On January 8, Betty Furness briefed NBC "Today" viewers on how good car bumpers could save money by limiting car damage in accidents. Though admitting there was no safety issue involved and that it was only a matter of repair costs, she still praised a California law requiring car manufacturers to disclose the strength of their bumpers on the sale sticker. An industry spokesman told viewers that such stickers were misleading because they did not tell consumers how much the better bumpers added to the car's cost. This did not convince Furness who turned from reporter to explicit advocate when she said: "New York and several other large states have considered this kind of legislation and we can hope the trend continues." In effect, Furness assumed government was better equipped than consumers to decide the right balance between price and quality.

CREDIBILITY UP IN FLAMES:
The GM-NBC Controversy

Another assumption consumer reporters often made was that pursuit of profits prompted car companies to neglect the safety of their customers. The corollary assumption was that "public interest" groups were disinterested observers concerned only with safety.

Accepting both assumptions led to the most embarrassing network segment on any topic of the year: the November 17 "Dateline NBC" story, "Waiting to Explode," about an alleged flaw that caused some models of GM trucks to explode in side-impact crashes. Michele Gillen and her "Dateline" team set up a test crash of a GM truck for the segment. But instead of a fair, genuine test, they rigged the crash by placing an incendiary device near the truck's gas tank and putting the wrong cap on the gas tank so that it would fall off on impact. Nearly all other journalists were outraged that Gillen would mislead viewers in such a way.

Most revealing, though, is what did not outrage other journalists. Don Hewitt, executive producer of CBS's "60 Minutes," said on the February 9, 1993, "Crossfire": "They had a pretty good story up to that point [when NBC faked the explosion]. They had a smoking gun and they shot themselves in the foot with it." *Washington Post* Ombudsman Joann Byrd wrote that by the time of the crash test, " 'Dateline NBC' had told its story." The lesson she thought reporters should take from the incident: " 'Complete' and 'thorough' are on any short list of what we hope a news story will be. But 'complete' and 'thorough' may happen sooner than you think."

Was Gillen's story "complete" and "thorough" up to the point of the faked explosion? Like Lyons, who had reported on the GM trucks on October 15, Gillen told viewers that more than three hundred people had died in side-impact crashes in the trucks in question. What she failed to tell viewers was that the records of GM trucks, even in side-impact crashes, and Ford trucks were virtually identical. This surely could not have been Hewitt's smoking gun.

Like Lyons, Gillen spent an extraordinary amount of time (16.5 minutes) attacking GM, but gave the company only one minute to respond. Again like Lyons, Gillen relied on putative "public interest" groups as sources, including the Center for Auto Safety, the Institute for Safety Analysis, and Byron Bloch. And yet again like Lyons, Gillen failed to tell viewers that these groups had close ties to trial lawyers, who stood to gain from network attacks on car companies.

Consumer reporters of course should do safety stories; consumers need to be informed about such matters. But serious mistakes are so common among reporters that viewers are left with a terribly flawed impression of automobile safety. Example: Both

Lyons and Gillen gave viewers the number of deaths in GM trucks without relating that number to other trucks' safety records. Example: Thompson and Gillen spent most of their segments attacking car companies without giving the companies time to respond. Viewers would have been better served by fewer scenes of weeping relatives of accident victims and more questioning of the companies accused of neglecting safety.

More important, consumer reporters should advise viewers that "public interest" groups generally have their own agendas that sometimes go beyond consumer safety. Writes Walter Olson of the Manhattan Institute: "Lawyers and their [public interest group] associates have become the supreme negative sources in American journalism, all too often with no acknowledgement that they have their own interests in the way stories turn out." If there were truly a safety problem with an automobile's design, then an engineer without ties to the auto industry or trial lawyers should explain it to viewers.

LETTING OPPORTUNITIES SLIP AWAY

There were several issues of concern to consumers in 1992 that no consumer reporter covered.

⊠ **Free Trade.** Consumers should have been told that free trade above all was a consumer issue. Reduced or eliminated trade barriers have brought prices down for consumers while forcing American companies to improve quality. A consumer reporter could have picked a product to profile—coffee, for example—and explained the direct benefits to consumers from low trade barriers.

⊠ **Monetary Costs of Regulation.** Viewers rarely heard about the direct costs of regulations. Since cost obviously is important to consumers, a report on the costs of regulation would have been an appropriate topic for Hattie Kauffman or Paula Lyons. Even mentioning that regulations imposed costs during segments on specific regulations would have been an improvement.

⊠ **Other Costs of Regulation.** Noticeably absent from the year's reporting was any mention of the nonmonetary, unintended consequences of regulation. Every network was quick to criticize car makers whenever there was even a scent of a safety problem. But no consumer reporters told viewers how the Clean Air Act could cause highway deaths by mandating, in the name of fuel efficiency, smaller, lighter, and hence more dangerous cars.

⊠ **Product Quality.** Kauffman, Lyons, Thompson, and Furness all aired reports suggesting that government should regulate not just product safety, but also product quality. A story about the concomitant added costs and whether consumers were finding the supposed higher quality worth the cost would have been a useful topic for a consumer report. Similarly useful would have been a story about how higher-quality products consistently had been invented in countries with pro-free enterprise government policies.

⊠ **Government Programs' Effects on Consumers.** Completely ignored by consumer reporters was how some government programs cost taxpayers money at the store. Farm price supports, for instance, drive up prices for consumers.

PART IV

WHAT ENTERTAINMENT DOES TO FREE ENTERPRISE

CHAPTER TWELVE

ENTERTAINMENT: AMERICA'S MOST WANTED

* PETER STEWART ARRESTED FOR MURDER.

* MAX MURROFSKY ARRESTED FOR SELLING STOLEN CARS.

* JACK SYLVESTER ARRESTED FOR BANK ROBBERY.

* DWIGHT CORCORAN ARRESTED FOR MURDER.

* CARLOS DIGORIO ARRESTED FOR CONSPIRACY TO MURDER.

* MINTON KILLS YOUTH.

* LEON LAMARR ARRESTED FOR MURDER.

* GEORGE COSTAS CONVICTED FOR MURDER OF YOUTHS.

* PHILLIP MARIETTA ARRESTED FOR DRUG TRAFFICKING AND MURDER.

These are not newspaper headlines nor excerpts from local newscasts. They are a rogues gallery from entertainment TV 1992. And all of these rogues had at least one thing in common—they were businessmen.

Peter Stewart owned a casino; Max Murrofsky was a classic car dealer; Jack Sylvester and Dwight Corcoran were bankers; Carlos DiGorio owned a hotel; Minton was a liquor distributor; Leon Lamarr and George Costas owned jewelry stores; and Phillip Marietta was a petroleum trading company executive.

Anyone watching entertainment TV in 1992 would have assumed that businessmen were America's most wanted bad guys. As studies of prior years discovered, entertainment TV's first choice for a criminal, an evil-doer, someone hurting society was a businessman. Though businesspersons were nearly invisible on TV newscasts, they overpopulated TV entertainment's underworld.

MURDERS COMMITTED BY GROUP

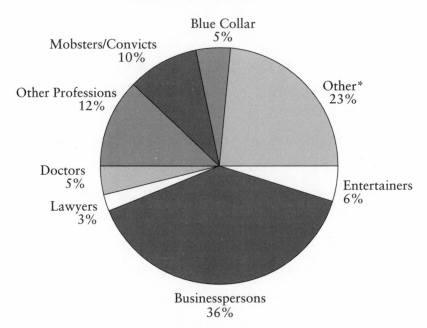

Based on a 12 week study of prime-time entertainment for 1992.
*Other includes: students, housewives, and unknowns.

They comprised 24 percent of all the main characters on entertainment TV in 1992. And they were 43 percent of the criminals and 36 percent of the murderers. Yet in the real world, businessmen commit a tiny percentage of crimes and murders.

For good reason, *New York Times* TV critic John Leonard declared, as cited in *Watching America: What Television Tells Us About Our Lives* by S. Robert Lichter, Linda S. Lichter and Stanley Rothman[1]: "On television . . . to be in business is to ride a monorail of avarice to disaster and bad sex." To which Tom Mankiewicz, former head writer of the program *Hart to Hart*, has added: "The businessman—the entrepreneur—is the kind of guy on television you love to hate."[2] And Lichter writes that TV drives home the "point that business at best serves no useful social function and at worst is a threat to a human social order. . . . Viewers rarely witness Horatio Alger stories of business success as the fulfillment of the American dream."[3]

When confronted with the statistics of how they have portrayed businessmen and business, TV executives only shrug. They claim that Peter Stewart, George Costas, Carlos DiGorio, and TV's other law-breaking businessmen break the law only in fictionalized entertainment. And, stress TV executives, viewers know that what they are watching is fiction.

These executives are correct. But only to a point. TV entertainment is designed to entertain, and the vast majority of Americans watch TV to be amused, diverted, mesmerized, engaged, and transported to other realms. That is why, presumably, Americans keep their TV sets playing an average of seven hours daily.

Yet while it entertains, TV does more—much more. TV also influences and educates. This is the near unanimous conclusion of experts. Said former Federal Communications Commission member Nicholas Johnson: "All television is educational. The only question is: What does it teach?"[4] One thing it teaches is that businessmen are murderers, drug dealers, bank robbers, and con artists; and that businesses sell stolen goods, destroy the environment, and cheat customers.

And when TV teaches, it is a mass teacher. According to the Nielsen ratings, 12.1 million Americans were told that banker

Dwight Corcoran was a murderer, 14.9 million that store owner George Costas was a murderer, 13.4 million that Phillip Marietta was a drug trafficker, and 11.9 million that Leon Lamarr was a murderer.

That these millions of viewers can be influenced by entertainment TV is really beyond dispute, confirmed by mountains of data by sociologists and others. Such studies, for example, have been used over the years to blame TV for contributing to violence and for stereotyping racial minorities, women, and gays. The notion that entertainment TV influences attitudes has become so accepted that some years ago Italian groups protested TV plots that linked Italians to organized crime. And in mid–1993, TV executives bowed to congressional pressure and pledged to curb onscreen violence.

TV's role in teaching violence has been long studied. It was the subject of a 1972 report by the Surgeon General's Scientific Advisory Committee entitled *Television and Growing Up: The Impact of Televised Violence*. The committee found a "preliminary and tentative indication of a causal relation between viewing violence on television and aggressive behavior."[5] Thirteen years later, the American Psychological Association declared that "television violence has a causal effect on aggressive behavior."[6] TV violence could cause aggressiveness, the experts argued, because, as the Task Force on Television and Society said, "Television is a subtle, continuous source for learning about the rules of life and society."[7]

Researchers have stressed that "even when producers and viewers do not intend it as a source of information, TV transmits messages about the world and society."[8] In *The Psychology of Television*, psychologist John Condry writes that "television serves as a source of occupational information" and that, for children particularly, "being exposed to the programs substantially alters selected perceptions of occupational roles."[9]

George Gerbner, Larry Gross, Michael Morgan, and Nancy Signorielli write in *Perspectives on Media Effects* that "Even when people recognize that the material they are viewing is fictional, its messages and images gradually shape expectations and beliefs about the real world."[10] Echoing this, the American Psychological Association said in 1992 that "even when [a TV program] is designed for entertainment . . . [it] has the potential for teaching children academic and social skills . . ."[11]

TV has done this by a process that some experts call the "drip model," explained by Michigan State University telecomminications professor Bradley S. Greenberg as the "subtle and gradual incorporation of frequent and repeated messages. . . . The more television individuals watch, the more they believe and accept its messages about society."[12] Condry agrees, writing: "Over a wide range of topics, dozens of studies have shown that the 'facts' of the world of television tend to 'creep into' the attitude and value systems of those who are heavy consumers of it, and it does this in a quiet, insidious manner. Most heavy viewers are not aware that their attitudes and values have been influenced."[13]

CASTING CALL FOR BUSINESSMEN:
Must be Criminal and Incompetent

If entertainment TV can influence viewers on racism, sexism, attitudes towards gays, and even Italian links to the mafia, then it is reasonable to assume that entertainment can influence what Americans know about their economic system, about businesses and businesspersons, and about the impulses, trade-offs, and other factors constantly at play in driving the American economy. Explains C. Clark: "Mass media encourage respect for social groups by showing them in roles that are sympathetic and positive. . . . Conversely, respect is denied when social groups are portrayed in stereotyped or negatively valued roles."[14]

TV entertainment in 1992 was loaded with negative stereotypes of businesses and businesspersons. This is clear from the examples on the following pages, based on data compiled from the Free Enterprise and Media Institute's comprehensive review of the content of entertainment TV in 1992. Randomly selecting one week in each month of the year, the institute staff monitored, analyzed, and codified every prime time non-news program on ABC, CBS, Fox, and NBC.

What this survey found is that entertainment TV in 1992 portrayed businessmen and women as unfeeling and cruel bosses and managers, as criminals or otherwise evil, and as taking advantage of the public. While viewers at times saw positive images of businesspersons, these seldom had much to do with business situations. Typically, moreover, they involved small businessmen and women.

Even an occasional viewing of TV in 1992 would have encountered a criminal or evil businessman. In total, businesspersons accounted for sixty-six of the 154 criminals, or 43 percent, in the twelve sample weeks analyzed by the Free Enterprise and Media Institute. Examples:

☒ A classic car dealer fronted for the thieves who stole Bonetti's car in the January 31 episode of CBS's "Tequila and Bonetti."

☒ Mr. Saxton, owner of a fertilizer company in the March 11 episode of NBC's "Quantum Leap," attempted to put poison gas into the asthma inhaler of a reporter who had discovered that Saxton's firm secretly was making chemical weapons.

☒ Developer Garcia, in NBC's April 12 movie *The Keys*, killed and otherwise intimidated those who refused to sell him property which he wanted for a hotel and casino.

☒ Van Adams, owner of Van Adams Industry in NBC's April 13 movie *Parker Kane*, dumped toxic wastes into a landfill and then killed the person who discovered that he was doing so. Adams also tried, unsuccessfully, to kill Parker Kane, the movie's hero.

☒ Mr. Valentelli, owner of an agency that cleaned government buildings in CBS's April 17 movie *Murder Times Seven*, sold the "mob" information which he obtained by rifling the district attorney's offices while he was cleaning them.

☒ Carlos DiGorio, owner of the Golden Sands Hotel in the May 13 episode of NBC's "Quantum Leap," planned to kill Mack, a comedian, because DiGorio liked Mack's girlfriend.

☒ Chloe, owner of the E-Lock company in the May 31 episode of "Quantum Leap," hired a corrupt cop to kill a pharmacist who wanted to stop supplying illegal drugs to E-Lock.

☒ Adam Logan, a prosperous cattle rancher in CBS's July 17 movie *Blood River*, burned a farm house and killed the family inside because it would not sell him the land that he wanted to expand his ranch.

☒ Minton, a liquor distributor in the August 8 episode of ABC's "MacGyver," was a gun supplier and a murderer.

☒ Mickey Stone, manager of Panther Studios in NBC's October 11 and 12 movie *Lady Boss*, allowed pornography to be shipped overseas by using the Panther label as cover.

☒ Pauly Thingpen, a developer in the October 16 episode of CBS's "Picket Fences," bribed city officials, broke the arm of an employee as punishment for filing a workman's compensation claim, broke the nose and an arm of a man who was going to testify in court against him, spat in a cop's face, and contemptuously justified these actions by boasting that he and his development projects had been the sole cause of the town's economic boom and that without him the town would go broke.

☒ Leon Lamarr, a jewelry store owner in the November 7 episode of ABC's "Columbo," killed his nephew Freddie to get the lottery money that Freddie had just won.

In TV's detective dramas, businessmen regularly turned up as criminals. Examples:

☒ On NBC's "Law & Order," the murderer in the May 12 episode was bank chairman Dwight Corcoran, the murderer in the July 17 episode was "respected businessman" Gary Wallace, the man identified as the real cause of a murder in the September 9 episode was businessman Ian Maser, the murderer in the November 11 episode was jewelry store owner George Costas, and the drug dealer responsible for murder in the December 9 episode was Nigerian Petroleum Company executive Phillip Marietta.

☒　On NBC's "Matlock," the murderer in the January 31 episode was bar owner Lucas Anderson, while a bank robber in that episode was bank president Jack Sylvester; and in the July 17 episode the participants in a money laundering conspiracy were Oak Creek's "pillars of the community" which included the owners of the town's hotel, gas station, and funeral parlor.

☒　On CBS's "Jake and the Fatman," the murderer in the January 29 episode was casino owner Peter Stewart, and the person who deliberately hooked rock star Dina on drugs in the March 11 episode was record producer Tony Stanza.

☒　On NBC's "In the Heat of the Night" in the January 31 episode, a towing company owner planned to kill his ex-wife; in the June 2 episode, the murderer was banker Dalton Sykes, and a potential witness to that crime who refused to cooperate with the police was chemical company owner Nolan Cantrell; and in the July 12 episode the drug dealer was moving company owner Barney Meechum.

☒　On ABC's "The Commish" in the April 11 episode, the wife-beater was corporate vice-president Richard Carver.

☒　On CBS's "Murder She Wrote" in the September 6 episode, the drug dealer and collector of stolen art was hotel owner Enrico Montejano.

Companies were also often portrayed as evil. Examples:

☒　On ABC's "Dinosaurs," business was routinely depicted as heartless. In several episodes, viewers saw the We Say So Development Corporation destroy a redwood forest to clear land for a housing development. In the January 29 episode, company manager B.P. Richfield declared that people should put their trust in corporations for only they could protect the "grapdelites," a small fuzzy animal facing extinction. After which Richfield ate the animal. In the August 14 episode, Richfield became a candidate for political office and promised to tax the poor, not the rich. "I call it my trickle down theory. Rich folks tend to live in big houses on the tops of hills. So, if we give them all of the money, some of it is bound to slip out of their pockets and roll down the hill where the poor folks are." When a reporter said, "You say you want to be the education elder and yet you favor the repeal of all child labor laws," he replied, "Absolutely. Children love to work. It's like a game to them. Getting all dirty down in the We Say So coal mine. And because they're small, you can fit more of them in a tight space." And in the September 11 episode, the company schemed to block introduction of an invention that would reduce what Mr. Ashland, the CEO, called the company's "obscenely profitable" energy division.

☒ On NBC's "Nightmare Cafe" January 29, a chemical factory dumped toxic waste into a harbor.

☒ On NBC's "In the Heat of the Night" January 31, a truck repair shop sold stolen trucks.

☒ On NBC's "L.A. Law" February 13, a company made four hundred farmers sterile by using chemicals banned by the federal government.

☒ On "L.A. Law" March 12, a logging company was described as having an "impeccable reputation for rape and pillage of the redwoods."

☒ On "L.A. Law" June 4, the owner of a health food and diet shake stand was accused of disguising high calorie shakes as diet shakes.

☒ On Fox's "Married With Children" September 6, a company advertizing time-share condominiums was operating a scam.

☒ On Fox's "Roc" November 8, Roc declared that "the utility companies will rob you blind."

☒ On CBS' "Hat Squad" December 9, a pizza parlor was a front for the mob.

When businessmen were not committing crimes, many were cheating or taking advantage of the public. On Fox's "The Simpsons," for instance, a yo-yo maker in the February 13 episode slickly used athletes to entice kids into buying yo-yos which then distracted them from their schoolwork. On the April 16 episode, Homer Simpson, in need of money, had to borrow from his boss at high interest rates; when Homer took a night job at a convenience store to pay back the loan, he discovered the store owner changing expiration dates on dairy products. And in the July 16 episode, Homer's boss secretly brought in professional athletes to guarantee that the company team would win the amateur league's championship softball game.

Ethics meant little to stereo equipment broker Brian Conover on CBS's "Middle Ages" September 10; he offered to "fudge" numbers for a client. Meanwhile, auto dealer Mr. Schmek, on NBC's "Different World" March 12, stole advertizing ideas from his employees.

On ABC's "Coach" March 10, Hayden told viewers that "All real estate agents are sharks. They don't care about you. . . . They're slimy, lying, greedy little parasites." The construction industry was slapped on "Murder She Wrote" July 12, when owner Michael O'Connor used his building business to defraud pensioners and young people. On "Murder She Wrote" April 12, the businessmen in the plot were unappealing members of an exclusive club where they schemed to do each other in. On CBS' "Fish Police" March 13, fast food restaurant owner Weenie King cheated his two brothers out of their share of the family fortune.

BOSSES AND OWNERS seldom were depicted as competent; and seldom too were they seen as contributing anything positive to their firm or the economy. Though Mitch and Kate in NBC's "Dear John" July 15 knew nothing about running a restaurant, they bought one with their life savings and retirement funds and then made a mess of the business by hiring an incompetent waitress who dumped food on the head of a food critic.

The owners in CBS's "Golden Palace" October 16, meantime, saw their hotel's insurance policy cancelled after coowner Rose covered the swimming pool while guests were still in it. Carol, in NBC's "Empty Nest" March 7, was another food-business failure; though a bad cook, she went into the catering business and made only $200 in four months.

Mr. Bracken, the boss on Fox's "Herman's Head" in the November 8 episode, invested in a hotel that turned out to be a wreck. A miscalculation by the resort owner, in ABC's "Family Matters" September 8, left all of his cabins with one wall missing. Flying service owner Joe Hackett, in NBC's "Wings" August 12, donated a plane ticket to a charity auction which was good for a trip anywhere that his service Sandpiper flew. But his brother and partner mistakenly omitted the qualifier on the ticket about "where Sandpiper flies" and thus implicitly promised to fly anywhere.

When not bumbling, bosses and owners often were portrayed as unfeeling and unpleasant. "Herman's Head" Mr. Bracken, for instance, intimidated his employees. Holling, the diner owner in CBS' "Northern Exposure," in one episode yelled at his cook until he quit. Another diner owner, on Fox's "Married With Children," told his waitress, "You are the stupidest girl I've had work here"— and then asked her to go out with him.

Mr. Burns, Homer Simpson's boss, had thugs toss Homer out on the street when Homer visited Burns' home. A nightclub owner on the May 13 "Quantum Leap" refused to give a pair of comedians a second chance, firing them after their act flopped one night. Also fired by an unfeeling boss were the radio station veteran staffers on the December 8 episode of ABC's "Full House."

Workers as well as bosses were depicted as incompetent. A real estate saleswoman in ABC's "Billy" was unable to make a sale; when she finally did, she almost sold her own house. Real estate agent Helen in "Wings" mistakenly included a $50,000 chandelier in the price of a house she sold. Ron, a used-car salesman in NBC's "Different World," also could barely make a sale and, what was worse, allowed a customer to drive away in a Mercedes.

The construction crew in Fox's "Vinnie & Bobby" routinely were depicted as lazy and inept. Bar waitress Delta in ABC's "Delta" routinely was late to work and pretty useless when she got there, while waitress Harriet in ABC's "Family Matters" was obnoxious and rude. And putative stock broker Vanessa, in ABC's "Hanging With Mr. Cooper," was afraid to invest her customers' money.

At Times, the Noble Businessperson ... but

Not all businesspersons were depicted by entertainment TV as criminals or cads. Some had endearing characteristics and even noble traits. By and large, these were owners and managers of small businesses—bookstores, diners, bars, dress shops, pawn shops, tattoo parlors, grocery stores, and so forth.

But their appealing characteristics generally were unrelated to their role as businesspersons. Mr. Peldicott, for example, a wealthy businessman in ABC's "Civil Wars," was favorably portrayed not because of anything related to his business (the nature of which remained a mystery), but because he gave $500,000 to the homeless. Bookstore owners Carl and Joan in NBC's "Heat of the Night" ran a free literacy class and gave books to the elementary school. Executive Otis Drexell in Fox's "Drexell's Class" became a teacher.

Entrepreneur Douglas in NBC's "Different World" paid for his employees' schooling if they earned A averages. Cafe owner Walt Turner, one of TV's rare black businessmen, in CBS's "Stompin' at the Savoy" was generous to his friends and faithful to his girlfriend. Commodity trader Dixon in ABC's "Burden of Proof" was honorable, even heroic, because of the sacrifices he had to make to keep his word to his deceased lover Clara. And the muffler shop owner in NBC's "Here and Now" was kind to and protective of his son.

One of the few opportunities viewers had to see a sympathetic portrayal of anything business-related was in the way businesspersons treated customers. Restaurant owner Phil on CBS's "Murphy Brown" was kind to them, as were a dress shop owner in ABC's "Young Riders" July 16, pawn shop owner Agnus in NBC's "Fresh Prince of Bel Air" September 7, grocery store owner Ruth Ann in CBS's "Northern Exposure" September 7, and restaurant manager Jojo Duncan in ABC's "Crossroads" October 10.

Occasionally viewers could glimpse, although fleetingly, entrepreneurs at work. The Davises, a black family on ABC's "Homefront" in the January 28 episode, struggled to earn extra money to open a restaurant; in the April 15 episode they had succeeded in doing so. Persistence, too, was the moral of the effort by Teddy in CBS's "Murder She Wrote" March 8, who dreamed of making a fortune by building roller coasters across the nation. Though he raised no money, he doggedly pursued potential investors. Larry, a writer for a newspaper in ABC's "Perfect Strangers" May 30, initially grumbled about being assigned to write captions for a new cartoon for the children's page of the Sunday paper, but soon began to appreciate the marketing possibilities of a new cartoon character.

Welfare mother Patsy in CBS's "Runaway Father" August 10, meanwhile, went back to school, graduated, and found a job with the federal government in what for TV was a very rare portrait of a person getting off welfare.

Quality was a rare message on entertainment TV, but it did appear. On CBS's "In Sickness and in Health" March 8, Jarred was the owner of a boot-making firm. Viewers saw him buying leather for its quality, not its price, just as, he explained, his father and grandfather had done.

Hard work and tough trade-offs were the unambiguous messages in the exchange between Mrs. Pack and the two detectives in the June 2 episode of NBC's "Law & Order." The cops who called on Pack in her Manhattan clothing plant found her extremely busy.

SHE: "It's the price of owning your own company. Twice a month to Hong Kong, sales meetings, lawyers, accountants. Sometimes I forget what it's all about."
COP: "And what's that?"
SHE: "Designing clothes. It's a tough business—24 hours a day—and then some."
COP: "So you don't spend much time with [your son] Roy?"
SHE: "Biggest regret of my life . . ."
COP: "I guess you're too busy."
SHE: "I work. Is that a crime?"

Viewers also saw business as hard work on a few other programs. Wally, for instance, in CBS's "Love and War" October 12, while preparing frantically for the Grand Opening of her restaurant was tough in dealing with tardy suppliers and exhorted her employees to work hard. Catalog company owner Ken, in ABC's "Room for Two" October 15, emphasized that he worked hard for his money and that competition was very brutal because "there are guys in this business who wouldn't mind breaking a few legs just to scare off the competition." Norman Demski, owner of Video Component Repair on ABC's "Overexposed" October 11, said, "I never dreamed I'd own my own business, let alone a place like this."

Viewers in 1992 seldom saw real business situations. Among the few times was a rare peek at the vagaries of the stock market. In ABC's "Hanging With Mr. Cooper" November 10, stock broker Vanessa was reluctant to invest her friend Robin's money in the speculative stock of MYCORP. Although Vanessa told Robin that she had purchased MYCORP shares, in reality she had put Robin's money in a low interest, but safe, six-month bank CD. Vanessa then invested her own money in MYCORP and made a killing when the stock soared. The stock market also enticed Carlton of NBC's "Fresh Prince of Bel Air" in the September 7 episode. He pawned his mother's diamond bracelet for money to buy an airline stock. The airline went bankrupt and Carlton lost everything.

The risks of starting a business were accurately described in CBS's "Davis Rules" June 3 when Davis and some friends invested in a clam-processing business. Davis's sister Gwen offered the sound advice that Davis "hasn't figured out the cost of processing and packaging. There's no distributor. And the whole thing seems to hinge on this clam advisor guy named Salty Jack." Davis ignored his sister and made a poor investment which he was able to recoup only by selling it to a naive, but trusting, friend.

That managing was not easy was a theme in NBC's "Out All Night" December 10. Nightclub owner Chelsea Page allowed Vidal Thomas, a pizza delivery boy, to act as manager for one night so that he could impress his girlfriend Hillary. From that, Vidal concluded that being a manager was not easy work. This was the same message in ABC's "Step by Step" November 13, which showed Frank, a contractor, having a very rough day fielding the complaints of customers.

One of the year's very few glimpses of business competence on entertainment TV was on CBS's "Bob" October 16. The owner of a comic book company succeeded because he always assembled a group of ordinary folks, including the shoeshine man, in his office building's lobby to judge new comic book creations. Competence too was the rare message in CBS's "Sexual Advances" May 10, when Paula, a saleswoman for athletic shoes, rescued a near-failed deal and kept a big customer that almost had been lost by another salesperson.

THE MESSAGE OF "SISTERS":
Hard Work a Virtue

The year's most consistently positive images appeared on NBC's "Sisters." This weekly saga involved four sisters who, in addition to encountering the romances and personal crises that typically punctuated TV dramedies, took their professional lives very seriously. Each week viewers saw the sisters working hard—with dialogue to emphasize the point. Said sister Georgie in the January 25 episode: "Hard work is always a virtue, even if it goes unrewarded." Later she observed realistically that "people work at their jobs because they have to, not because they love to. That's why it's called work." In the October 10 episode, sister Teddy worked all night filling orders for the clothing she had designed.

These hard-working women, moreover, were not the wooden workaholics, oblivious to family and other personal concerns, who typically populated dramas and sitcoms when entertainment TV put successful executives on the screen. Each sister, rather, was portrayed sympathetically, even in tough situations.

Frankie, the sister who was a corporate vice-president, in the January 25 episode, was seen agonizing over how to deal with a client who had sexually harassed another staffer. In the September 5 episode, she was agonizing over how to fire a nice, but incompetent, associate. In both situations, Frankie did what was necessary—confronting the harasser and firing the incompetent, but doing so in an appealing way. Sympathetic too was Teddy. In the

October 10 and November 7 episodes viewers saw her standing loyally by a competent assistant even though he was an ex-convict.

To be sure, "Sisters" occasionally packed political wallop—but aimed it at both ends of the spectrum. In the February 8 episode, for instance, Alex's daughter wrote about a feminist activist and extolled "the workers' timeless struggle." But instead of making this statement an ode to class warfare, "Sisters" writers mocked it by painting its source, the daughter, as the program's least pleasant character, a spoiled, irritating brat. And in the April 11 episode, when Georgie heard about her sister Alex not being paid by a company which had declared bankruptcy, Georgie snickered: "Hey. Don't look at me. Talk to your Republican friends."

"Sisters" even managed to slip a supply-side theme into the January 25 episode. Teddy, who had trouble making a living as an artist, took a job selling Mary Kay-type cosmetics to women at afternoon kaffee klatches. To her dismay, no one seemed interested in buying the cosmetics. But the women were enthralled by the sweatshirt which Teddy was wearing and had designed. Demonstrating that supply of a good product creates its own demand, Teddy found herself taking orders to make sweatshirts and other clothes and thereby discovered that she might have a profitable future in the clothing business.

An Economics Lesson:
Mixed and Misleading

At times, entertainment TV in 1992 gave the viewer an explicit lesson in economics. One useful lesson was that get rich quick schemes rarely delivered. This Arnie learned in ABC's "Commish" February 8. While visiting Tahiti, Arnie bought two hundred cases of a "revolutionary" new sunscreen used by the natives, which he intended to sell back home at a large mark-up. But when he tried some of the product, he got sun poisoning—and was stuck with his two hundred cases of the potion.

Another useful, albeit seldom seen, lesson was that there were limits to what government could do. In Fox's "Beverly Hills 90210" August 12, Jack, who had lost his job and was homeless, said to a sympathetic Brandon: "There's a recession on, kid. Uncle Sam can't force companies to stay in business, or hire vets."

THE MOST IMPORTANT economics lesson on entertainment TV probably concerned work and the work ethic. Here TV's record for the year was mixed. Some programs signalled that hard work and tenacity were virtues; others ridiculed work.

The message was strong and positive in ABC's "Roseanne." In the June 2 and August 11 episodes, Roseanne and husband Dan both insisted that their children get jobs to earn money for the Nintendo game, the car, and other things they wanted to buy. In NBC's August 14 "I'll Fly Away," a schoolboy bought a car with the money he had earned by working all summer. Kevin of ABC's "Wonder Years," in the March 11 episode, was proud of how hard his father worked, while Michelle of ABC's May 12 "Full House" sold lemonade for the money to buy an ant farm. From Georgie on NBC's January 25 "Sisters," viewers heard the sound advice that "people work because they have to" and from Peggy Anne in NBC's "Cry in the Night: The Taking of Peggy Anne" July 12, they heard that "there's nothing wrong with cleaning other people's houses."

Despite these positive lessons, overall entertainment TV's messages were the wrong lessons. Good signals about work, for instance, were offset by episodes mocking it. In NBC's "Seinfeld" January 29, George boasted that he had just been fired from his job. In CBS's "Evening Shade" October 12, Taylor got the money he needed for a date from his father after Taylor had said that he could not get a job because it would cut into his free time.

A second serious problem with entertainment TV's depiction of work was that almost no one did any serious work.

A third problem was the erroneous information conveyed. NBC's "Different World" January 30, for instance, gave viewers misleading data on benchmarks for high investment returns. In the episode, Whitley, a sympathetic and competent young executive, tried to sell a painting. Stressing its potential as a good investment, she promised that it would double in value over ten years. In the real world, such a return would be acceptable, but probably not qualify as a "good investment." It would take only a 7 percent annual increase to double the value over ten years. The episode erroneously taught viewers that doubling money in ten years would be impressive.

The "Different World" February 13 episode made two false didactic points about the economy. In the first, Whitley said that companies should contribute to charity because "the private sector must give back what it has received." In fact, the private sector is constantly giving back by creating jobs, raising living standards, inventing products and processes that improve health and extend life, devising products that entertain, and so forth—in addition to vast private sector contributions to charities. Even the way Whitley's statement was phrased misled viewers because it implied that the "private sector" was some entity that "received" something for which it should be grateful. In fact, the private sector mainly gives rather than takes; it gives by being society's sole creator of wealth. By contrast, the government (the "public sector") mainly takes—by collecting taxes—which it then spends. Government does not create wealth.

The second economic mistake made by the February 13 episode was the depiction of Mr. Gains, owner of the campus restaurant The Pit. After losing his lease to a national chain, he said, "I put in the highest bid I could, but I can't compete with the big corporations." Ultimately, executives of the national chain were persuaded to help Mr. Gains by underwriting The Pit's lease. The message of this was that small businessmen could not compete with giant corporations.

The truth has been just the opposite. Across the nation, big corporations have been in trouble and under siege from small, new firms. Often, moreover, local companies outcompete national chains. The "Different World" episode would have been much more accurate, and thus useful to viewers, had it shown Mr. Gains beating the national chain and saving The Pit—by innovating, introducing new products, and improving service.

The private sector also took a hit from a pair of sympathetically portrayed characters in CBS's "Stompin' at the Savoy" April 12. Talking about capitalism, they said that it keeps working people poor. Yet as the experience of Eastern Europe and the Third World long have demonstrated, it is government-run economies that have kept people poor. Capitalism, for all of its faults, has created wealth and jobs for a greater share of people than any other economic system.

The dealmaker was the one who caught the flak in NBC's "Law & Order" May 12. McFadden, a merger and acquisitions expert, had made millions from engineering hostile takeovers of companies. In this episode he was described as having laid off some people and sold unprofitable operations after taking over a company. This prompted one character to say: "You ask me, the press is giving them all a bad rap. They are calling them sharks and barracudas. They are more like angels—less waste, more profit." A labor leader disagreed, saying that McFadden forced down wages. Phil Cerretta, a police officer, then said, "McFaddens of the world leave a lot of wreckage behind."

That was another flawed economics lesson for viewers. In fact, there would have been more wreckage without McFadden; failing companies would have continued to sink until they stopped operating altogether. Then everyone would have lost their jobs. Viewers ought to have heard Cerretta say, "Mcfaddens of the world anger a lot of people. But that's what happens when you come in and clean up someone else's mess."

Raising funds for new ventures was the theme in a couple of programs. In real life, typically, small businesses obtain their start-up money not from banks, but from personal savings, family members, and friends. But in CBS's "Hearts Are Wild" January 31, when Mickey and Sammy wanted money to open a pizza parlor, they went to Las Vegas to win it gambling. Though they lost everything at first, they eventually bought a winning keno ticket and collected the money they needed to start their restaurant. Here viewers learned that budding entrepreneurs raised capital at the Las Vegas gaming tables.

Bankruptcy was addressed April 11 by Alex, the interior designer in "Sisters." When a client refused to pay her, she said: "Bank-ruptcy. Have you heard about this latest fad? You can run your business into the ground, not pay any of your bills, and then start up again with a clean slate—legally." The truth is, of course, that bankruptcy leaves no business with a clean slate. Obligations to former creditors may be wiped clean, but the slate remains clut-tered with a dreadful credit rating which makes it difficult for a business to obtain credit at market rates or, while still in bank-ruptcy, to operate without supervision from a court.

THE ABOVE EXAMPLES of entertainment TV's depiction of eco-nomic matters in 1992 were drawn from the twelve sample weeks, one randomly chosen from each month by the Free Enterprise and Media Institute. If the examples are representative, as they probably are given the large sample, then TV's forty other weeks in the year would yield similar evidence that entertainment TV in 1992 poorly instructed viewers on how the American economy functions.

If sociologists are correct when they talk about the "drip model" and if they and other experts are correct when they say that enter-tainment educates even when the viewer knows that what is being watched is fiction, then entertainment TV in 1992 miseducated viewers. For every accurate and positive image of a kind business-man or woman, of a business producing a product, or of someone working hard, entertainment TV dripped persistently into viewers minds the lesson that businesses and businesspersons not only are evil and nasty, but that there is no connection between what they do and how the economy performs.

It would not have taken much effort to make that connection. Mrs. Pack's impassioned statement on the June 2 "Law & Order" demonstrated that neither drama nor story line need suffer by accurately depicting a business situation. Pack surely was not a sympathetic character. Yet from her, viewers heard and saw that entrepreneurs were harried, worked hard, and made sacrifices.

Neither plot nor drama would have been degraded, nor produc-tion costs increased, if the murderers on the January 29 "Night-mare Cafe" had been government officials instead of chemical company executives; if the murderer in the January 31 "In the Heat of the Night" had not been a truck repair shop owner; if the murderer in the May 13 "Quantum Leap" had not been a hotel owner; if the drug dealer in the May 31 "Quantum Leap" had not been the owner of a company; if the murderer in the November 7 "Columbo" had not been a jewelry store owner, or if the drug runner in the December 9 "Law & Order" had not been a petroleum company executive.

NOTES

1. S. Robert Lichter, Linda S. Lichter and Stanley Rothman, *Watching America, What Television Tells Us About Our Lives* (New York: Prentice Hall Press, 1991), p. 130.
2. Ibid., p. 154.
3. Ibid.
4. John Condry, *The Psychology of Television* (Hillsdale, New Jersey: Lawrence Erlbaum Associates, 1989), p. 85.
5. Althea C. Huston et al., *Big World, Small Screen*, p. 2.
6. Ibid.
7. Ibid., pp. 57–58.
8. Ibid., p. 130.
9. John Condry, *The Psychology of Television*, p. 137.
10. Althea C. Huston et al., *Big World, Small Screen*, p. 22.
11. Ibid., p. 4.
12. Ibid., pp. 6–7.
13. John Condry, *The Psychology of Television*, p. 141.
14. Althea C. Huston et al., *Big World, Small Screen*, pp 21–22.

PART V

THE YEAR'S WORST— AND BEST

CHAPTER THIRTEEN

THE WORST
OF 1992

THE MOST MISLEADING TV stories in 1992 on business and economic issues illustrated weaknesses that appeared in other stories and magnified them in ways that might alert all reporters to possible flaws in their own presentations. The Free Enterprise and Media Institute staff, reviewing all of the year's newscasts, nominated the ten most misleading news stories on business and economic issues. The institute then assembled a jury of well-known free market economists: Bruce Bartlett of the Cato Institute, Christopher Frenze of the Joint Economic Committee of Congress, Edward Hudgins of the Joint Economic Committee of Congress, Marvin Kosters of the American Enterprise Institute, and Stephen Moore of the Cato Institute.

The jury met on June 28, 1993, to view videos of the stories, analyze the stories' transcripts, and render their verdicts. Each jury member rated the stories on a scale of minus one to minus ten (with minus ten the worst) using as criteria the extent to which the stories answered the questions: (1) What solution does the story propose for economic problems? Is it government-based or market-based? (2) Does the reporter understand basic economic principles? (3) Is the reporter accurate in reporting economic statistics?

THE VERDICT

ABSOLUTE WORST:
NBC's Keith Morrison—Minus 49 Points

The TV newscast segment that most misled Americans in 1992 regarding their economy was Keith Morrison's report on NBC "Nightly News" February 7. Anchor Tom Brokaw had promised viewers that Morrison would answer the question: "How good, really, were the good old days [of the 1980s]?"

In answering Brokaw, Morrison caricatured most of TV's mistakes in reporting about America's free enterprise economy. He chose unrepresentative examples, used flawed data and invoked highly charged language.

Specifically:

1. To portray the entrepreneur of the 1980s, Morrison selected Mike Glickman. Said Morrison to viewers: "Who is Mike Glickman? He is the image of the eighties, superentrepreneur, who by the time he was twenty-five had built a huge and gaudy real estate empire. And he was the prince of laissez-faire who could do no wrong—until it all came crashing down when houses stopped selling on a dime."

To be sure, in the 1980s (as in other decades), great fortunes were made and great fortunes were lost. Morrison's use of Glickman as the paradigm of the 1980s told viewers, however, that entrepreneurs of that decade lived high and ultimately lost everything. This was absolutely untrue.

In fact, in the 1980s, record numbers of Americans became entrepreneurs and record numbers succeeded in keeping their businesses. The paradigm for the 1980s was not the fast-living Glickman, who boasted to viewers of his "brand new home. Beach house. Cars. It was the greatest." The paradigm was the African-American or Hispanic or woman entrepreneur, all of whom, in record numbers, started and continued running their own business.

2. To make his point criticizing the 1980s, Morrison used shrill language which had little basis in reality. He said: "Oh, there was a party [in the 1980s] all right. One of the biggest, most avaricious displays of ostentation in a hundred years. . . . The amazing thing is that most people are content to believe that almost everybody had a good time in the eighties. A real shot at the dream. But the fact is, they didn't. Did we wear blinders? Did we think the eighties only left behind just the homeless? The fact is that nine in ten Americans saw their lifestyle decline. Agriculture was lousy, mining in a depression, manufacturing, except for defense, in a terrible slump."

On hearing Morrison say this, juror Stephen Moore declared: "That's just plain false. The fact is that the great majority saw their lifestyles climb. Did Morrison just make up the numbers?"

Other jurors agreed that if anyone was wearing blinders, it was Morrison. Said Christopher Frenze: "The Glickman case demonstrates that the American economy is one of income mobility, not a caste system. The Glickmans can come down as well as go up. And by indirectly acknowledging mobility, Morrison really undermines the whole premise of his segment." Frenze added that "Morrison was inexcusably wrong on his numbers. The median family income went up in the eighties, as did income across the board." As to Morrison's claim that manufacturing was in a terrible slump in the eighties, Frenze said: "That's incorrect. American industry in the 1980s regained its world competitive stance. Where did Morrison get his silly statistics?"

Edward Hudgins pointed out that Morrison's segment ignored two of the most dramatic economic developments of the eighties: record job creation and rising real purchasing power. "This was inexcusable," as was the lack of any "attempt at all to show the other side," Hudgins said.

SECOND WORST:
NBC's Jeff Madrick—Minus 45 Points

Runner-up dishonors went to a September 7 NBC "Nightly News" segment in which Jeff Madrick reported that America's poor were getting poorer in the 1980s. As with Morrison, Madrick chose unrepresentative examples and used flawed data. He also interviewed biased sources without offering viewers contrary opinions.

Madrick's peg for the story was a study by what anchor Deborah Roberts called a "Washington research center." Said Madrick: "A new report from the Economic Policy Institute shows that, adjusted for inflation, 80 percent of all American workers are earning less today than they earned in 1979." Later Madrick returned to EPI statistics saying: "The new report on the working poor shows that one in five workers earned near-poverty level wages in 1973, one in four workers in 1979, and in 1991 it was almost one in three."

Juror Stephen Moore pointed out the first problem with the segment: "The Economic Policy Institute is an explicitly liberal and pro-big government organization. But Madrick did not tell the viewer this. Thus the impression was that EPI had no agenda. It does." Moore gave Madrick more demerits for his use of numbers. Explained Moore: "All the drop in income was between 1979 and 1981, during the Carter years. After that there was a steady climb until Reagan left office. The bad situation in 1991 was the result of the Bush recession."

Christopher Frenze concurred, pointing out that Madrick's analysis gave the false impression of a steady drop in income from 1973 through 1991: "The truth is, the poverty rate for low income workers fell during the 1980s. Poverty was on the decline in the 1980s. All Madrick had to do was call the Commerce Department to find out."

Madrick claimed that the allegedly low wages were a result of foreign competition and a low minimum wage. Bruce Bartlett took Madrick to task for such economic illiteracy: "This is nonsense. Every economist knows that the cause of low wages is low productivity."

Madrick then interviewed what was supposed to be a typical working-poor person. Said Madrick: "Thirty-seven-year-old Nitza Vera leads the life of the working-poor every day in New York City. Though she recently got a promotion at a local community help organization, this mother and grandmother still only takes home about $300 a week."

Jurors argued that Vera's case was not typical of working families in the 1980s since their incomes rose during the decade. This led Edward Hudgins to conclude that Madrick had missed an important angle: "Nitza Vera is one of the struggling poor of New York City. That's a valid topic. But why didn't Madrick explore some reasons why she was poor? Where's the mention of New York City's economic policies, such as job-killing high taxes, housing-killing rent control, and so forth?"

Bartlett saw another angle: "Madrick failed even to note that Vera apparently has serious social problems to grapple with, which largely explain her economic situation. Where is her husband and where are the parents of her grandchildren? Whatever the answer, it is obviously critical to any discussion of this woman's situation."

THIRD WORST:
ABC's Jack Smith—Minus 44 Points

Ranking third worst for the year was the ABC "World News Tonight" February 1 report on health care reform by Jack Smith. Anchor Carole Simpson introduced the segment by correctly going to the heart of health care problems: "Running number two to the economy in this political season is concern over spiraling health care costs. And, as ABC's Jack Smith reports, a lot of that cost has nothing to do with health care."

To illustrate the mounting administrative costs of health care, Smith took viewers to a doctor's office and explained that the doctor last year "dealt with 631 different insurance companies, with dozens of different forms and different procedures all entombed in manuals and rule books." Smith said the doctor "now spends more time on paperwork than with his patients. And of his forty-five employees, fifteen do nothing but paperwork." Smith ended his segment with a call for action, implicitly endorsing the idea that America's many insurance companies be consolidated into one health insurance provider which then would require that doctors fill out only one form. Said Smith: "So the next time you see a candidate on the stump ask him about it. If there were not just one form, but just one insurance provider, the savings would be even greater—$100 billion. Enough to make health insurance coverage affordable to everyone."

The Free Enterprise and Media Institute jury thought that the story began with the potential to inform, but then veered irresponsibly off course. Said Moore: "Smith was right in diagnosing the problem, but got the treatment all wrong. A single-payer plan—the one provider with one form—would eliminate competition. Doesn't Smith know that it's only competition that keeps down prices?" Kosters said: "Smith had no appreciation for competition. The idea also seemed to be that Americans won't mind waiting in lines endlessly, but do mind multiple insurance forms."

Hudgins also thought that "the story started out with some promise, mentioning paperwork problems faced by doctors. But then it ignored the source of most excessive paperwork—federal and state regulations—and went on to blame insurance companies." Hudgins asked: "How many of these companies simply were following government orders?" Bartlett echoed Hudgins: "My guess is that the paperwork involved with Medicare and Medicaid is a very significant share of the paperwork burden."

FOURTH WORST:
ABC's Ned Potter—Minus 43 Points

The jury chose Potter's "World News Tonight" December 15 ode to Japan's environmental industrial policy as the fourth most misleading story of the year. Potter told viewers that environmental protection would be the biggest new industry of the future. He said that while America was leading the world in environmental cleanup technology, "Japan is mounting a major offensive to be the new leaders in what they call an eco-industrial revolution."

Potter described a Japanese government plan called "Earth 21." It was designed, he said, to coordinate and direct companies to work on such projects as solar energy, wind turbines, and technology for cleaner coal and oil plants. Potter explained a Japanese project called "Genesis," saying that it "would be a worldwide network of massive solar power farms connected by cables across continents. When night falls over China, it would get its power from Africa where the sun would still be shining."

The moral of Potter's story: "[Genesis] shows how far ahead the Japanese are looking. And that's the challenge for America. With the new administration seeking an economic revival, how can it best help U.S. industry compete with Japan for the environmental marketplace?"

Bartlett found a conspicuous error in the story. Potter had said that the Japanese private sector alone spends more on research and development than the United States as a whole. "In fact," Bartlett said, "it is exactly the opposite. In 1989, U.S. private industry spent $57 billion on R&D, while Japan as a whole spent $46 billion."

Two of the jurors spotted Potter's affinity for big government liberalism. Said Frenze: "This story is really propaganda. It shows how obsessed Potter is with planning. Government has to have a plan for everything." Hudgins agreed: "So the Japanese philosopher-kings are pouring money into new technologies. There's no mention of how it is they know which technologies of the future will work and which will not. There's no mention of how risky and even foolhardy it may be for them to think that they can pick the winning technologies better than the market."

Kosters and Moore also found a common big government theme underlying the story: that government should lead the way into a wondrous, Buck Rogers-type techno-future. Both jurists mocked Potter's effusive praise of Japan's Genesis project. Kosters called it "gee-whiz technobabble." Moore said it was "high-tech nonsense." Asked Kosters: "Why couldn't Potter tell viewers that almost all

Japanese government efforts to help industry or push technology have been flops?"

At one point in the story Potter said that the smokestack scrubber industry, which was developed in America, was now dominated by Japan. To which Hudgins responded: "Sure, America might have lost the lead in smokestack scrubbers. That's not the real problem. What Potter should have noted is that because government mandates the use of certain technologies, like smokestack scrubbers, it cuts off the development of better, less costly means of doing the same job. Why didn't Potter give the audience a chance to hear from some free-market environmentalists? They would have pointed this out."

The jurors remarked that Potter did not mention how America already had tried versions of Earth 21 and Genesis; these were the synthetic fuels project, windmills, and similar efforts. On all of them, the results were disastrous. The jurors also said the story failed to examine the record of the Japanese government in subsidizing energy production. Said Kosters: "For outright economic illiteracy, Potter is amazing."

FIFTH WORST:
NBC's John Chancellor—Minus 41 Points

The July 7 John Chancellor commentary on how Reaganomics supposedly bankrupted America was judged the fifth worst story of the year. Chancellor reported on the findings of a Federal Reserve Bank of New York study that "says the [recession] has its roots in the economic policies of Ronald Reagan." Chancellor said that "federal spending on vital infrastructure, including schools and highways, declined" and that "in the year 1990, supply-side failures cut the economy's productive capacity by a full 3 percent, which caused an enormous loss of $165 billion in national income, just in that single year." Chancellor also claimed that "during the Bush administration none of the Reagan administration's mistakes have been corrected."

Chancellor's assertion that none of Reagan's policies had been reversed got the biggest response from the jurors, for it got to the heart of whether Reaganomics could be blamed for the economic woes of 1992. Hudgins said: "Reagan followed one set of policies. Those policies were fundamentally changed in Bush's 1990 budget scheme, and they were reversed by Bush's reregulation explosion. Thus it's difficult to blame economic conditions in 1992 on Reagan's policies, which were no longer in effect." Hudgins said that any loss of output was due to Bush's reregulation and higher taxes, not the supply-side policies of the Reagan administration.

Frenze agreed, pointing out that the 1990 budget deal between Bush and Congress raised taxes, significantly reversing Reagan's low-tax approach. Stephen Moore was surprised by Chancellor's comment that government spending declined during the Reagan years. Said Moore: "Spending kept going up. How could Chancellor say we didn't spend enough?" Other jurors concurred, pointing out that spending on almost all programs increased during Reagan's two terms.

Bruce Bartlett, however, moved to acquit on the grounds that Chancellor was giving a commentary, not a story. Bartlett also pointed out that, unlike Morrison and others, Chancellor was at least referring to a real study, however flawed it might have been.

SIXTH WORST:
ABC's Sylvia Chase—Minus 40 Points

This long Sylvia Chase report for ABC's "Prime Time Live" January 9 deplored the lack of tougher regulations for truck safety guards to prevent "underrides"—accidents caused when autos crash into the rear of trucks and plow under them. The results of the accidents are particularly grisly and could include decapitation. Chase spent most of the story with relatives of underride victims. She also talked to "safety experts" and said: "Experts at the National Highway Traffic Safety Administration who proposed the new safety guard have been overruled at the highest levels of government, where cost effectiveness has been put ahead of human life. Safety advocates point the finger of blame at the White House."

Jurors faulted Chase for taking statistics out of context, perhaps deliberately to alarm viewers. She said that two thousand had died in truck underride accidents in twenty years but did not tell viewers that this was a tiny fraction of the approximately 1 million traffic deaths in that same period. It seemed that Chase was more interested in finding a way to slap the trucking industry than highlighting a serious cause of accidents. Had she truly been concerned with accidents, she could have reported on a type of accident responsible for a larger share of highway deaths than the truck underrides.

What was worse, Chase failed to alert viewers to potential bias in sources. Chase, for instance, interviewed Byron Bloch, whom she identified as a "safety expert." She did not tell viewers of Bloch's close ties with trial lawyers, a group which gains enormously from taking defendants' sides in traffic accidents.

Chase used emotionally charged language, such as "cost effectiveness has been put ahead of human life." Yet cost effectiveness routinely has been put "ahead of human life." Limiting highway speed to five miles per hour, for instance, probably would save nearly fifty thousand lives per year, but Americans could ill afford such a low speed limit. It would not be cost effective. Chase also spent a great amount of time attacking the trucking industry, without giving the industry much time for rebuttal.

Said Kosters: "What really struck me about this story was the highly partisan nature in terms of the way she attacked the Republican administrations." He pointed out that Chase did not question why President Carter and a Democratic Congress had not enacted stronger regulations for trucks while they were simultaneously in power for four years.

Along this line, Bartlett wondered why Chase did not question Joan Claybrook, whom she had interviewed for the segment, more aggressively. "[Claybrook] headed the agency which oversaw truck safety regulations in the Carter administration," Bartlett said. "Pointed questions should have been asked about why she didn't fix this alleged problem when she had the power to do so."

Complaining that no deregulation expert, such as Fred Smith of the Competitive Enterprise Institute, was interviewed, Hudgins said that "much of the story hangs on an 'ABC consultant [Bloch].' He is a paid gun for the anti-auto industry folks."

SEVENTH WORST:
ABC's Paula Lyons and NBC's Garrick Utley—
Minus 39 Points

Tying for the seventh worst story of the year were Paula Lyons' ABC "Good Morning America" July 9 report about the threatened Women, Infants and Children (WIC) program which gives coupons to welfare mothers to buy produce, and Garrick Utley's NBC "Nightly News" December 13 report about Germany's apprenticeship program.

Lyons interviewed farmers and mothers who benefitted from the WIC program and WIC program administrators, one of whom said: "Everybody wins. I can't imagine who would be against such a program." Lyons agreed: "Who indeed?" To which juror Stephen Moore asked: "What about taxpayers?"

Jurors argued that if Lyons had interviewed a critic of WIC, viewers could have learned that many believe that the program has encouraged dependency. Bruce Bartlett spotted an incongruity in Lyons' numbers: that $3 million would benefit 500,000 households. "The idea that a $3 million program is going to provide all these benefits to 500,000 people is ridiculous," Bartlett said. Frenze added that the story was incomplete because it did not mention "government policies that drive up food prices, like agricultural marketing orders." Hudgins noted that this was an example of the "give us money and we'll do some good" attitude of big government proponents.

Utley's report focused on Germany's "government-industry partnership" that trained workers who did not have college educations. Declared Utley: "Skilled workers. Motivated workers. In

Germany they are not in short supply. The reason: Germany's apprentice training program, the ticket to high-paying jobs." He explained that the process began when tenth graders reported to government work information centers where they applied to work with a firm.

Utley interviewed a student in the apprentice program who said that there was no discrimination in Germany between those who went to college and those who went through the program. Then Utley said: "The program works and keeps Germany competitive in the world. Could it work in the United States?" To answer this he turned to a German vocational school director who said it would work in America, but would be expensive for both government and industry. Utley's message to viewers was: The German government works with German industry to train those who do not go to college. It works. Too bad America won't try it.

The Free Enterprise and Media Institute jury concluded that Utley understood little about either the German or American work force. Explained Moore: "In terms of work force quality, it is the Germans who should be imitating us. We have a far more productive work force than Germany." Utley's statement that apprentices in Germany made $500 to $600 a month prompted Kosters to wonder "why Utley failed to explain that this would be below poverty-level wages in America."

Bartlett, Frenze, Hudgins, and Kosters concurred that Utley owed it to viewers to explain that the German system was extremely elitist; it decided the career path of a German at age fifteen or sixteen by putting him or her on rigid job tracks. Said Hudgins: "Why didn't Utley tell viewers that one big price Germany pays for its apprenticeship system is a lack of social and economic mobility? Americans would and should never tolerate such class rigidity." Frenze and Hudgins added that Utley forgot to mention that German job creation had been much slower than America's for years and that its unemployment rate higher. Said Hudgins: "Didn't Utley see what was going on in Germany? It's in a deep and structural economic mess. Maybe, in fact, one cause is the rigidity typified by this government-industry job training thing. This is no time for Utley to hold up Germany as an example."

Ninth Worst:
ABC's Jim Hickey—Minus 37 Points

Ninth place was awarded to an ABC "World News Tonight" January 26 report by Jim Hickey about the Americans with Disabilities Act, which was about to take effect. He interviewed disabled advocate Sharon Mistler and together they reassured viewers that the law would not be too intrusive. Said Hickey: "Reasonable alterations must be made to give the disabled greater access to goods and services. Lowering drinking fountains or installing bars in hotel bathrooms. Providing menus in braille, or, for the deaf, installing strobe lights on fire alarms."

When a small business representative argued that the vagueness of the law could lead to lawsuits, Hickey said: "Disabled activists say it is not their intention to force anyone to go to court." Mistler added: "Disabled people do not want to file suits. Let's face it, all we want to do is get in the grocery store." To Hickey, "it is a matter . . . of the disabled working with the business community to come up with workable solutions, something they've been trying to do for years. Now they are backed up by the law."

Both Moore and Hudgins pointed out that Hickey and Mistler turned out to be very wrong. By mid–1993, for instance, the law already had spawned many lawsuits. According to Hudgins: "Even before the law took effect, lawyers were telling personnel managers, 'We don't know what this means. The courts will figure it out.' " Hickey could have reported this. Moore added: "The examples cited by Hickey of changes businesses would have to make were the changes that would be least onerous. He ignored the really costly changes, such as the retrofitting of buses or the mandatory hiring of an extra employee to read to each blind employee."

Hudgins found bias by omission, explaining: "The story did not mention that a major concern during the ADA debate was that there was no attempt at all to allow the most cost-effective means of helping the handicapped to be used. For example, chauffeur-driven vans, in many cases, would cost a fraction of the ADA mandate to re-equip every bus in a city with wheelchair lifts, and would provide better service. Hickey never mentioned this, nor did he say anything about the huge, unnecessary cost of the ADA."

TENTH WORST:
CBS's Bob Schieffer—Minus 33 Points

Just slipping into the Irresponsible Ten was the CBS "Evening News" January 18 story by Bob Schieffer about "considering a national industrial policy." According to Schieffer, "federal seed money . . . could help develop high risk, new technologies." He argued that "government has worked with businesses for decades: mobilizing to fight World War II, building the first atomic bomb, landing on the moon, and Star Wars." Almost all of Schieffer's Talking Heads supported the idea of a government industrial policy. For example, Jeff Faux of the Economic Policy Institute: "The question is which industries are so important. That's what the Europeans and Japanese are arguing about. That's what we ought to start arguing about."

At one point Schieffer said, "[A]irplane builders see the efforts of Taiwan to buy the troubled McDonnell Douglas Company as a serious threat to American dominance in that field." This caught the attention of Bruce Bartlett: "My recollection is that the Taiwan government was not the buyer, but a private firm based in Taiwan. If this were the case, the distinction should have been made. Moreover, Shieffer himself admits that McDonnell Douglas was 'troubled.' If so, how could Taiwan threaten U.S. dominance of the field if the alternative was that McDonnell Douglas would go bankrupt?"

All the historical examples cited by Schieffer in favor of industrial policy were actually extremely costly and inefficient, justified only because of pressing national security concerns. In peacetime, with the hot and cold wars over, Schieffer's examples of the atomic bomb or moon program had no relevance. Another problem with the segment, as Hudgins noted, was that it "completely ignored the cause of industry's problems: government regulation and taxes." He said that Schieffer "treats business problems as either some kind of act of nature that can only be changed by government or the result of lack of government intervention."

Other jurors pointed out that the story ignored the pathetic record of the American government in picking winners and losers. "Where was the mention of synthetic fuels? What about the SST airplane?" Hudgins asked. Frenze saw the story as another example of the liberal reflex—"having a plan" rather than letting the market, with the intelligent choices of millions, decide which industries to support. Bartlett argued that the private sector plans for the future and adjusts its plans with new information. "Government, on the other hand, tends to stick with its plan no matter what," he added.

Dishonorable Mention

Some stories that did not quite make the ten most misleading of the year merit mention:

☒ CBS's Robert Krulwich, in his "This Morning" June 23 interview with Harry Snyder of *Consumer Reports*. Krulwich endorsed the idea that having single-payer health care would save $70 billion in administrative costs. He did not note that in no area has government been more efficient than the private sector. Why, therefore, did Krulwich assume that government would be more efficient than health insurance companies? In the segment, moreover, Krulwich ignored the problems that other nations have had with socialized, or quasi-socialized, health care.

☒ ABC's Bettina Gregory, in her "Good Morning America" September 9 report about product liability reform. Aside from interviewing George Bush, Gregory gave viewers only reform opponents, such as "consumer advocate" Joan Claybrook, an accident victim, and two Democratic senators. To give equal credibility to both sides, Gregory should have interviewed an expert favoring product liability reform who was not a Bush administration official. And when Gregory interviewed victims, she gave viewers only those on one side of the issue. An interview with a small businessperson who had been forced out of business because of a frivolous lawsuit would have helped balance her story.

☒ CNN's Anne McDermott, in her "World News" September 5 report about teacher strikes in California. She interviewed several teachers who declared that higher taxes to fund more spending on education was the only solution to California's education problems. McDermott never explored possible solutions, such as school choice, that did not require more spending. Nor did McDermott tell viewers that many states that spend relatively little on education do better than most of the states that spend much more.

☒ Reports questioning the freshness of fish by ABC's Paula Lyons on "Good Morning America" January 16, NBC's Lea Thompson on "Today" January 16, CBS's Hattie Kauffman on "This Morning" January 21, and CNN's Brian Barger on "World News" August 12. Each reporter violated journalism's *habeas corpus* dictum: to show evidence of a problem before reporters proclaim it a problem. None of the reporters could point to anyone who had become ill from eating fish.

☒ ABC's "Nightline" National Town Meeting on health care reform February 6. The program's long, 2½ hour format allowed for a large panel of experts and an audience. Yet there was no time, apparently, to give viewers a peek at free market approaches to health care reform. Rather, the panel was dominated by those seeking government intervention in health care. When a small businessman in the audience, two hours into the show, brought up such reforms as medical savings accounts, the panel ignored his point.

☒ ABC's Don Kladstrup in the "Nightline" June 1 report about the environmental problems of Madagascar. "Nightline" gave Kladstrup the entire show. His theme was that Madagascar's population growth was threatening the country's unique environment. Kladstrup and those he interviewed depicted the problem as one of helpless peasants having no choice but to harm the environment in order to survive. Kladstrup failed to interview a free market environmentalist who could have told viewers that free market government policies could see Madagascar's poor prosper and simultaneously preserve the island's environment.

CHAPTER FOURTEEN

THE BEST OF 1992

IT WAS NOT all bad on TV in 1992. The Free Enterprise and Media Institute's jury of economists found ten stories that merited commendation as the year's most balanced and informative on how the American economic system functioned. The criteria for judging these stories were the same as for the ten misleading stories; how, that is, the stories answered these questions: (1) What solution does the story propose for economic problems? Is it government-based or market-based? (2) Does the reporter understand basic economic principles? (3) Is the reporter accurate in reporting economic statistics?

THE VERDICT

ABSOLUTE BEST:
ABC'S John Stossel—49 Points

The best economics and business story of the year, according to the jury, was the ABC "20/20" January 24 report by John Stossel about workplace regulations. Stossel looked at proposed regulations that would prevent companies from firing or deciding not to hire those who were smokers, drinkers, and others engaging in activities considered unhealthy, even when such activities were indulged on the employees' own time. Among those interviewed by Stossel were ex-employees who complained of being fired unjustly and one boss who claimed that the firings were just.

As Stossel developed the story, its theme was that employers needed flexibility in hiring and firing. Stossel made three arguments for this: (1) "The competition of the market will prevent abuses. Employers with restrictive policies will have to pay more to hire their ideal worker. That will create opportunities for smokers and others." (2) "How can American companies compete if every time they make a personnel decision, they have to consult a labor lawyer to wade through the laws?" (3) "Smoking costs money. So who should pay? If the employer must treat everyone the same, you're really saying nonsmokers must subsidize smokers. Is that fair?"

The jurors applauded Stossel for his grasp of free market principles and, specifically, for recognizing that the market has built-in remedies against discrimination. They also praised Stossel for understanding that even compassionate-sounding regulations, such as those protecting worker privacy at home, have costs and could make American companies less competitive.

At one point Stossel pointed out that privacy-rights arguments for such regulations were not applicable because the Constitution protects citizens from government, not companies. "There's a difference because we have just one government. We must obey its laws. With employers we have a choice. We could quit." Juror Stephen Moore said that this point was "excellent in that it illustrates that employment is a voluntary association."

SECOND BEST:
NBC's John Gibson—48 Points

The year's second most successful story in teaching viewers about America's economy was the NBC "Nightly News" September 11 report by John Gibson on how California's generous workers' compensation system was forcing businesses to flee the state. Gibson interviewed four small business owners, all of whom said that the costs of the system were driving them out of business.

Gibson told viewers: "California is one of only six states that pays stress claims and in ten years those claims, many fraudulent, have risen 700 percent. Fraud is fueled by constant advertising on television and radio by lawyers and doctors. Under the California system, doctors and lawyers are paid automatically even if the worker's claim is ultimately denied." Then Gibson gave viewers useful insight into how a free market worked. He said: "Businesses big and small do have options: they can go to Arizona, Nevada, or Mexico. Until workers' compensation is fixed, every day somebody's employer is giving up and leaving California."

The jurors praised the story for showing that regulations imposed costs and that this regulation was particularly expensive. Said Moore: "The story did a good job of showing how taxes and government regulations cost jobs and how businesspeople vote with their feet." Bruce Bartlett added that Gibson hit the economically correct note on why businesses were leaving. "That businesses were fleeing California could have easily been misportrayed as greedy businessmen trying to find cheaper labor to exploit," said Bartlett. "Instead, Gibson showed that it was regulations driving them and jobs out of the state."

One of the businessmen whom Gibson interviewed was an African-American restaurateur in South-Central Los Angeles. He told viewers: "I can survive riots. I can survive crime. I can survive a lot of things. But I cannot survive workers' compensation." Juror Moore was particularly impressed that Gibson found "a black spokesman for the free market," considering how the vast numbers of new minority-owned businesses are routinely ignored by TV.

THIRD BEST:
ABC's John Stossel—46 Points

Stossel also grabbed third place honors with his ABC "20/20" October 16 story about the high costs of Social Security and other entitlements. The jurors praised Stossel's report for telling viewers things about such programs that they might not have known: (1)

That $70 billion in Social Security and Medicare benefits went to households with incomes higher than $50,000 a year; (2) That entitlements made up almost half of all government spending; (3) That seniors were getting back all their lifetime contributions to Social Security, plus interest, in three years; (4) That the retirement age for seniors had remained the same since the program started, even though life-expectancy had increased dramatically; and (5) That the Social Security Trust Fund was empty except for IOUs, the government having borrowed the Social Security money to finance general spending programs.

Stossel spent considerable time interviewing seniors about entitlement reform. He was able to illustrate that most seniors did not know what a windfall Social Security was for them, and that, when they found out, most were willing to consider cuts. He also outlined ideas for changes, such as Medicare reform, means-testing, or delaying the retirement age.

The jurors were pleased, as Moore said, because "Stossel's story focused on the point that the federal debt problem is one of overspending, not that the government gets too little in taxes." One place where Stossel was wrong, according to Moore, was his statement that "only entitlements are big enough to make a difference" in cutting the deficit. Explained Moore: "That's not true. We can cut other programs and we can balance the budget without touching Social Security."

FOURTH BEST:
ABC's James Walker—41 Points

The fourth best story was the report by James Walker on ABC's "World News Tonight" January 15 about how unnecessary medical waste regulations were driving up health care costs.

Walker began by recalling the summer of 1988, when medical waste had washed ashore in New Jersey causing public panic. This panic, Walker reported, led to a stringent EPA pilot regulation program on medical waste disposal in New York and New Jersey.

Said Walker: "As a result, hospital disposal costs shot up as much as 700 percent ... The question now is, should all states be required to adopt these strict and costly procedures? Scientists say no, that the new regulations were an overreaction."

Walker interviewed a microbiologist who said that household waste was 100 percent more contaminated than most hospital waste and that "the Environmental Protection Agency now acknowledges it was pressured by the public's worry about AIDS and its belief that all medical waste was infectious to enact rules based more on fear than fact." Walker observed that "with scientists maintaining that only 6 percent of hospital waste requires special handling and with health care dollars short, the question is: Should limited resources be spent to appease popular misconceptions?"

Jurors Christopher Frenze and Stephen Moore both noted that the story gave insight into how regulations often rest on political passions rather than scientific data. Moore said that Walker did a good job of "showing the costs of regulation and how this one thing increases medical costs."

FIFTH BEST:
ABC's Bob Jamieson—37 Points

Rounding out the top five is Bob Jamieson's "World News Tonight" December 14 report about a Bill Clinton proposal for an investment tax credit. Jamieson visited Cooper Industries, which made spark plugs and oil well valves, to see how the credit would affect it. Jamieson explained that Clinton's plan only allowed credit for investment above the previous year's level. This aspect of the Clinton plan caused a problem, said Jamieson, because "many companies like Cooper have invested year after year to improve their factories without any special tax credit. . . . They worry the greatest benefit would go to companies which only begin investing now."

Jamieson also illustrated the proposed plan's weakness in allowing the credit only for American-made equipment. Cooper had bought a machine that increased enormously the speed at which valves were produced. Said Jamieson: "The problem is the machine was made in Italy. No comparable machine was made in America. Clinton's plan would not give Cooper a tax break for buying the Italian machine because it is targeted to create American jobs in American factories."

Jurors agreed that the story was, as Marvin Kosters said, "really quite well done." According to Moore the story correctly emphasized the restrictiveness of Clinton's version of the credit: "The story shows the stupidity of an investment tax credit for only American purchases. The story was informative about how a credit would work."

SIXTH BEST:
CNN's Jamie McIntyre—36 Points

The sixth best story of the year was the CNN "World News" April 14 report by Jamie McIntyre about a free market health care reform proposal called "medical savings accounts." McIntyre introduced viewers to Pat Roony, an insurance company CEO who had come to Washington to lobby for the reform. McIntyre explained that with the reform, employers would buy less insurance than previously for their employees and the deductible would be increased. The money employers saved would go into a special account for health care expenses that, if unused, would roll over into an Individual Retirement Account for the employee.

"The idea is to get people to shop for minor medical services the way they shop for groceries," McIntyre said. "Imagine if employers paid 80 percent of the grocery bill. How many consumers would bother to check prices and compare before buying? The problem, argue critics of today's system, is that too many health care purchases are made with other peoples' money."

McIntyre then interviewed two critics of the Roony reform who said that it would discourage people from seeing a doctor when they were sick and probably not save as much as Roony claimed.

Noting that Roony had convinced several congressmen to take up his cause, McIntyre ended by commenting: "But even if a Medical IRA law were to pass Congress, employers would still have to be convinced any savings should go to their workers."

Jurors agreed that McIntyre had done a good job of outlining the rationale of medical savings accounts. They said that he made a valuable observation of the market by comparing health care to grocery shopping. This, jurors said, showed that any health care reform needs to make health care more like a free market. There was disagreement, however, over McIntyre's final statement. While Moore said it was legitimate to suggest that employers might not want to give up health care savings to employees, Kosters thought McIntyre had exaggerated the danger.

SEVENTH BEST:
ABC's Steve Shepard—31 Points

Voted seventh best was the Steve Shepard story on ABC's "World News Tonight" January 26 about the luxury tax's disastrous effects on the American boating industry. Shepard reminded viewers that Congress had passed a 10 percent luxury tax on yachts in 1990. The result, reported Shepard, was that "over the last year, the boating industry has gone into a tailspin. Builders have gone broke, yards have closed, and boating industry workers have been laid off. Boat dealers say the luxury tax has been the main culprit."

Shepard interviewed Bush White House chief of staff Samuel Skinner, who told viewers that the tax had actually lost revenue for the government by forcing many taxpaying boatmakers and boat repairmen out of work. The jurors liked this last point, saying that Shepard had demonstrated to viewers that taxes influenced behavior in ways that Congress usually did not foresee. Still, Hudgins said: "Shepard should have interviewed a defender of the tax, if for no other reason than to see what he would say about a tax that has had such a destructive effect."

EIGHTH BEST:
CNN's Ed Garsten—29 Points

This went to the CNN "World News" March 8 story by Ed Garsten about a proposed regulation on replacement parts for autos and other products. Garsten explained that the regulation would require consumers to buy replacement parts only from the original manufacturer for up to ten years after the original purchase. In an interview, a mechanic told viewers that the regulation would almost quadruple the cost of a transmission part. Garsten also interviewed several warehouse managers who said the bill would throw them and their employees out of work.

While many of the jurors said Garsten was a bit garbled in delivering the story's message, they agreed that he showed viewers that regulations could destroy industries. Said Moore: "This story gives viewers an example of how regulations are often anticonsumer."

NINTH BEST:
ABC's Stephen Aug and NBC's John Chancellor—21 Points

Two stories tied for ninth best of the year. Jurors selected an ABC "World News Tonight" January 29 report by Stephen Aug on George Bush's proposed tax credit for first time home buyers and a NBC "Nightly News" March 25 commentary by John Chancellor about how bloated entitlements threatened America's financial future.

Aug interviewed two young couples who said that the tax credit might well prompt them to buy a house, and two home builders who said that the credit would help their industry create jobs. Said Aug: "Other businesses could benefit as well, like appliance makers, furniture producers, moving companies, mortgage bankers, real estate lawyers."

Jurors gave Aug points for acknowledging that taxes influenced behavior. They had trouble, however, with other aspects of the story. Moore called it an "oversell." He said: "The story makes home-buying seem like the silver bullet for the economy, when it is not." Frenze said the bill was "a bad idea to start with and Aug thus was misleading viewers with his rosy view of the bill."

Chancellor began his commentary by telling viewers that Warren Rudman of New Hampshire was not going to run for reelection to the U.S. Senate because of his frustration that government was not "functioning." Said Chancellor: "What's wrong in his view is the incredible growth in entitlement programs like Social Security, Medicare, federal and veterans pensions—programs that will eat up the whole federal budget and make the United States a penniless Third World borrower in just a few years, unless they're brought under check."

Chancellor's commentary triggered disagreement among the jurors. Moore thought Chancellor served viewers well by telling them that entitlements were out of control and driving up the federal deficit. Frenze nodded agreement, pointing out that most of the massive increase in government spending over the past two decades had come from entitlement spending. Said Frenze: "It was good that Chancellor stressed entitlement increases."

Other jurors, however, were not so pleased with Chancellor. Kosters said there was "very little useful information about the problem given." And Bartlett objected to Chancellor's shrill language about America becoming a "penniless Third World borrower in just a few years."

THE BEST OF THE REST

Some stories that did not make the cut for the ten most informative reports, but still gave viewers valuable insights into free enterprise, were:

☒ An ABC "20/20" January 3 report by John Stossel on workers' compensation fraud in California. Like Gibson, Stossel told viewers how high rates for workers' compensation insurance were driving businesses and jobs out of the state. Stossel pointed out that the cost was not merely reflected in higher prices, but that "we also pay more taxes for this. . . . You want to be generous when people are really hurt. But the more generous you are, the less incentive there is to come back to work."

☒ A Charles Gibson interview on ABC "Good Morning America" May 12. Gibson visited Portland, Maine, where the hot debate was about developing the waterfront. One guest wanted to restrict waterfront business activity. Gibson asked: "Why shouldn't the market determine what's on the waterfront?"

☒ The ABC "Good Morning America" June 2 story by Michael Guillen about scientific disagreement over global warming. His report was one of the rare instances in 1992 in which doubts were raised about the alleged dreadful condition of the planet. In this story, Guillen told viewers that some scientists thought that burning the rain forests might not be so bad because it could slow global warming by creating a cloud cover.

☒ The CBS "60 Minutes" June 28 report by Mike Wallace about the "Mississippi Christmas Tree," a scam involving federal farm subsidies. Wallace interviewed economist and congressman Richard Armey, who told viewers that most agriculture subsidies went to the wealthy, that the subsidy program was easily abused, and that farm subsidies in general hurt the economy.

☒ The CBS "60 Minutes" July 5 report by Steve Kroft about the Rural Electrification Administration. Said Kroft: "Once a government project gets started, it is nearly impossible to shut it down." He pointed out that almost all rural areas now had electricity and that the program was kept alive as "welfare for the wealthy."

☒ The CBS "This Morning" August 14 interview of author Martin Gross by Harry Smith. They talked about maddening examples of government waste detailed in Gross's book, *The Government Racket: Washington Waste From A to Z.* Smith endorsed the findings in Gross's book: "If you want to see some numbers that will really knock your socks off, this is the book where they are all located."

TV JUST DOESN'T GET IT—AND WHAT IT AND VIEWERS CAN DO ABOUT IT

THE FREE ENTERPRISE and Media Institute's analysis of 1992 network television newscasts and prime time entertainment leads to one conclusion: Network TV has a problem when it covers the American economy. It just doesn't get it. And, as a result, it distorts the portrayal of the economy.

Morning after morning, night after night, and one newsmagazine segment after another, viewers of network TV saw and heard a distorted picture of how their economy functioned and those who made it function. The American economy, they learned, was a tale of catastrophes, bankruptcies, fraud, and ineptness, which was dominated by white businessmen (and a few businesswomen) who were criminals and con men and by consumers who were stupid, gullible, and powerless. The tale was a litany of problems for which, inevitably, government was the preferred solution.

This, in a nutshell, is what American viewers saw and heard on TV in 1992. It is no wonder that Americans understand so little about their economy. The economic and business tale told by TV bore little resemblance to the real story of the American economy and business. It bore no more resemblance to reality than did TV's depiction of the tarantula.

That is the bad news.

The good news is that there is little evidence that network TV executives intentionally distorted economic and business coverage. Indeed, polls have found the vast majority of TV executives strongly supporting capitalism and free enterprise. If this is so, then TV's distorted and unbalanced depiction of the American economy and business probably results from unfamiliarity, ignorance, inattention, and even some sloppiness.

If so, then the further good news is that the networks can do something about their problem. They can improve economic and business coverage. Indeed, TV reporters in 1992 demonstrated that when they personally knew something about an economic topic, they tended to get it right. This was the case with two major stories: silicone breast implants and taxes. On both topics, TV reporting did not reflexively call for government action and regulation. On the contrary, most of the reporting was unfriendly to taxes and unfriendly to tougher government regulations of implants, dealing skeptically with claims that government action was necessary. On these issues, the reporters sought proof from those calling for higher taxes or a government ban on breast implants.

What prompted reporters to get it right on taxes and implants? Probably that reporters had real world, rather than hypothetical, experience with both issues. Since journalists paid taxes, they probably knew that the level and kind of taxes affected their spending and saving behavior. As for breast implants, many reporters probably knew women who had implants or knew and agreed with feminists who argued that women had a right to control what happened to their bodies.

That TV reporters can get it right on taxes and breast implants raises the intriguing possibility that they can get it right on other issues relating to economics, business, and government regulation of the marketplace. And they can do so without dramatically and expensively revamping the newsroom.

First, however, TV must recognize that it has a problem—just as for a long time it had a problem covering African-Americans, women, and gays. In essence, network producers, writers, and reporters need to stand up and declare: "I'm a network journalist. I've got a problem with economic issues. I want to solve the problem."

Network TV then can attack its problem by asking itself—and answering—sixteen questions involving its coverage of the American economic system.

QUESTION ONE—
Am I Being Accurate?

This question would not have to be asked had TV reporting in 1992 always had its facts right. But it didn't; it made errors that easily could have been checked. Surely TV should be able to verify its facts as rigorously as do magazines with their crews of persistent, if ornery, Fact Checkers. If the press of meeting broadcast deadlines prevents adequate fact-checking, then facts should be reviewed after the broadcast so as not to repeat the mistakes.

Even more distressing than factual inaccuracy was the way newscasts used controversial studies without alerting viewers to the controversy and without giving the other side of the controversy a chance to explain its views. This happened repeatedly when TV covered capital gains taxes, distribution of the income tax burden, alleged dangers of foreign investment in America, and the assertion that the economy had been creating mainly low-paid, low-skilled jobs.

QUESTION TWO—
Am I Defining Economic Terms?

This is another question that no one should need to ask. The journalist's primary responsibility may well be to make the complicated world comprehensible to readers and viewers. This is what transforms the journalist into a medium through which complex and vast amounts of data are gathered, analyzed, and then organized into a form understandable to laymen and women.

When it has come to economic and business stories, however, TV reporters have often failed the viewer by not defining terms. While there was considerable reporting on the capital gains tax in 1992, for instance, reporters rarely told their audience what a capital gain was. Reporters also blamed junk bonds for a host of problems, from the savings and loan crisis to the collapse of companies. Yet reporters never explained what a "junk bond" was.

And while viewers heard much during the year about infrastructure, reporters defined the term solely as public projects like roads and bridges. Reporters never told viewers that infrastructure also was private—like telecommunications, shopping malls, office complexes, express mail, rail, air, and truck distribution networks, and so forth—and that such infrastructure not only had become as important to the modern economy as government-paid infrastructure but that the private infrastructure had been modernized and expanded ambitiously in the 1980s.

QUESTION THREE—
Am I Asking "Why" and "How?"

This is still another question that should not be on the list. After all, every journalism student in his or her first day of class is told that the core of a good story is what teachers for generations have called the five W's and one H—Who, What, When, Where, Why, and

How. On the first four W's, TV economic and business reporting did fairly well in 1992; on Why and How it often failed.

Example: When NBC's Mike Jensen reported a credit crunch faced by small businesses, he omitted the Why and thus failed to inform viewers that the main reason for tight credit was the zealous enforcement of federal regulations in the wake of the savings and loan problems. Such enforcement had made banks extremely shy of lending to any but the most solid borrowers.

Example: CBS's Ray Brady and reporters on other networks throughout the year repeatedly told viewers that the economic recovery was creating few new jobs. But no reporter asked Why? Had they done so, they probably would have interviewed economists who could have suggested that the higher federal taxes and increased regulation imposed after 1990 had discouraged businesses from expanding payrolls—just as taxes and regulations had curtailed West European job growth for almost a decade.

Example: CNN's Anne McDermott and other reporters covering education stories typically called for more government outlays to solve education problems. No reporter asked How increased spending would help. Had reporters done so, they would have discovered little correlation between levels of education spending and performance. Asking the "How" could have led reporters to tell viewers about the states, like North Dakota and Utah, that spend relatively little on education per pupil yet consistently rack up the nation's best school test scores.

Obviously, telling the viewer why and how an event occurred adds enormous value to a story. Just as important, it becomes a self-audit mechanism for the reporter. Seeking answers to Why and How forces a reporter to test the implicit premises and hypotheses on which the story rests. From this, the reporter might discover that some facts are false, that some facts contradict each other, that the marshalled evidence no longer supports the story's conclusion, or that a dimension of the story has been overlooked.

QUESTION FOUR—
Am I Putting Statistics into Perspective?

Network newscasts were larded with statistics. Yet most conveyed
limited meaning and could have misinformed and even panicked
viewers because the statistics stood in isolation. Reporters typically
made no attempt to give the statistics context and place them in
perspective.

Example: CNN's David French reported that fast food restaurants were the most dangerous workplaces for teens; some 139
had died at such establishments in 1990, he said. What was the
viewer to make of such a statistic? Should parents forbid their
children to work in fast food restaurants? Such a question would
not arise had French added perspective by saying: "Very few teens
die in the workplace. Of those who do, more die while working at
fast food restaurants than anywhere else. Of course, this simply
may be because more teens work at fast food restaurants than
anywhere else."

Example: ABC's Sylvia Chase breathlessly reported that two
thousand Americans had been killed over twenty years when their
cars had plowed under the backs of trucks in what have become
known as "underride" accidents. This was another alarming statistic and could be used to justify tough government regulations
to prevent underrides. Chase's use of gruesome visuals and interviews probably increased viewer alarm even more. What she
did not use was perspective. For one thing, Chase did not tell
viewers whether underrides were a serious cause of highway
deaths or whether the numbers of underrides were growing. For
another, she did not explain that in that twenty-year period highway accidents of all kinds took more than 1 million lives. Had
Chase done so, viewers might have concluded that though underrides were a dreadful way to die, they comprised just two-tenths
of 1 percent of highway fatalities and thus did not warrant new
regulations.

Example: Almost daily, network news reported economic indicators released by government agencies or private organizations which, in the aggregate, painted a picture of the economy. The trouble was that viewers never heard the statistics summed up nor saw them pulled together in a composite economic picture. Reporters could have done so, perhaps once a month, and also could have attempted to explain why some economic statistics contradicted others.

QUESTION FIVE—
Am I Sufficiently Inquisitive and Skeptical?

Hollywood accurately portrays journalists as tenaciously (if not annoyingly) inquisitive and skeptical, traits that ferret out information from elusive sources. Curiously, though, these traits were not evident in the stories on economics and business in 1992. Only rarely did reporters push and probe an assertion or grill a Talking Head expert. The result of such low voltage inquisitiveness was that questionable and false statements and invalid interpretations were presented to viewers as unchallenged fact.

Example: In covering the bill to reregulate cable TV, reporters unquestioningly accepted assertions by bill advocates that cable deregulation in the mid–1980s had led to unreasonably high rates. At the same time, reporters noted that the number of cable subscribers had soared since deregulation. Simple inquisitiveness should have nudged reporters to ask an expert: "Doesn't the increased number of subscribers refute the assertion that rates are too high? Why would so many new households subscribe if rates are unreasonable?"

Example: In the many instances when government regulations were prescribed to solve problems, reporters rarely questioned whether the regulations would work. Yet even mild doses of journalistic inquisitiveness on how existing regulations had fared and skepticism about their efficacy would have prompted reporters to tell viewers that regulations often failed to achieve their intended results and almost always imposed an unanticipated price.

The most serious suspension of journalistic curiosity was in their reporting of Rio's international environment conference. Despite vast coverage, little attempt was made to introduce to viewers new or different perspectives of the issue. Nor did anyone attempt to inform viewers that scientists were deeply divided over the extent to which the world's ecology was threatened. Instead, with no probing and no apparent skepticism, network reporters accepted the dire assessments and draconian prescriptions offered by environmental extremists. Elementary inquisitiveness should have prompted reporters to ask whether nonconventional approaches could save the environment and whether, in fact, huge Rio-like global conferences ever had accomplished anything.

QUESTION SIX—
Am I Giving Viewers Balance?

Balance, of course, is the hallmark of good journalism. While exact balance may be impossible, so many 1992 economic and business stories were seriously imbalanced that it raises the question of whether reporters even sought balance. On as straightforward a matter as the Talking Head count, for instance, reporters presented to viewers far fewer free enterprise advocates or economists than they did champions of state intervention in the economy. From such a skewed lineup, viewers would probably have concluded that market solutions to problems had few supporters (outside the Bush administration and Republican party) while government solutions were generally accepted.

The year's most glaring imbalance was the reporting from the Rio conference. In the session's first week, of the thirty persons interviewed by the networks who were not government officials, only two suggested free market means for addressing environmental issues; the other twenty-eight were all environmental extremists and supporters of extensive government controls.

The same ratio seemed to hold for the rest of the year's environment coverage. On TV, scientists and other experts who strongly advocated only a government solution to environmental problems were rarely balanced by scientists and experts suggesting other answers—or raising doubts about the seriousness of the alleged environmental problem. With the exception of one report on tradeable "rights to pollute," the networks carried no story that even hinted at how nongovernment forces of the marketplace could be mobilized, in some fashion, to protect the environment.

Ditto for regulatory matters in general. Though at times described as bothersome, costly, and even inefficient, regulations were accepted by reporters as prescriptions for society's difficulties. Network reporting almost never balanced that by stating, or even implying, that nonregulatory actions merited a try. On health care, meanwhile, the networks painted an overall picture of crisis; viewers could never have learned about the American health care system's enormous strengths or about problems with government health plans.

QUESTION SEVEN—
Am I Avoiding False Dichotomies and False Synonyms?

Balance is not achieved if reporters offer viewers a choice of alternatives that, in fact, is no choice. This happened in 1992 when reporters used false dichotomies, portraying as opposites or alternatives matters that were not.

Example: CBS's Bob Schieffer reported that "President [Bush] seems to favor new emphasis on old programs that favor tax breaks to help inner-city poor to own their own homes and open up businesses. Others in Washington want more emphasis on putting people back to work." Schieffer's dichotomy was "tax breaks" versus "putting people back to work." That was a false dichotomy. Not only are "tax breaks" and "putting people back to work" not opposites, many economists argue that lowering taxes puts people back to work.

Example: NBC's Bryant Gumbel, questioning a "Today" guest about the Clinton economic summit, asked: "What is your best guess on Clinton's top priority: cutting the deficit or creating jobs?" Gumbel's dichotomy was "cutting the deficit" versus "creating jobs." That was false. If the deficit were cut by trimming government spending and reducing government share of gross domestic product, the economy would have more resources with which to create jobs.

Example: The many reports on the environment that framed the issue by pitting business against the environment. The two were not in contradiction. Reporters could have cited examples of how free market approaches, such as trading pollution limits or creating a property right in a resource, could make it profitable for businesses to protect the environment.

As misleading to the viewers as false dichotomies were false synonyms. Among the most frequent were the words "wealthy" and "business," which network reporters generally treated synonymously. A typical newscast phrase was "a tax break that benefits the rich and business." While some businessmen and women indeed are rich, the vast majority are not. They run the small businesses which, though they are the economy's most dynamic component, were widely ignored by TV reporters. A tax measure good for the wealthy, therefore, was not necessarily good for small business.

QUESTION EIGHT— Am I Tilting Credibility?

A report ostensibly balanced actually becomes slanted if one side of an argument is presented in ways making it more credible than the other. Genuine balance, for instance, pits a Republican against a Democrat, a corporate executive against a union official, or a liberal against a conservative. Each side's credibility is about equal since the viewer probably expects each to advance a partisan, ideological, or biased position. Here one assumed bias would balance the other.

But balance is not achieved when a corporate executive is pitted against a "consumer advocate" or when a government official is pitted against an "environmental activist." In these cases, viewers are likely to see the "expert" and "activist" as unbiased and without a self-serving agenda. By contrast, the executive and official are likely to be seen as advocates for their firm or industry or for their administration. "Consumer advocates," "activists," academics, and other ostensibly public-interest sources simply carry more credibility than government, business, and political officials. Tilting credibility to one side in a story destroys balance.

Network reporting in 1992 at times tilted credibility sharply. In stories on the Rio environmental meeting, for example, reporters pitted Bush administration official William Reilly against "environmental activists." Viewers were much more likely to trust and believe the activists than they were Reilly. It would have been much fairer to pair free market environmentalists against environmentalists who insisted on tough government action and big government programs.

Credibility was also tilted when reporters failed to identify the affiliations and hence potential biases of the experts whom they interviewed. When ABC's Sylvia Chase and other reporters covered alleged auto safety defects, they seldom interviewed neutral engineers. Instead they went to self-proclaimed "safety experts" like Byron Bloch with his close ties to groups such as trial lawyers that had much to gain from undermining auto industry credibility. Since reporters did not mention those ties, what viewers saw was a supposedly unbiased expert paired against a self-serving auto company official.

ABC's Bettina Gregory, CBS's Hattie Kauffman, and other reporters in their stories about efforts to change product liability laws tilted credibility by introducing victims on only one side of the argument. Watching victims, understandably, heightens emotions and intensifies feelings about an issue. Instead of balancing one set of victims with another, in the product liability stories the reporters showed viewers only those victims who opposed changing the law. These victims naturally defended the existing liability laws by saying that they gave victims of flawed products the ability to collect appropriate damages for their suffering. The proposed law, they argued, would deny victims the awards they deserved. What viewers did not see or hear were the victims who favored changes in the laws; they could have explained how frivolous law suits and astronomical damages awarded by courts and juries were forcing businesses to shut, destroying jobs and keeping products and services off the market.

QUESTION NINE—
Am I Interviewing Enough Economists and Businessmen?

Photos of economists and business executives should start appearing on the milk cartons in TV network cafeterias because these people are missing when it comes to newscasts. In all the coverage of the federal budget, the viewer saw scarcely any economist. Nor were they seen in stories about the product liability bill, mandated child care, mandated family leave, Bush's proposed tax cuts, and the Americans with Disabilities Act.

Though economists probably would have disagreed on these and other issues, the viewer would at least have benefitted from witnessing the disagreement. If nothing else, it could have made the viewer suspicious of network newscasts' simplistic answers to issues. Beyond that, viewers could have learned some basic facts and principles about their economy.

QUESTION TEN—
Am I Interviewing Enough African-Americans,
Hispanics, and Women?

The honest answer would have been "no" from just about every network and reporter in 1992. In the year's economics and business stories, African-Americans, Hispanics, and women were even less visible than economists—unless they headed activist groups or were government officials. A rare exception was Stephen Aug's May 7 comment about the growth of the largest black-owned businesses. From TV's coverage, viewers could conclude that African-Americans, Hispanics, and women played no role in the economy. This was untrue. Their entrepreneurial activity had been booming and the number of African-American, Hispanic, and women's businesses had grown faster in the 1980s than that of any other group.

What viewers did see of African-Americans and Hispanics were representatives seeking expanded welfare and other government programs. This probably reinforced the false stereotype that African-Americans and Hispanics economically were failures.

QUESTION ELEVEN—
Am I Observing the *Habeas Corpus* Standard?

Journalism needs an explicit *habeas corpus* standard. This Latin term, meaning "having the body," refers to a core imperative of Anglo-American legal tradition: the state cannot prosecute a crime unless the body, which is evidence of the crime, is produced. Applied to journalism, this would mean that a reporter could not declare that a problem exists without producing evidence of the problem.

Journalistic *habeas corpus* was ignored often in 1992. Reporters warned viewers, among other things, of tainted fish, flawed automobile bumpers, unhealthy Canadian beef, and poorly labelled bottled water. In each case reporters explicitly or implicitly called for government action to remedy the putative danger. Yet in each case reporters failed to produce any evidence of danger—that anyone had become ill or been hurt from the fish or beef or weak bumpers or bottled water. Without evidence of a problem and danger, the reporters should not have said that there was a problem or danger. And without the problem or danger, there would have been no need for a solution.

Were journalists routinely to invoke a *habeas corpus* standard, they would be less likely to exaggerate dangers (as many did during the Rio environment conference) and less likely to panic. They also would be less likely to call for government regulations if there were no evidence of a problem for regulations to solve.

QUESTION TWELVE—
Am I Recognizing Trade-offs?

Every reporter at one time or another probably has repeated Milton Friedman's famed quip about no free lunch. Yet reporters of economic and business matters often implied that lunches *could* be free. They particularly did this when they ignored the concept of trade-offs—that benefits are offset to an extent by costs, and costs are offset by benefits. Thus CNN's Brooks Jackson saw only the dark side of the office building glut; he did not see how economic forces, triggered by the glut, pushed down rents and thus enabled tenants and start-up businesses to benefit.

Recognizing trade-offs, moreover, would have prompted reporters to note that while a government regulation might address one need, the regulation's cost might create a new need. Thus though autos could be designed to weigh less so that they polluted less, this also might make them less safe in collisions. While a tariff on a product might, in the short run, help the product's manufacturer and workers, it would also raise costs for consumers and erode American competitiveness. Ultimately, the tariff would hurt even the protected industry; shielded from competition, the industry would become less competitive.

The notion of trade-offs could teach reporters as well to be suspicious of proposals that assume that enough regulations and mandates can create a risk-free society. Each attempt to eliminate a subsequent unit of risk typically costs more than the attempts to eliminate earlier units. The concept of trade-offs could prompt reporters to question whether society can afford or would want to pay for still more schemes to eliminate risk.

QUESTION THIRTEEN—
Am I Squandering Chances to Educate Viewers?

TV newscast executives and reporters should explicitly recognize that, unavoidably, they teach economic lessons. In acknowledging this, they should recognize further that it would be appropriate for them to look for opportunities to educate—even by adding just a phrase or sentence to a story so that viewers could learn something about their nation's economic system.

In Stephen Aug's January 3 ABC report of fourteen thousand retailers going out of business, for instance, he could have inserted an economic lesson simply by adding: "But entrepreneurial optimism, apparently, keeps blooming because last year more than 900,000 new businesses opened their doors—their eager owners obviously confident that they could avoid the mistakes and potholes that doomed the others."

In Irving R. Levine's January 10 NBC story on government-funded job retraining programs, he could have taught viewers something had he mentioned that retraining by American businesses accounted for almost all retraining in the country and was more effective and less costly than government programs.

In the networks' stories about Macy's bankruptcy filing, viewers could have learned, had they been told, why that kind of bankruptcy was a useful device and better than shutting the doors altogether, which would throw everyone out of work, lose everything, and pay creditors almost nothing.

In Bob Jamieson's ABC report on Macy's bankruptcy, he told viewers that all major New York department stores were in trouble—but did not explain why. Had he done so, viewers could have learned how established institutions had grown bureaucratic and slow to adapt and thus had become vulnerable to competition. In Keith Morrison's NBC report that city authorities had barred Pam Resch from giving piano concerts in her San Jose, California, home, he could have taught viewers, by using Resch as a paradigm, how regulations imposed huge burdens on business and creativity.

In Noah Nelson's NBC story on home repair horrors, he could have inserted a lesson by adding that the home repair business created tens of thousands of jobs and entrepreneurial opportunities for upwardly mobile minorities and those with limited schooling.

In Kathleen Koch's CNN story on new rules for de-icing airplanes, she could have included a lesson by noting that without any government regulations airline companies had enormous incentives to de-ice planes. She or a Talking Head expert could have explained that poor maintenance would result in airplane accidents which, in turn, would drive away customers and soon drive the airline out of business. This would have taught viewers that marketplace competition typically is much more effective at much lower cost in protecting the consumer than regulation by government bureaucracies ever could be.

How easy it was to add a lesson to reports and educate viewers was demonstrated by CBS consumer reporter Hattie Kauffman when, as a kicker to her "This Morning" June 3 segment on the trend towards clear products, she said that "every day at the checkout lane we cast our votes. If we want our mascara clear or wine coolers clear, that's just what the manufacturers will give us." With this she reminded viewers of the enormous power of choice in the free enterprise system and how this ignites the dynamics of competition.

QUESTION FOURTEEN—
Am I Reporting the Most Important Economic and Business Stories?

Producers periodically should step back from the torrid pace of covering daily news events to ask themselves if their newscasts have caught the most important (though not necessarily most urgent or dramatic) stories. Had producers done so in 1992, they would have given viewers an occasional three- or four-minute segment offering key insights on business and the economy. These would have included stories on:

• America's continuing reign as the world's most competitive and top trading country. Viewers would thus have learned that despite problem areas, like consumer electronics and automobiles, America continued to export more goods and services than any other country, while America's labor force continued to work more efficiently and productively than that of any other country. The storyline of the segment could have been an examination of how America had managed to remain the world's top exporter and what it would take to keep the lead.

• Free enterprise as consumer protection. Here reporters could have sketched how the free market's fierce competition penalized companies that ignored consumer tastes, whims, and safety.

• The jobless economic recovery. Though reporters and candidates for office repeatedly and correctly told viewers that the year's economic recovery differed from its predecessors because it was creating few new jobs, viewers were not told why. A segment on this would have allowed reporters to explore how taxes, regulations, education, demographics, and other factors might have retarded job growth.

• The true saga of IBM's troubles—and the triumph of America's computer industry. While reporters gave viewers an almost week-by-week update on IBM's deepening woes—unprecedented layoffs, cutbacks and management purges—newscasts missed 1992's biggest economic story: the exciting triumph of American upstart computer companies over giant International Business Machines Corporation. TV could have described how the creativity and competitive drive of America's computer hardware, software, and marketing midgets had brought IBM low and also had recaptured the world computer market for America. If anything could be, the story was a free enterprise morality play showing that the American economy was so dynamic and offered so many opportunities for new entrepreneurs (in contrast to Western Europe and Japan's rigidities) that brash newcomers could assault and even beat long-entrenched firms as seemingly invulnerable as IBM.

QUESTION FIFTEEN—
Am I Following-Up on Earlier Stories?

In December 1976, the *Argo Merchant* oil spill off Cape Cod became one of that year's biggest stories with TV newscasts and documentaries exhaustingly covering what was called massive environmental damage. Three months later, the National Oceanic and Atmospheric Administration announced that there would be "minimal biological and aesthetic damage from the spill." The press ignored the story.

Nearly two decades later, the *Argo Merchant* episode remains a paradigm for newscast coverage of disasters, crises, and other big splash stories. Reporters seldom return to the scene of the crisis to ask: How did things really turn out? Reporters seldom revisit yesterday's dire predictions to check whether they were fulfilled. Were they to do so, viewers would gain enormously.

In 1992, for example, a key theme in reporting the Americans with Disabilities Act was that the new law would not trigger an avalanche of lawsuits. In a typical report, ABC's Jim Hickey told viewers that "disabled activists say it is not their intention to force anyone to go to court." Yet almost immediately after passage of the act, attorneys for disabled Americans started filing suits. Neither Hickey nor other reporters covered this.

Follow-up coverage was also missing on the airlines' summer fare wars. Ray Brady, among others, warned that the price wars and the fact that deregulation was driving airlines out of business would mean higher prices for consumers down the road. Yet when Brady and the others arrived down the road, they failed to ask whether their predictions had turned out to be correct. Had they checked, they would have told viewers that start-up regional airlines and no-frills airlines were picking up the slack for the failed airlines and keeping prices low.

QUESTION SIXTEEN—
As a Producer and Writer of Entertainment Programming, Am I Aware I Am a Teacher?

Entertainment TV's writers and producers should recognize that their stories and the characters in them teach viewers lessons about life, including about how their economy functions. While entertainment surely need not be explicitly didactic—viewers would hardly find that entertaining—when it does teach about economics and business it might as well reinforce a culture that nurtures economic growth and mobility.

It may well be, of course, that entertainment's writers and producers know little about how the American economic system functions, and they may also assume that a plot would lose its punch if businessmen were not pegged as culprits. But if unfamiliarity with economic and business concepts is indeed the problem, the entertainment TV community could take specific steps to correct it. It could learn enough about America's economy to recognize which lessons entertainment TV should teach.

Beyond that, just as writers and producers have agreed to discuss scripts and plots with minorities and gays to avoid depicting them inaccurately (and even offensively), writers and producers could recruit a panel of businesspersons and economists to review programs depicting economic and business situations.

TEACHING THE TEACHER:
How Viewers Can Help TV

Viewers, of course, need not wait for TV executives, producers, writers, and reporters to ask themselves, and act upon, the above sixteen questions. If Americans want TV to be fairer, more balanced, and more enlightened in covering economic and business matters, various actions can be taken. Viewers can:

1. Alert ABC, CBS, CNN, and NBC network headquarters when their programs misrepresent and unfairly cover economics and business issues. Letters and calls receive most attention when addressed to the president of the network, the vice-president for news policy, the network news director, the executive producer of the show, the producer of the story, and the reporters themselves. Such letters should describe in detail the program's mistakes and even suggest possible remedies which could be drawn from the sixteen questions. As has been evident from the response to African-Americans, women, those concerned about violence on TV, and other groups, network TV eventually bows to popular pressure.

2. Alert the owners, boards of directors, and general managers of the local affiliates and other stations carrying the network programs that misrepresented economic and business issues. Local station owners particularly do not want to offend local audiences. And though station owners and managers are not responsible for the content of network broadcasts, their views carry great weight at network headquarters.

3. Alert national and local firms whose advertisements appeared on newscasts and other programs that distort and otherwise unfairly treat economic and business matters.

4. Organize a group of local businesspersons and economists to discuss with local TV executives, reporters, and producers ways of improving coverage of the local economy and business issues.

5. Organize a national Economists TV Advisory Council to review the economic and business themes in entertainment TV and to suggest to newscast producers, writers, and reporters how their stories could be more informative and balanced.

6. Organize TV economic literacy training courses for children and TV awareness courses for adults. Known as a "media literacy curriculum," this already has been suggested by the American Psychological Association as a way to blunt TV's "potentially negative effects of programs" dealing with minorities and violence.[1] Explains the association:

> In the lesson on prejudice and stereotypes, the children were asked to describe the kinds of people who were portrayed unrealistically in television programs, including the handicapped, minorities and men and women of different ages and occupations. Possible homework assignments included being a "stereotype detective" by looking for stereotypic characters on commercials and programs, or drawing pictures of people in nontraditional roles.[2]

Surely courses along these lines could teach children and adults how to be knowledgeable about TV coverage of business and the economy. A "stereotype detective," for instance, could spot unfair stereotypical depictions of businesspersons on entertainment and stereotypical use of businesspersons on newscast interviews. A "balance detective" could spot false dichotomies, tilted credibility, and other cases of imbalance.

7. Devise a Free Enterprise Index for TV, similar to the Violence Index proposed by George Gerbner, former dean of the University of Pennsylvania's Annenberg School of Communications. To measure violence on TV, Gerbner devised the formula: $VI = (\%P) + (2R/P) + (2R/H) + (\%V) + (\%K)$ which means that the Violence Index equals the percent of Programs containing violence plus two times the Rate of violence incidents per Program plus two times the Rate of violent incidents per Hour plus the percent of characters involved in any Violence plus the percent of characters involved in a Killing.[3]

A Free Enterprise Index need not be so complicated as Gerbner's Violence Index but it still could measure how accurately programs portray America's free enterprise economy, the frequency of false data and interpretations, and the opportunities used or squandered to teach Americans something about how their economy functions. Free Enterprise Index for entertainment, meanwhile, could equal the percent of criminals who are business characters plus the percent of those who are portrayed negatively minus the percent portrayed positively.

IF NETWORK TELEVISION recognizes that it has a problem with its economic and business coverage, if it takes seriously the sixteen questions that it should ask itself about this coverage, and if it pays attention to viewers who want to improve coverage, then TV could begin to solve its problem and get it right.

If TV starts getting it right, TV no longer would make the mistakes of Diane Sawyer (who told viewers that banks "reward" depositors by paying interest) or of Ray Brady (who told viewers that economic improvement depended on businesspersons' "liking" Bill Clinton's proposals) or of Keith Morrison (who told viewers that "nine in ten Americans saw their lifestyle decline" in the 1980s) or of Bryant Gumbel (who told viewers that there was a conflict between cutting the deficit and creating jobs).

If TV starts getting it right, reporters no longer would assume that problems are solved by new government programs or more government spending or that a risk-free society is a realistic goal. While government can address some of the nation's problems, the burden of proof should be on those seeking government action. Reporters should recognize which side has the burden of proof.

If TV starts getting it right, it will offer to viewers businesspersons who are black or female, corporate executives who are struggling to protect the environment while saving (or creating) jobs, investors who are pursuing profits without being labelled greedy, and small businesses that are triumphantly bringing down their large, bureaucratic competitors by offering better goods at better prices with better service.

If TV starts getting it right, it will echo those reporters in 1992 who brought balance and inquisitiveness to the silicone breast implant controversy and in so doing taught American viewers some economic basics—that well-intended regulations could have very painful consequences, that life was full of intelligent risk-taking, that striving for a risk-free society inflicted an extraordinary price, and that agonizing and complicated trade-offs were inherent in all economic decisions.

If TV starts getting it right, viewers can begin to conclude from coverage of the economy and business that if government does not address a genuine need the private sector generally could, that private firms would not do this altruistically but in their own self-interest to increase productivity and competitiveness and profits, and that such actions could benefit society.

If TV starts getting it right, it can inform viewers of the genuine strengths and weaknesses in the American economy, identify genuine problems and inequities, and thus allow Americans, who get 79 percent of their information about the economy from TV, to begin monitoring knowledgeably the decisions and actions of their officials and representatives.

If TV starts getting it right, its reporting will stop distorting what viewers see of the American economic system.

Notes

1. Althea C. Huston et al., *The Role of Television in American Society* (Lincoln: University of Nebraska Press, 1992), pp. 6–7.
2. Ibid., pp. 103–105.
3. John Condry, *The Psychology of Television*, p. 61.

APPENDIX ONE

ANALYSIS
METHODOLOGY

THROUGHOUT THIS STUDY there are references to the amount of time TV newscast reporting bolstered understanding of free enterprise and the amount of time it undermined understanding of free enterprise. These calculations are the result of analysis by Free Enterprise & Media Institute researchers of all news on ABC "World News Tonight," ABC "Good Morning America," ABC "Prime Time Live," ABC "20/20," ABC "Nightline," CBS "Evening News," CBS "This Morning," CBS "60 Minutes," CNN "World News," NBC "Nightly News," NBC "Today," and "Dateline NBC" in 1992. For each news story dealing with a free enterprise issue, researchers logged every second as either bolstering free enterprise, undermining free enterprise, or as background information.

Researchers counted seconds as bolstering free enterprise if reporters or those whom they interviewed spent those seconds (1) calling for less government intrusion in the free market, (2) making arguments against policies of more government intrusion, (3) making arguments for policies that would limit government intrusion, or (4) citing the goals or rationales for policies that would limit government intrusion.

Researchers counted seconds as undermining free enterprise if reporters or those whom they interviewed spent those seconds

(1) calling for more government intrusion in the free market, (2) making arguments against policies of less government intrusion, (3) making arguments in favor of policies that would increase government intrusion, or (4) citing the goals or rationales for policies for more government intrusion.

The vast bulk of seconds in most news stories were spent on background information. This included time reporters spent explaining the details of how a policy would work. In such cases researchers would only count the seconds as bolstering or undermining free enterprise if the reporters weaved the goals or rationales for policies into their explanations of how policies would work.

The issues on which the institute counted seconds were health care, taxes, regulation, government spending, and environment. Although environment and health care could fall under other categories, there were enough stories on these topics to warrant separate treatment. Some examples of how researchers classified reporters' statements:

—The CNN "World News" April 14 story by reporter Jamie McIntyre. It covered medical Individual Retirement Accounts as a free enterprise-based alternative to government health care reform proposals. "Here's how it would work," McIntyre began. "Roony says group insurance costs employers an average of $4,500 a year per family, and typically comes with a $150 to $250 deductible. But, he says, for $1,500 annually, the same policy could be purchased with a $3,000 deductible, and the money saved could go into a special fund to be used by the employees to pay medical bills. Any leftover funds could be rolled over into an Individual Retirement Account." Saying this took McIntyre 37 seconds. Researchers counted these seconds as background information, since he only outlined how a medical IRA would work.

McIntyre then explained the rationale behind medical IRAs for 20 seconds; researchers counted these as bolstering free enterprise: "The idea is to get people to shop for minor medical services the way they shop for groceries. Imagine if employers paid 80 percent of the grocery bill. How many consumers would bother to check prices and compare before buying? The problem, argue critics of today's system, is that too many health care purchases are made with other people's money."

McIntyre then cited some of the arguments against this free enterprise-based proposal for 29 seconds; researchers counted these as undermining free enterprise because they implicitly called for a government health care plan: "But critics say the plan is far from a cureall, pointing out it will do nothing to help the 35 million Americans who don't have insurance, or people who can't get it because of preexisting conditions, not to mention convincing Americans to stay healthy in the first place."

—The NBC "Nightly News" March 27 story by chief financial correspondent Mike Jensen. He first explained presidential candidate Jerry Brown's plan for a flat tax and a value-added tax. Researchers counted Jensen's 6-second explanation as background information: "In place [of other taxes] Brown would have identical taxes of 13 percent on all individuals and businesses."

Jensen then gave viewers a 14-second denunciation of the flat tax, which researchers counted as opposed to free enterprise because it opposed lower taxes: "But most economists don't think it will work. They say Brown's tax rate of 13 percent is so low it wouldn't produce enough revenue, and that his plan would help the rich, but hurt the poor and middle class."

Then Jensen illustrated the shortcomings in the value-added tax, using 9 seconds that researchers counted as bolstering free enterprise: "Again, it sounds good, but companies would raise their prices to cover the new taxes, and the consumer would end up paying."

—The CBS "This Morning" September 24 story by economics correspondent Robert Krulwich. In his whimsical style, Krulwich catalogued all the regulations imposed on businesses (he had a mock businessman say, "Who's gonna pay?" as an off-screen voice listed all the regulations). Since Krulwich had not yet made judgments about the regulations, researchers counted these seconds as background information.

Then Krulwich outlined the objections to over-regulation:

"Now you add all these programs together. That's a very big bill you're handing that business executive. One analysis found that for many companies, just two of these programs—job training and health care—would double the payroll tax, which is the tax that businesses have to pay for every worker they've got. Well, if these new laws mean that businesses have to lay out more money for the workers they've already got, what will the boss say when he's asked, 'How do you feel about hiring new workers?' " Researchers counted these 29 seconds as bolstering free enterprise because Krulwich used them to demonstrate the cost of regulations to the economy.

Krulwich then gave arguments for the regulations: "They [Democrats in Congress] say a secure worker, who is not afraid he'll get fired if he goes home to take care of his sick parent, an insured worker, who is not afraid that if he gets sick he'll be devastated, a trained worker, who is regularly given new skills, will work harder, be smarter, and by that fashion the business will be more productive and will produce, in the end, more jobs. And they say, if you're still a bit skeptical, 'If this is so hard to do, how come some of the best companies in America and the richest companies in America are doing it, and by their count seventy-two other countries in the world, including the Scandinavian countries, Germany, France, are doing it as well?' They're not getting poorer." Researchers counted these 36 seconds as undermining free enterprise because Krulwich used them to counter arguments that the regulations would cost the economy.

—The CNN "World News" August 6 story by reporter Bob Franken about a bill in Congress to increase spending on food stamps. Franken said that the act "expands food stamps to feed hungry children. The act would pay for itself by imposing a 10 percent surtax on millionaires." Researchers counted these 10 seconds as background information.

Later in the story Representative Tom Downey, a New York Democrat, argued that "the president [Bush] wants to engage the nation in a discussion about family values, and today we are talking about family values." Since Downey was equating support for expanded government spending with support for families, researchers counted these 8 seconds as undermining free enterprise.

But Franken also aired part of a speech by Representative Dan Burton, an Indiana Republican, who was once a child abuse victim: "I know a little bit about that, because I grew up with it. And I'm telling you, the approach you're talking about, throwing more money from the federal government at the problem, is not the solution." Since Burton distinguished between support for government and support for families, researchers counted these 11 seconds as bolstering free enterprise.

—An ABC "World News Tonight" April 20 environmental story by reporter John McKenzie. He told viewers about proposed regulations on the fishing industry. He explained: "There is a controversial five-year plan to rebuild the stocks [of fish]. It would require fishermen to reduce their days at sea by 10 percent a year, make fewer trips to some of the prime fishing grounds, and use a larger mesh to ensure only larger, older fish are caught." Since McKenzie was merely outlining the proposed new regulations, researchers counted these 17 seconds as background information.

"But here in ports like Gloucester, Massachusetts," McKenzie continued, "the fear is that regulations designed to save the fish could put many fishermen out of business." Since McKenzie reported that regulation imposes a cost, researchers counted these 8 seconds as bolstering free enterprise.

McKenzie finished the story with a 24-second argument that researchers counted as undermining free enterprise: "And everybody pays a price. As the catch continues to fall, the cost of fish continues to rise. No one denies the plan to restock these waters will force some fishermen to pull up their nets for good. But conservationists say sacrificing some fishermen now may be the only way to ensure a fishing industry in the future."

Since none of the institute's researchers, and most likely none of the network reporters, is trained in environmental science, environmental stories were handled as follows: Predictions of impending environmental catastrophe, no matter how far-fetched, were counted as background information. Researchers only counted statements that called for more government action as undermining free enterprise. In some cases, proposals for solutions with minimal government interference in the market, such as the buying and selling of a "right to pollute," were counted as bolstering free enterprise.

TO SELECT THE target weeks used for intensive analysis of TV coverage (Chapters I through IV) the year was split into four 13-week groups, and one week was randomly selected from each group.

To gather the data on entertainment television's treatment of free enterprise, researchers first analyzed all the network prime-time programming from the four target weeks. Then, to get a representative sample of the entire year, researchers analyzed all the prime-time programming from the second week of each of the eight remaining months.

APPENDIX TWO

WHAT TO READ & WHOM TO INTERVIEW

Several books can broaden journalists' understanding of free enterprise. Among them:

Capitalism and Freedom, by Milton Friedman
Economics in One Lesson, by Henry Hazlett
Free to Choose, by Milton Friedman
Losing Ground: American Social Policy from 1950–1980, by Charles Murray
Revolution, by Martin Anderson
The Seven Fat Years, by Robert Bartley
Wealth and Poverty, by George Gilder

To attain genuine balance in their reporting, TV journalists should give viewers a chance to hear and see many more experts who advocate free market solutions to problems. Among the experts available to reporters:

General Economy

Martin Anderson *Hoover Institution*
Doug Bandow *Cato Institute*

Bruce Bartlett *Cato Institute*
Christopher Frenze *Joint Economic Committee of Congress*

George Gilder *Discovery Institute*

Edward Hudgins *Joint Economic Committee of Congress*

Marvin Kosters *American Enterprise Institute*

Arthur Laffer *A. B. Laffer, V. A. Canto & Associates*

Daniel Mitchell *National Empowerment Television*

Stephen Moore *Cato Institute*

William Niskanen *Cato Institute*

Alan Reynolds *Hudson Institute*

Paul Craig Roberts *Center for Strategic and International Studies*

Fred Smith *Competitive Enterprise Institute*

Norman Ture *Institute for Research on the Economics of Taxation*

Walter Williams *Center for Economic Education, George Mason University*

Health Care

Doug Bandow *Cato Institute*

Rita Ricardo Campbell *Hoover Institution*

Michele Davis *Citizens for a Sound Economy*

John Goodman *National Center for Policy Analysis*

Brink Lindsey *Cato Institute*

Merrill Matthews *National Center for Policy Analysis*

William Niskanen *Cato Institute*

Budget/Government Spending

John Cogan *Hoover Institution*

Scott Hodge *Heritage Foundation*

Dana Joel *Citizens for a Sound Economy*

Paul Merski *Citizens for a Sound Economy*

Daniel Mitchell *National Empowerment Television*

Stephen Moore *Cato Institute*

Dan Murphy *Citizens for a Sound Economy*

Jim Miller *Citizens for a Sound Economy*

William Niskanen *Cato Institute*

International Trade

James Bovard *Cato Institute*
Edward Hudgins *Joint Economic Committee of Congress*
Brink Lindsey *Cato Institute*
William Niskanen *Cato Institute*

Bryan Riley *Citizens for a Sound Economy*
Jim Sheehan *Competitive Enterprise Institute*
Fred Smith *Competitive Enterprise Institute*

Taxes

Bruce Bartlett *Cato Institute*
Steve Entin *Institute for Research on the Economics of Taxation*
Sam Kazman *Competitive Enterprise Institute*
David Keating *National Taxpayers Union*
Arthur Laffer *A. B. Laffer, V. A. Canto & Associates*
Charles McLure *Hoover Institution*
Paul Merski *Citizens for a Sound Economy*

Tom Miller *Competitive Enterprise Institute*
Daniel Mitchell *National Empowerment Television*
Stephen Moore *Cato Institute*
William Niskanen *Cato Institute*
Paul Craig Roberts *Center for Strategic and International Affairs*
Norman Ture *Institute for Research on the Economics of Taxation*

Environment

Jonathan Adler *Competitive Enterprise Institute*
Terry Anderson *Political Economy Research Center & Montana State University*
Robert E. Gordon *National Wilderness Institute*

Kent Jeffreys *Competitive Enterprise Institute*
Donald Leal *Political Economy Research Center*
David Ridenour *National Center for Public Policy Research*

Robin L. Birett *Pacific Legal Foundation*
John Shanahan *Heritage Foundation*
Jane Shaw *Political Economy Research Center*

James R. Streeter *National Wilderness Institute*
Richard Stroup *Political Economy Research Center*

Regulation

Doug Bandow *Cato Institute*
Wayne Brough *Citizens for a Sound Economy*
Orrin F. Finch *Pacific Legal Foundation*
James Gattuso *Citizens for a Sound Economy*
Marvin Kosters *American Enterprise Institute*
Brink Lindsey *Cato Institute*

Nancy Mitchell *Citizens for a Sound Economy*
Tom Moore *Hoover Institution*
William Niskanen *Cato Institute*
Walter Olson *Manhattan Institute*
Fred Smith *Competitive Enterprise Institute*
Ronald Zumbrun *Pacific Legal Foundation*

Labor Issues

Richard B. Berman *Employment Policies Institute*
Anthony T. Caso *Pacific Legal Foundation*
Bill Custer *Employee Benefit Research Institute*
John H. Findler *Pacific Legal Foundation*

David Kendrick *National Right to Work Legal Defense Foundation*
Ed Lazear *Hoover Institution*
Timothy McConville *National Right to Work Legal Defense Foundation*
Dallas Salisbury *Employee Benefit Research Institute*

Addresses of Organizations Listed:

A. B. Laffer, V. A. Canto &
    Associates
4275 Executive Square,
    Suite 330
La Jolla, CA 92037
(619) 458–0811

American Enterprise Institute
1150 17th Street, NW
Washington, DC 20036
(202) 862–5800

Cato Institute
1000 Massachusetts
    Avenue, NW
Washington, DC 20001
(202) 842–0200

Center for Strategic and
    International Studies
1800 K Street, NW, Suite 400
Washington, DC 20006
(202) 887–0200

Competitive Enterprise
    Institute
1001 Connecticut Avenue, NW
Suite 1250
Washington, DC 20036
(202) 331–1010

Citizens for a Sound Economy
1250 H Street, NW, Suite 700
Washington, DC 20005
(202) 783–3870

Discovery Institute
1201 3rd Avenue, 39th Floor
Seattle, WA 98101
(206) 287–3144

Employee Benefit Research
    Institute
2121 K Street, NW,
    Suite 600
Washington, DC 20037
(202) 659–0670

Employment Policies Institute
607 14th Street, NW,
    Suite 1110
Washington, DC 20005
(202) 347–5178

Center for Economic
    Education
George Mason University
Fairfax, VA 22030
(703) 993–1140

Heritage Foundation
214 Massachusetts
    Avenue, NE
Washington, DC 20002
(202) 546–4400

Hoover Institution
Stanford University
Stanford, CA 94305
(415) 723–0603

Hudson Institute
5395 Emerson Way
P.O. Box 26–919
Indianapolis, IN 46226
(317) 545–1000

Institute for Research on the
　Economics of Taxation
1331 Pennsylvania Avenue,
　NW, Suite 515
Washington, DC 20004
(202) 347–9570

Joint Economic Committee of
　Congress
805 Hart Senate Office
　Building
Washington, DC 20510
(202) 224–5171

Manhattan Institute
52 Vanderbilt Avenue
New York, NY 10017
(212) 599–7000

National Center for Policy
　Analysis
12655 N. Central Expressway,
　Suite 720
Dallas, TX 75243
(214) 386–6272

National Center for Public
　Policy Research
300 Eye Street, NE
Washington, DC 20002
(202) 543–1286

National Empowerment
　Television
717 Second Street, NE
Washington, DC 20002
(202) 546–3000

National Right to Work Legal
　Defense Foundation
8001 Braddock Road,
　Suite 600
Springfield, VA 22160
(703) 321–8510

National Taxpayers
　Union
713 Maryland
　Avenue, NE
Washington, DC 20002
(202) 543–1300

National Wildlife
　Institute
25766 Georgetown Station
Washington, DC 20007
(703) 836–7403

Pacific Legal Foundation
2700 Gateway Oaks Drive,
　Suite 200
Sacramento, CA 95833
(916) 641–8888

Political Economy Research
　Center
502 S. 19th Avenue,
　Suite 211
Bozeman, MT 59715
(406) 587–9591

INDEX